Live love every day.

Agni

Cosmic Library Publishing LLC
2838 Beach Blvd. S
Gulfport, FL 33707
CLPcontact@gmail.com

Published by
Cosmic Library Publishing LLC,
St Petersburg, FL 33707

Library of Congress Control Number: 2009905970
ISBN: 978-1-936060-26-9
SAN: 8 5 8 – 1 5 2 5

Second edition March 2010

You can find us on the Internet on the following sites:

www.cl-publishing.com

www.jesus-the-book.com

Jesus
The Book

Durga Holzhauser
Frank Eickermann

Cosmic Library Publishing

Contents

Dedication

We have written this account for you, my Lord Jesus Christ, as we have ourselves experienced it with you, and as your mother, Mary, and other friends and acquaintances have recounted it to us. Therewith we have fulfilled our promise to you.

We already knew at that time that your chronicle, and those of your companions, would be mislaid in the course of the centuries. Hence, since these are our experiences, we have saved them for you, in order that they may one day again see the light of day: to recount your life story, together with the records of those who were with you at that time.

I remember precisely my first encounter with him. I was a young girl, perhaps three years old. My parents lived on the outskirts of the city of Jerusalem. My father and mother were both priests in the Essene tradition, in an Essene community on the edge of the city. I had been born in this community and grew up with this tradition. Our life in the suburb was somewhat separated from that in the city of Jerusalem. I remember when my father took me with him to the town center, where the markets were situated. Sometimes he had an appointment or some business to do. Everything seemed so different from the small community in which I lived.

Jerusalem was noisy and turbulent and I was continuously surrounded by its hustle and bustle. Soldiers in leather armor added to the turmoil, which scared me at first. My father called them "Romans." Amongst the Romans were also men to whom my father referred as "the Old Jews." They wore long cloaks and long beards and their eyes seemed cruel; I felt intimidated by them. Since childhood, I had had the gift of perceiving the colors of the auras surrounding people, and I sensed the sharp contrast between the cold, hard grayness of the citizens of Jerusalem and the warm, clear colors that I saw envelop the people from our community. At home, everything was lighter and more transparent, in stark contrast to Jerusalem. In our village, my soul had space to expand freely.

My father often took me with him into the city, but my mother did not join us. Many a time we would jostle down the narrow alleys, my father conversing with the bearded men. I would observe the stalls, the buildings and the passers–by, haggling as they went about their business. Everything was in a state of permanent turmoil. As a child, I was unable to describe the feeling, but later, as I grew up, I recognized describe the feeling, but later, as I grew up, I recognized that these impressions were those of the violence, cruelty and insurrection that were a constant shadow upon the city's inhabitants. Their words were hurtful and rude, their voices loud and coarse and their movements in the markets were violent and clumsy. I missed the gentleness and tolerance of our community.

I found the men my father met unpleasant, and I didn't care for them one bit. I had no idea what my father's business with them was, but it always seemed very serious and he never appeared very pleased afterwards; his brow would become wrinkled and I could sense the weight of his worries on his shoulders, which was unusual for him. In those days, I was too young to ask him to explain and instead would just cuddle up to him so that he could protect me from this world. Then I would sense the warm green–golden light of his heart, which I loved so much.

As I grew up, I discovered that our Community had separated from the Essenes in the desert, who lived quite differently from us and who were one of several Essene splinter–groups. Instead, my father was true to the "Original Essenes," as he called them. Much of his time was spent in negotiations with the higher councils of the old Jews, arguing for our traditions and beliefs, and pleading for peace and for mutual recognition between us. This became apparent as I grew older.

I always felt relieved and more at ease when my father, who was equivalent to a high priest in our community, got back home and was able to devote himself to our daily religious routine. I loved our simple life and our traditions. My father performed his rituals and prayers and attended to the needs of our community. Then, ruby–colored and golden light would rise out of the ground and ascend to the sky, between Heaven and Earth. Visitors from outside the community would come, appearing gray and dejected from the burdens of life but, after my father's ceremonies, they returned home, their souls unburdened and their hearts enlightened.

My mother was also a priest of sorts but she was concerned with other matters; her colors were beautiful and gentle. I also had an older brother who was difficult and rebellious, and my father had to keep a close eye on him. But I had my own world. It was connected with the colors in my father's aura, which filled me with delight and pleasure. Our life was as simple as my father's room, but the gentle simplicity of that time was a gift from Heaven to enjoy and play with. I loved plants and animals, whose language I understood and had learned from my mother.

My mother, a successful and respected healer, visited the sick and radiated a wonderful light from her heart and from her hands. As it flowed into the bodies of the sick, I could see the burden of illness clear away and the light become bright and radiant. I loved my mother for her abilities and I was always allowed to attend whenever she created prayers out of her love and filled the room with her radiant colors. Sometimes, precious stones would appear, radiating as divine lights to cure disease. When we had left the houses of the sick and were alone again, she would look upon me with her warm, brown eyes and say, "My little girl, I will teach you all of this, since it is our tradition. And, one day, you too will help and serve in this tradition. I see your wonderful heart and know that Heaven sent you to me. I can see that you will one day be even greater than I. You may not understand now, but time will show!"

I must have been three or four years old when my father first allowed me to accompany him on a long journey. We travelled on foot with our donkey, whose name was Little Benjamin. I was very fond of our donkey, and was very happy that he accompanied us. My father said to me, "Come with me, my little daughter, so that you can meet the leaders of our tradition."

The countryside in which we travelled became increasingly dry the farther we travelled, with fewer trees and sparse greenery. It was hot and we travelled over scorching desert sand. My father taught me a method of creating a layer of light under my feet so that the burning heat of the desert sand could not reach them, even when we were almost roasting in the hot midday sun. The dust on which I walked was like gold, and I was amused that it was not burning the soles of my feet. I really liked that, and I walked on the sand imagining that I was walking in complete safety on golden light.

Sometimes the sun was so hot on our way that my father let me drink out of his little leather flask; it contained a mixture of water and our divine potion, which we'd always drunk at home. Then I had the strength to continue our journey. I had never noticed the magical effect of this drink at home; I went from being hot, tired, and mildly dehydrated to almost immediately feeling refreshed and content. The sun no longer bothered me; it had become my friend, and accompanied me with its benevolent beams showing me the way.

I had no idea how long the journey would take. Sometimes, we joined groups of Bedouin and other travellers. They shared their food with us and we even slept three nights in different oases. I admired the camels and the very different people we met. My father explained that they came from foreign lands. Some of them looked very strange to me: they wore exotic clothes, which I found very interesting. I asked myself, "What do these foreign countries look like?" But I did not communicate with these strange people. I just watched in fascination. When I needed my father's support, I would make inner contact with him, whereupon he would envelop me in his green–golden light. Then we would continue on our travels.

Only later did I realize that, although I seldom conversed with people, I was always somehow in contact with them. When I didn't like them, I felt an invisible wall between us, and nothing inside me would induce me to make contact with them. I didn't look for a reason.

I don't know how long our journey lasted. By night, we slept in the desert and admired the heavens, full of stars. We had warm blankets and my father would tell me about the stars; this was the first time that he'd done so. I would look at this glittering drama late into the night until I fell asleep and his stories continued to echo within me. He described, in simple words, distant worlds full of wisdom that existed above and sometimes made contact with us. My father told me, "I know many people in our home village, Qumran, and you will get to know them too. They are our sages, our wise teachers, who visit these worlds. I too was chosen to be their pupil and to learn from them, but I was destined to take another path.

Nevertheless, you can learn a lot from them, my daughter. You'll experience all this for yourself." But I also remember, in the course of my star–gazing, that I would hear sounds and perceive spirits which pleased me far more than all those colorful characters who came and went on our travels in the desert. I sensed that more fascinating beings were above us. Sometimes, the heavens appeared to flash with colored lights, as if another world were greeting me. But none of the beings came near enough for me to recognize them. I could sense them from a distance, and that filled my heart with joy. As I slept, I felt completely protected and lost all fear.

One day we stopped and my father said, "Look over there. You can see the walls of Qumran. That's our destination." As we drew near, I was surprised that there were no guards as there were outside Jerusalem, where the doors were locked and protected by armed soldiers. The town we approached was bathed in a wonderful light that could be seen from far away. The light was golden and radiated up to the heavens, in sharp contrast to Jerusalem, which was clad with gray and severity. I was so happy to be here. We reached a large wooden gate and my father spoke to someone on the other side who replied, "What news have you for me, stranger, that you may enter our holy community?" My father answered with words that I had never heard before and the doors opened to let us in.

A current of warm light met me and enveloped my whole being. I cannot describe what happened to me. My whole body tingled such as I had never before experienced, and I was drawn into the town as if by magic. The whole place oozed tranquillity and the inhabitants looked quite different from the people of Jerusalem. They were quiet and introverted.

They were simple and modest and in prayer. Hardly a word was spoken. As we passed the inhabitants, I saw that they were inwardly reflective but nevertheless radiated their light far and wide. They were not locked into their world, as the travellers in the desert had been. This world was open and radiant, as if it contained a nucleus of heavenly light that reached all inhabitants. I heard no arguments and sensed that here were agreement and tolerance.

My father and I followed a path until a woman met us. He called her Mary. She wore a headscarf and was very beautiful. She had the kindest eyes that I had ever seen, so full of love. I discovered later that she was Jesus' mother. She said to my father, "Zodiac, my old friend. How wonderful that you have received my call and that you have heard the message of my heart across the desert to Jerusalem. Please come in." Then she saw me and said, "So this is your little daughter, whom we have awaited. She is just as beautiful as your wife, Magda." She regarded me for a while, which seemed forever. Her heart emitted a wonderful loving light that streamed over me. I had never experienced anything like it! It was incredible to see how a doorway to the heart could be suddenly opened, flooding everything with its golden–rosy light. I looked at her and was slightly intimidated, since the light of her aura was powerful and all–pervasive. I lowered my eyes.

She turned to me and said, "Look at me. You don't need to be afraid of me. I know you well and I'm happy that you have found your way to me again. It is good that you have returned." Then she pulled her cloak around her shoulders and said, "Follow me. I've prepared some food for you. You will certainly be hungry. The Essenes here have brought bread for you. It was baked fresh today and it'll restore your strength after the long journey."

She led us into a room where there was space for many guests. The wooden tables were very plain and Mary invited us to sit down. She offered my father wine and passed me bread, dates and some kind of fruit that looked like those we had seen on the cacti. We ate, and I saw how my father's face changed — the worry–lines around his mouth and brow softened and disappeared. His face became relaxed and the light in the room seemed to calm him and restore his strength. I was astonished to see the change, something I had never seen before. His whole being radiated joy, as he only did when he performed his rituals at home. He became simultaneously strong yet gentle. We all smiled, conscious of the similarity of our thoughts. We had both learned something very important, without words and without any other communication between us.

My father and I sat eating, silent and content. I'd never enjoyed such a delicious feast, so different from the meals I was used to. The food was so full of vitality and I filled myself up with dates. My strength returned and gradually I recovered from the long journey. Then Mary came back in and said to my father, "Come Zodiac, the Council awaits you." My father looked at me and said, "Come with me. I'll show you a place where you can occupy yourself until I'm finished; it may take some time, but I don't know how long. You don't mind being alone for a while, do you?" I shook my head by way of agreement, since I had no difficulty in being alone here, and, anyhow, I found everything in this village so exciting that I was happy to investigate everything that was happening around me. He led me to an open space in front of a hall and said, "Wait here until I return. I'll be here as soon as the Council releases me."

I sat on the steps facing a forum and wondered about what "the Council" might be. I was sure all the same that my father would explain it on our way home and that I would get to understand a bit more. I felt the sun above me and took pleasure from this wonderful place. I became aware of an inner tranquillity, which aroused my curiosity and led me instinctively to some of the surrounding buildings in which various crafts were being exercised in silence. The movements and activities in the various houses of the vilage fascinated me. In front of the steps was a fountain, and I sensed that this was where the citizens assembled; the atmosphere here was full of lightness and peace.

While I was reflecting, someone approached from behind and I felt an incredible beating and strength in my heart. I had an extraordinary feeling that I was unable to describe. Children arrived, spreading out over the area. I was suddenly afraid and drew back. I began to feel as though my father had deserted me and was surprised to find somebody standing in front of me. I looked up into the most unbelievable pair of eyes I had ever seen. I perceived a being so immense that I had neither words nor thoughts to describe it, but all I could make out was the silhouette of the boy, a few years older than myself — perhaps ten or eleven years old. His aura was so incredibly large and consisted entirely of light. His eyes seemed to look into my soul. And then he smiled. I neither knew what was happening to me nor where I was. An infinite expanse opened up before me and I was carried momentarily out of this world. I found myself transferred to the heavens, amongst

14

the stars. An instant later, I returned to my original spot, and found myself once more captured by those eyes. He just smiled but didn't speak.

Another boy came up to join him, and his energy, by contrast, seemed rebellious, striving and vigorous. The boy took his arm and said, "Come on, Jesus!" Then the young Jesus fixed me again with his incredible eyes before running off with the others and I was left alone, quaking, for I was no longer of this world! Only the sound of my heartbeat reminded me that I was still on Earth. The sun began to set and, with it, the warmth of the day receded. Then I realized that I was cold and began to shiver. I pulled a woollen scarf from my pocket, a gift from my mother, and wrapped myself in it, remembering my mother's words: "I made this for you, my little princess. When you are cold, wrap it around you; it will always keep you warm." I cuddled myself into the scarf and felt completely protected and secure. I thought of my mother and missed her.

Suddenly I heard a wonderful sound from afar: beautiful vibrant tones, filled with harmony. Later, I discovered that the Essenes of the village gathered at this time for evening prayers. All the houses vibrated, as if in resonance, and the air began to shimmer with a golden light. It was all so powerful and moving, accompanied by the sun setting gently into the desert sands. Images all melted into one another to become a single picture of great beauty and strength. Then I sensed my father approaching me from behind. He sat down next to me on the steps and looked at me. "I've loved these evening prayers here in Qumran too," he said. "Every evening, they thank God for their lives and their vitality, which they continue to celebrate until deep into the night."

15

His voice had changed, as if he had become immersed in recollections of ancient times, buried in his memory but still very much alive. I sensed that he had a special memory in his soul, one that was revived and stimulated by the wonderful vibrations which filled the village. His whole being seemed to change: he appeared larger and more powerful than normal. He was suddenly so clear and pure, as I have seldom seen him. He said, "We'll stay here for a few more days." At first, I was not sure whether I should rejoice or cry. I missed my mother so much. On the other hand, the prospect of remaining in this wonderful village was exciting and pleasant. My father immediately laid his warm cloak over my shoulders against the chill of the night and I cuddled up to him, enjoying the warmth of his body. "They have asked me to wait just a few moments, until their most devout prayers are finished", he said. "Then they will find accommodation for us. You'll see, my little princess, the nights here are even more wonderful than in the desert."

A few minutes later, a man appeared and greeted us: "Shalom! Follow me. I'll show you where you can sleep." He brought us to a small house at the end of the street. "You can stay here, Zodiac, until you have completed your business with the Council." It seemed to me that this person did not know much about my father's business with the Council, and did not seem curious about it. This surprised me. Everyone I had met before had always seemed curious and wanted to know what was happening and why. This man seemed different, content with what he had and what he knew, but not striving for things beyond his understanding or responsibilities. We went into the room and my father said, "Make yourself comfortable and don't be surprised if you wake up in the night and I am sitting up beside you. While we're here I'm going to take up my old habit of meditating through the night again. I must gather myself together, since the Council and I have important decisions to make."

In the meantime, the night had turned completely dark. The village was absolutely still. When the sun set the villagers turned in, as if they were completely in rhythm with the heavens. The small window above my bed was covered with a thick woollen curtain, which I drew to one side to stare out at the moon. My father had gone out again and reassured me saying, "Don't be afraid if I leave you alone for a while. I'm going to join the others for ablutions. You can stay here." He showed me a bucket filled with water, and said, "You can wash here. I'll be back again when you are asleep." Then he regarded me with warm, loving glance, with which I was so familiar, and said as encouragement, "Everything is all right." I nodded and he left.

I drew the curtain farther to one side and looked up at the moon. It seemed to me that I'd never seen the moon so bright. It spoke to me in a thousand tones and I felt as if I had a home there, one I had never previously known. I became immersed in its rich silvery light. I dropped the curtain and washed myself in the tradition of the Essenes, as my parents had taught me. In my prayers, I asked God to wash away the burdens of the day, so that my body and soul might be cleansed of my experiences and prepared for the night. That way I could ascend to my heaven, in which I'd envelop myself, and wake up the next day with new strength for the tasks ahead. My mother had taught me this ritual since I was a baby. When I was very small my mother washed me, but she soon taught me to wash myself. With this feeling of protection

17

and safety, I lay down on the sleeping mat, covered myself with the warm blanket and lay awake.

I was a bit frightened at first, since everything was new and strange; in particular, the vibrations were eerie. Nevertheless, I sensed their power and I knew that my father wouldn't leave me in an unsafe place. So I ignored my fears, and gradually fell asleep. I can vaguely remember that I awoke after only a brief sleep, and for a moment did not know where I was. I realized my father was next to me. He was covered in a dark blue light, and was deep in meditation, but the incredible blue halo around him was completely new to me. His whole being seemed to radiate into his aura, appearing as a dark blue sky filled with stars. I didn't dare to speak to him. Then I heard the sound that had woken me: singing and prayers. Everywhere there was a ruby-red light. I sensed that the villagers were moving about in the night — or was it already the next morning? I really did not know. I lay quietly in my corner and sensed the movements and listened to the songs and prayers as some of the town folk moved out of the village.

Later I learned that each day, a group of the Essenes set out at four o'clock in the morning — the leaders of the devout, and those that they had chosen the previous evening, left the village in the direction of their holy grottos, chanting their prayer to God. They would remain until sunrise, combining their prayers with the Holy Light of God, which they dispatched all over the world. Only when the sun appeared above the horizon would they return. I was amazed that nobody was disturbed by the nightly journeys through the streets; in Jerusalem there would have been great protests by citizens demanding silence during the night and an end to these disturbances, but there were no such protests here. It seemed that the villagers here either were not disturbed and did not awaken, or they awoke and were in complete resonance with the devotions on the street. I sensed, yet again, all of the inhabitants, although I had seen only a very few of them so far. I felt that they were always in resonance with any new spiritual occurrence. I was carried into the ruby–colored prayer and became immersed in the experience that was so familiar to me. Finally I went back to sleep in a sitting position, and only awoke when the sun tickled my face with its beams.

My father was already up and, as I opened my eyes, he said, "Good morning, my little princess!" He laughed and was in excellent spirits, such as I'd not seen him for a long time. His happy disposition, which was powerful and contagious, radiated throughout the room; I could only respond by jumping up from the bed, happy and ready to face the day. He said, "When you have finished your ablutions, I'll collect you and then we can eat." Once again, the water was ready for me; I had not even noticed it. Later, when I had been with the Essenes for some time, I discovered their aptitude for providing things lovingly and discreetly, going unnoticed. One received their service, without hearing or sensing it, or without even perceiving who had rendered it. I loved this Essene quality right from the beginning. Outside my family, in my home village, people always enthusiastically demanded something in return once they had performed a service. The Essenes here were different. Everything they did was unconditional, and without expectation of payment, reward or other compensation. I would get to know this mentality more intimately, but my first acquaintance with this sort of friendship and love was, nevertheless, somehow familiar and moved me deeply — the unconditional giving and taking.

I completed my morning ablutions and recited my morning prayer to the sun and moon, a ritual which united their energies in me, as my mother had taught me. I sat for a while and emptied myself of all thoughts and feelings, as was our tradition at the beginning of each day. My mother had explained to me, "When you begin the day completely empty, it can be filled with marvels, since you are an empty container that has room for God's divine presence every day. But when you are filled to the brim with thoughts and feelings, there is no room for wonders. So empty yourself every morning and you will be able to experience God's grace and His miracles to the fullest." I loved it when my mother closed her eyes, withdrew into her innermost self and spoke like this. She would appear so beautiful to me, as full as the moon, without a blemish in her soul or in her aura. I remembered her words and rejoiced at the new day ahead of me.

Then my father came for me, calling "Come on, let's eat." We entered a room full of people and I held my father's hand even tighter. He comforted me saying, "You must get used to this. The Essenes traditionally eat together. Every morning you will see all the villagers here; they dedicate their meal to God and delight in the communal repast — even though the room is full. Every person here is filled with good will, since this is our home. Did you know this is my father's house? I'm so happy that I can show it to you. In Jerusalem, we have lost almost all these traditions, since they are not practiced as they are here. Here is the inheritance of my parents and grandparents. These are our origins ... yours too!"

20

Then he was silent and I sensed a deep train of thought, which he kept to himself. Silently, we approached a table, where people I had never seen were already sitting, but where two places had been kept for us. These were devout men and women, the strength of whose souls was so obvious. My father bowed to them and said, "Masters, it is an honor that you permit my daughter and I to sit at your table." The word "Masters" stuck in my memory. I had never previously heard the word, but I knew that it must signify something very important. I sensed the power of these people, although I was not at all scared. Their eyes were completely calm, powerful and radiant. I thought to myself, "Perhaps they are kings and queens, and I am permitted to sit at their table."

We sat down and I sensed them staring. Under the table, I counted the pairs of feet: it must have been seven or eight. I lowered my eyes, since I'd noticed how they were looking at me. We were served a warm porridge. I enjoyed it, just as I had on the previous day, since the meal was indeed something special — so full of living energy. I ate without looking up and my father also ate in silence.

The thoughts at the table were all perceptible to me, since they came from the heart and needed no words. I was aware of the energies which were transported backward and forward, exchanged as in a conversation and was a little disturbed by the glances of the villagers at our table — as if they were looking deep into my soul. Nobody had ever looked at me like that. At first I did not know how to protect myself, until it became clear that there was nothing intrusive or unfriendly in their intent; it was just that I had never experienced this before. Then one of the men spoke. "Your daughter has not lost her gift to completely enclose and seal her soul when she doesn't wish to be discovered. I wonder how many of her gifts she will rediscover in the course of her stay here." My father swallowed. "Of course," the man continued, "we know her origin and the potential that she brings with her." But one of the masters was not to be distracted. "It is really astonishing," he began, "that someone so young does not permit us to see into her soul. She is able to completely protect her soul." His voice was pleasant and I found his tone very agreeable.

Then suddenly all at the table began to speak, one after the other. A woman with an enchanting tone, like a bell calling the faithful to worship, spoke. "Your daughter is a bit afraid to look directly at us." My father replied somewhat guiltily, "She's not used to having so many people around her. We live fairly isolated from others. As you know, where we live, the last remnants of our tradition are disappearing, or are modified by mixing with other influences. So we live withdrawn in many ways from the community around us. My daughter isn't accustomed to being confronted by so many people at one time."

The woman with the bell–like voice spoke again. "I would love to see your wonderful eyes again. Apart from Jesus and John, I've seldom seen such a heavenly gleam in anyone's eyes." I don't know what I said, but I dared to raise my eyes and saw nothing intimidating in the twinkling green eyes of the woman. She seemed so happy and open that I got more confident. She looked straight at me with a friendly gaze, full of love. "It's good," she said, "that you're willing to respond to me, because we'll be seeing each other frequently when you come to learn with me."

I looked at my father and suspected that something had been decided without my knowledge. My father drew back within himself and said nothing. I sensed from the vibrations from his heart that he was telling me that I could trust him, but that he'd just not been able to discuss the matter with me yet. He'd discuss it with me in detail when he knew more. The woman noted the shock I had experienced in my heart. She'd obviously noticed that I could perceive the meaning behind every spoken word. The woman spoke again. "Have no fear. It will all be to your advantage." Then the villagers that my father had addressed as "Masters" stood up, bid us farewell and one of them said, "We shall meet in a new phase of the sun." My father and I remained sitting there for a while. Gradually, everyone left the hall and went about their daily work.

Then the room was empty except for my father and me. After all, we were guests. My father said, "I'd like to show you more of the village of Qumran, if you'd like." I agreed and was happy and excited. To see the village would be a great adventure. There were so many things that seemed fascinating which I did not yet understand. "But first," he continued, "I have to go to a meeting of the Council. I will have to leave you again, but today it'll be a good bit livelier."

I went to sit in the same place again, but today there was much more activity. People were constantly coming and going. The spring was an important source of water for the village, where the villagers washed their clothes and also where they gathered together before going their various ways. I observed people's movements until my father came back. As he approached, I saw he was troubled. It wasn't our habit to ask immediately what was wrong. We always knew within ourselves when the right time was to discuss delicate matters. I felt in my heart that he was mulling over something that he did not yet wish to let me know.

He gave me his hand and said, "Come with me. I've got permission to show you round Qumran. You should know that this is a great privilege. The community doesn't open its doors for many people. We are not permitted to enter the rooms where the villagers work and live, but they would like you to become familiar with the village and get to know it a little. But we have to wait just for a little while. We're honored that Mistress Sumaja herself is going to come with us to show us around." An instant later, Mistress Sumaja appeared and I ventured to look at her and perceive the light she was emitting: it was an incredible ruby–colored radiation straight from her heart, reflecting in the silver and gold in her aura.

We followed the Mistress and, despite my being so young, I was able to follow the conversation. It made a deep impression on me and I'll never forget it. We turned into a narrow alley and it occurred to me that the buildings were simple and clean. There was no dirt in the air or on the ground, as if they'd been washed by God's hand. Mistress Sumaja spoke. "Come with me. First we would like your daughter to see the places where we bring up our children." She looked at my father. "I am sure you can remember," she said. While we walked through the village, I noticed that it wasn't very large, yet had a wide–open feeling of freedom. We reached a square where she began to explain, "Here are our schoolrooms." Looking at me, she continued, "Here in Qumran, the children acquire the traditional knowledge of the Essenes, which we have carried with us for a very long time. We relay everything to our children, so that they can themselves pass our heritage on." Sadness appeared in her eyes, which puzzled me at the time.

The building had many rooms and I could sense the children within. Amongst my various impressions, I could feel the all–pervading light of the boy I had met the day before. In my heart I knew that the essence of his being flooded through all the rooms and reached all people. My attention was completely drawn to him. To avoid disturbing the lessons, we didn't enter the classrooms. The Mistress indicated that we should move on. We then came to another building, this one completely covered with signs and symbols, which fascinated me. It appeared to me that it attracted light from all directions – from Heaven and Earth. Sumaja smiled and said, "That's our library. All of our assembled knowledge is there, recorded in writing. We store it on scrolls. The signs and symbols attract living knowledge from Heaven and Earth to endow our scrolls with the divine message. Our knowledge is living, animate and dynamic. It is perpetually renewed and nourished from the font of all knowledge."

We were then permitted to enter the library. The inner room was full of shelves, in which shiny, metallic scrolls were stored. There were no windows, just oil lamps and wooden tables, at which people were working with great concentration. Sumaja looked over at my father and said, "We are trying to record in writing all our traditional knowledge, which has, up until now, been retained and passed on only verbally, according to the energy and light content. We've requested many of our scribes and monks to help us preserve our knowledge before the time comes when we can no longer do so."

25

As she explained this, it seemed for just a moment that an alien energy forced its way out of the floor, trying to permeate the room. I sensed immediately that Sumaja spread her love so that the alien energy was repelled.

"We have only a little time to conserve our copper scrolls in order that the knowledge will not be lost before we have to leave here." She cast a meaningful glance at my father, as if they both knew and shared something. Again, this puzzled me. Sumaja asked me, "Would you like to touch the scrolls?" I nodded nervously. She encouraged me, "Just put your hand out and touch them." I laid my hand on the metal rolls, and it was as if light was emitted and they spoke. Light, signs and words appeared. She smiled and said to my father, "Not many people come into the library, and, even among those who were born here, few possess the ability of your daughter to see and read the light of the divine language. She seemed satisfied and I enjoyed the game — every time I touched another scroll different signs, sounds and colors appeared above me.

Later, I would learn to understand the meaning of all matters relevant to the scrolls. In my subconscious mind, I understood when Sumaja said to my father, "We now have a method, developed by Master Metachion in distant Persia, that enables us to encode our texts. That way we can guarantee, in the event that the scrolls should ever fall into the wrong hands, that nobody will know that we have recorded our secret knowledge concerning the future of the world. But everyone who possesses the knowledge of divine light will still be able to rediscover and read our secret messages." That conversation remains fixed in my memory even today.

Sumaja went on, "I had a vision that in some distant era, when Qumran no longer exists, our Scrolls will be rediscovered. Our store of knowledge is powerful and extensive; we must be sure that it doesn't fall into the wrong hands. Should anyone indeed find the scrolls, they will just think we are just recounting our history. In fact, the secret of our Light is being locked away within them, so we can rest assured that all our most treasured secrets will be extremely well concealed for all time."

We left the library and proceeded up a hill, which afforded us a view of the sea. We looked down and I heard the Mistress sigh quietly. She looked at my father and I could sense that that she saw something in the depths of the sea which disturbed her. The light of the sea was so different from that of the village, which was bright and radiant. Although discreetly hidden, I detected the anxiety in her, and it even seemed dark and threatening to me. I began to feel quite scared. She looked at me and said to my father, "Your daughter is an exceptional person. She's even sensing the vestiges of Sodom and Gomorrah, which lie at the bottom of the sea, upon which we pray every day for peace."

She sighed again. "You should know, Zodiac, it has become a heavy responsibility, keeping these energies under control. With the unrest in the world outside and the epoch that is beginning, great disturbances are appearing under the Red Sea. They have been quiet for a long time now, but recently I have begun to sense the shocks vibrating from the depths. I'm not sure how long we can keep them under control. The effort costs us so much strength. Even when we go down into our caves every night to pray, we have the feeling that our authority and powers are disappearing. A new era is beginning."

She added, "I only hope the Messiah will come to support us, since the load is getting harder to bear every day. All our hopes rest on him now. We really don't know what to expect. So far, God has given us no sign." She was silent again, and I sensed her worries surfacing despite her efforts to maintain her divine inner tranquillity.

After a while, Sumaja regained her composure and said, "Come. It's time to return to the High Council. There's a resolution to adopt." We made our way back and it occurred to me that there were no flowers anywhere to be seen on the streets, yet there definitely was a floral aroma about. The village was indeed pleasantly scented but I did not like the look of the water I had seen. Inside myself, I felt that I didn't want to return to this place.

We then came to a building, where Sumaja said, "Let me go into the temple quickly before the Council reconvenes. I'll light the sacred lights, so that we'll have every support to take the decisions which have to be made." My father wanted to ask her something, but she had already entered the temple.

We waited outside this wonderful place. It glowed brightly with a golden light, completely in harmony with the village. I could sense the flames of divine fire that filled the room inside. Next to me, my father was absolutely still. The stillness affected me too. It had a sense of absolute emptiness, but it did not calm me at all; it was like waiting for something formless and indefinite that my imagination just could not grasp, so I leant against my father for support, and gradually my trust returned. He stroked my hair, his hand resting on my head and peace and calm flowed out of his hand. I felt secure once again. Nevertheless, I could not shake off a slight feeling that left me ill at ease.

The Mistress returned from the temple and her aura shone even stronger than before. It was as if she were clothed in flames. Her appearance was terrifying and very powerful. Still I was by no means afraid; in fact, I was spellbound by the way she came toward us, swathed, it seemed, in fire. "Come. The Council has decided that your daughter may be present during their deliberations, even young as she is."

We entered a very pleasant room with a long stone table at its center. It was simple but appeared to me very noble and, naturally, I showed great reverence. I recognized all the Masters and Mistresses I had met that morning. This time I looked more freely around at them. The first was a young man in whom a joyous fire was burning. He smiled at me and I was filled with the all the joy which his heart emitted. My gaze moved on to a slim, tall woman, whose long hair fell about her body. She had wonderful eyes and a slim face. She showed no particular qualities except for purity and a curious inaccessibility. A crystalline fire in her heart reached out to me.

Next to her was a man with a long white beard, who radiated wisdom, tranquillity and dignity. My parents had often spoken of God the Father, and it was as if God shone through this dignified man. I liked him immediately. He was so fatherly. His Aura was radiant white and I sure his long white robe began to radiate even more when I looked at him. Later, I would come to learn his name: Joseph of Arimathea. Today he had been called to the Council as an extra eighth member, to support the seven permanent members from Qumran. I couldn't take my eyes off him, since I felt so safe in his light. I was touched deeply by the sense of his benevolence.

My eyes moved on, coming to rest on the next person at the table, a slim, tall woman with dark eyes, more thoughtful, if it's possible, than those I had seen up until then. She seemed strong-willed and of a very serious nature, which impressed me. The strength and purity of her character were immediately apparent; she would, without doubt, be incorruptible. She embodied a black fire, which was different from the dark fire of the sea — and which did not disturb me here. Nevertheless, her love outshone her other qualities and tempered the fire around her. She greeted me with a generous smile. Another woman, who was small with thinning hair, did not appear quite as impressive as the others, but a gentle gold-white light radiated from her, which came to me in waves. There were two other men in the room, but they withheld their energy and didn't attempt to make contact with me.

We were invited to take our places on the stone seat. I touched the seat before I sat down, and was fascinated. It was made of stone but not at all cold, and emitted warmth and light. The discussion commenced and I conditioned myself to ignore the words and focus only on the meaning. I sensed that my father disagreed with the Council; something was unacceptable to him. I only heard the words superficially, for my inner being left the room and wandered out into the village, to one particular boy, as if his heart had called me. A golden ball of light appeared out of my body and floated through the alleyways until I had reached him. This was a sensation completely familiar to me. I longed to be there. In this globe of fire I was happy and felt completely at home. Then, just as suddenly, I had detached myself from him and was drawn back into the Council meeting. My body was noticeably present again, as if I had awakened and returned to myself.

My father stood up and said, "I cannot accept your plans unconditionally. I'm going to take my daughter back home and see how your visions for Qumran develop. I know I had given you my permission to seek knowledge of my daughter in the stars, but I cannot just agree to your plans at present; it is my duty to protect her. I don't know whether what you have suggested protects her adequately. I appeal to the Council to accept my decision as a father. In two years I will return, and we will see how matters have developed. I implore you to concern yourselves with worldly matters. I understand your anxiety and your change of heart. Please give me some time. I promise you that I'll continue to educate her in the name of our tradition, but I am still her guardian and her father. With respect, I am not completely at peace with our forefathers and am not yet willing to just hand her over to you."

It was suddenly very quiet in the Council Chamber. At this moment Mary appeared, as I had seen her yesterday. Her light had already preceded her arrival. She brought love and security into the chilled atmosphere. Her warm, soft voice spoke into the emptiness. "Zodiac, permit me to visit every now and again. You know that that I am a high priest of the White Order, as is your daughter. You cannot give her all the knowledge that she can acquire from me. So let me come, say twice a year, at the time of the high moon, so that I can start teaching her. I can't see that there is anyone else to inherit the knowledge of the White Sisters. Would you allow that?"

My father answered, "Mary, you know that I trust you. It would be an honor for my wife and for me to receive you in our home and have you stay with us while you educate our daughter." And after a moment's silence, he added, "So that is now decided!" My father regarded the members of the Council, and it seemed to me that the two reticent men, who had earlier withdrawn into themselves, darkened as if a black cloud was above them. A chill ran down my spine. The amicable unity of the five who had earlier made contact with me was in sharp contrast to the darkness of the other two; their energy seemed to divide the room. Mary intervened and said, "Come Zodiac, it's time to go." My father asked me to go outside and wait; he'd follow shortly.

When Mary and my father did emerge from the room, I saw that the boy Jesus had appeared and came toward us. He stood before us and for the first time I heard his voice, which was clear and affectionate. He said, "I know you wish to leave, and I would like to come with you to the gate with my mother." A great joy surged through me, since I liked him better than any of the others we had met there. Every time I looked at him, my heart raced and I was overwhelmed with joy. My father answered, "We'll need just a few minutes to pack our things." I then watched as he purposefully strode ahead to kneel before the boy and continued, "Permit me, Lord, to prostrate myself before you. It would be a great blessing for me."

Jesus remained standing, as if unaffected by my father's words. Young as he was, he exuded dignity. He simply accepted my father's love, as he first knelt then lowered his head before Jesus' feet and, for a moment, was freed from time and space. I observed all this and withdrew into myself, since I was unable to do anything but gaze blissfully at Jesus. My father got to his feet and I watched Mary, who just continued to smile. My father then recovered himself and said briskly, "Right. Let's collect our things. Come on." We went back to the room where we had slept, retrieved our belongings and then we walked along the streets to the gate through which we had entered. Jesus and Mary were waiting for us. Jesus looked at me and for the first time addressed his words to me. "I will be very happy when you return." I wondered how he knew that I would return.

Mary turned to my father and said, "In the two holy full moons this year, I shall come to stay with you for three days, if I may." My father bowed and indicated with a gesture that I should do the same, so I folded my hands and bowed too. Then Mary leant down and wrapped her arms around me, after which Jesus did the same. A blissful happiness spread through my body and my heart jumped. Then they bade us goodbye with the words, "May your ways be filled with joy and may you be warmly welcomed in Jerusalem." As they spoke, Sumaja appeared out of an alley, accompanied by a man with a loaded donkey. She approached and said, "You should not return without accompaniment and should avoid joining any of the Bedouin tribes. This is Jahor. I'm giving him to you as a guide. You will find he is a loyal attendant. He knows the way to Jerusalem and where the oases are. The provisions should be sufficient for your voyage home. I feel better knowing that he's going to be with you for the journey."

Our guide was different from the Essenes, most of whom have light skins. He had very dark skin, dark eyes and dark hair with black curls. He was obviously from another tribe, probably another race, but he had dignity and radiated a protective strength of character. I felt secure with Jahor as our guide for the journey. After all that I had experienced in Qumran, I didn't really want to be exposed to the disturbing energies of other travellers on the way home.

And so our journey home began. Father and I walked for many hours in silence, side by side, and he asked me more than once whether I would like to ride on the donkey. I shook my head and told him it did me good to walk, and I really wanted to carry on like that. Later, my father told me that he was astonished that I kept walking, uphill and downhill, despite my being so young. I was always a very boisterous child, always ready for any new activities. I knew he was very proud of me. We walked the whole day, into the evening sun which encompassed us in its rays. The route just seemed to flow by, under our feet. Our guide strode ahead of us silently. His incredible strength encouraged us to continue. Eventually we stopped at a water source, and he informed us that we would spend the night here. He unpacked the blankets and gave us food. Then he withdrew some distance from us and prayed, kneeling in the sand.

For some time my father and I were silent, until I asked him, "Father, who was that boy?" He paused before answering: "He is the Messiah, my daughter." "Messiah?" I asked. My father continued, "Our people have prophesied for a long time the coming of the Messiah; it's in visions and in our writings. Our responsibility to prepare the way for him is part of our heritage. He carries the Kingdom of God in his heart. We have been promised his arrival for such a very long time. Now he is really here!" I saw tears rolling down my father's cheeks. "You don't know how much hope he has given us, and will give us in the future. We have waited so long." "Father, he is so different. He is so full of light and love." "That's how it is when God comes to us and lets us see His face," replied my father. "By the grace of your ancestors, you have been permitted to see Him. You yourself are a present from God too, and I am so thankful that you have come to us."

We both went to sleep that night without another word. The next day, we continued our on our way. It was a quiet journey for several days, during which we did not speak much to one another. Finally we reached the gates of Jerusalem, after which our guide bade us goodbye. My father thanked him and gave him a gold piece from his purse, as is our tradition, and said, "God bless you." Whenever my father gave someone money he blessed it and a wonderful light flowed out of his heart. Our guide acknowledged the thanks without a word, but with reverence and respect, and made his way back the way we had come. I wondered where he would go; would he return home or go to another place? But we did not discuss this.

We returned to our home and I noted at once the wrinkles returning to my father's brow. One of our servants came straight out to us and said, "Thank God that you're back. The mistress, your wife, Magda, Sir, took ill while you were away. Please, I think you should come and see her straight away." For a chill moment my heart stood still and I found I could hardly breathe. The whole word seemed to be spinning around me. I began to suspect something very serious. My father said, "Go and find your brother. I'm going to visit your mother." I went to my bedroom and crouched on the floor. I was so very afraid and I shook all over, waiting until my father said I could see my mother. The day was unusually dark and gloomy, and the servant lit the oil lamps very early. Eventually my father came and said, "Your mother would like to see you." Shaking again and with a trembling heart, I went to her.

My mother was not in her bed but lay on her straw–filled mattress which been raised up on a couple of benches on the rooftop so she could catch the evening breeze. She lay completely surrounded by a wonderful light. She was very pale and her cheeks were white, unlike the healthy rosy cheeks I was used to. She said, "Come to me." She gave me her hand and stroked my head. "My little princess! I don't know why the Lord has chosen it so. Now that you have been recognized, I have to go ... You ascend and I descend! I cannot follow the thoughts of the Lord, but I will follow His call. I'll always be with you, wherever you are. But I don't think I'll be in this body much longer."

I couldn't understand what she was saying, but still I wept uncontrollably. The world around me disappeared. I was in deep despair, since I sensed that this wonderful light of my mother was gradually moving away and even her voice was fading. I sensed my father behind me, holding my brother's hand, and I could feel how their hearts were just growing so heavy. A great sadness crept into the room. I just wanted to follow the light and go with my mother. Then I heard her voice, firm and resolute. "No, little one. Where I am going, you cannot come. My way now is through the stars, and no living thing can get there. You must go on learning and trying your best to understand life. You have a purpose in this world and I want you to throw yourself into it completely. I'm going to be looking down on you from the starry home of our ancestors. I'll always be watching over you and I'll never, ever leave you alone, I promise. But now you're going to have to let me go. You know if you don't let me go, I'll remain here and I'll never get on my great adventure through the stars, baby ... "

I understood every word she said. Because I trusted her so completely, I decided I had to let her go. Then she was gone. Her hand gradually cooled and the essence of her being slowly ebbed out of her body until she was lifeless. Her body was empty. Nothing that I knew lived in it. It was just a shell. My father crouched over her body and wept pitifully. I could read some of the words in his heart: "Why have you left me so soon? How will I look after the children without you?" I know too, that there were also unspoken thoughts between a man and his wife. A female servant came to lead me away. My father said, "Take her to the bedroom and look after her. I can't deal with them right now. I need to get over this, to grieve." The servant took my brother with her too. I could feel him shaking. I went to my room.

As I went in, a most wonderful golden light met me. I felt that our servant, who had known me all my life, was unable to sense it; she walked through the light, but I could tell she just didn't see it. But I could see it. It became more and more distinct, more beautiful, warmer and it was taking hold of me, transporting me with it. I unrolled my bed and sat right in the middle of it and let the light permeate into my inner being and console me. Suddenly the image of my mother was with me, but she was only light, bright and radiant. Her image said, "Everything is in order. Trust me. Life is full of gifts even though we do not comprehend them. When you understand this, we will always be together. With my eyes I will accompany you on your way." Then the image faded away but in the comfort and tranquillity of her message, I was able to sleep.

The following years went by as in a dream. I can't say I was unchanged, but in my home changes always occurred only gradually and almost imperceptibly. My father withdrew into his own world and my brother went to a boarding school of the Old Jews, an old tradition each learned, eastern mystic of the Magi of lore would have gone through. I lived from day to day, relatively emotionless. Over the next couple of years, the only stimulating times were when Mary visited us twice annually for three days. During this short time, I lost my apathy and enjoyed life again. In those few days she swathed me in her light, which flowed continuously to me. New information came to me without effort, as if by accident. My father was happy to give me over into her care on these days. Nevertheless, the pain deep in my heart at the loss of my mother remained.

So Mary taught me, and my father had also appointed an elderly teacher for me. He taught me to read and write and instructed me in foreign languages. I learned Greek and Roman. When the teacher spoke to my father, he told him what a teachable child I was; never had he known a pupil who was able to learn writing and languages so rapidly. Father was always enthusiastic whenever I learned something of my own accord without his having to teach me. At five years old, I could read. I absorbed all the writings he gave me eagerly: stories from far-off countries, information on foreign peoples. But I came to notice that, whenever a book from our Jewish people came into my hands, he would quietly remove it. It was as if my own father did not want me to read it. I felt there was something that he just could not be reconciled with. I never spoke to him about it, since I sensed that it probably wasn't a good idea. I loved him as ever, although he was never the same after my mother died. The world of literature and scripts was now my world, until the day when Mary appeared unexpectedly and astonished my father.

When I saw that Mary had arrived that fateful day, I ran to her, hugged her and she held me in her arms. She received me with her characteristic love and benevolence, and stroked my head and ran her fingers through my dark, curly hair. I was so happy to see her again. Although we hadn't met often, I had come to regard her as a kind of a mother figure. Carefully and gently she said to me, "Leave us alone for a moment. I have to speak to your father." They withdrew to discuss some matter alone, but my curiosity was so great that I hid myself and listened in on their conversation.

Mary said to my father, "Zodiac, the time's come when I have to take your daughter with me. You yourself have witnessed all the tension and the disturbances. Essenes won't be able to live much longer in this community. Two of the Masters have already left Qumran, and now there's a counter–movement. Everything's beginning to disintegrate and Jesus is going to have to travel with his uncle, Joseph of Arimathea, soon, so he can complete his education abroad. I'm begging you, please let me become her guardian and take her with me. We can still get to Qumran safely and stay there for a while. If we wait too long, it may become difficult for me to pass on any knowledge to her. The Essenes are requesting that you permit her to learn what she'll need on her way. We sense danger, and there are so many signs confirming it that we're sure that at some point soon we're all going to be dispersed over a large area, our communities scattered."

My father stood with his back to her. Her request had been truly heartfelt, yet my father remained still. I sensed him becoming even more severe and melancholy than usual. His feelings were in complete turmoil. Even so, I hoped that he would agree to what Mary wanted, since I would have loved to go with her. The house that my mother left behind had changed and I just couldn't bear to stay there any longer. After a long pause, my father finally replied, "You know, Mary, that I have allied myself with the Zealots. Our people are tearing themselves apart. The king of the Jews rules us and he's just stopped being a friend to us. He doesn't protect the old Essene traditions anymore; worse, he's trying to destroy our world. This destruction has to stop and I've decided to join the fight. So, all in all, I think it would be better if you did take her with you. There's going to be turmoil here in Jerusalem. At least this way I can champion our cause without worrying about my children, especially if it's going to end up costing me my life."

I was shocked. I had absolutely no idea what my father's intentions were, and I was suddenly afraid that this might be the last time I would see him. As I would learn later, my fears were not unfounded! It was my fate it seemed, to become an orphan at an early age. Completely composed, Father asked me, "When would you like to like to leave with Mary?" Mary answered for me, "Let me stay here one night; tomorrow someone will come and fetch us and bring us safely to Qumran." My father said, "Please ... you are my guest. I'm going to have a meal prepared for us. I know you and I don't always see eye to eye, but I'm sure you know how much I value your friendship. Whatever happens, I know in my heart your understanding and your goodwill. Let's make this last evening a sacred time for all of us." That evening, we ate together and my father had my older brother join us. I loved my brother, but we had over the past years become almost strangers. I regarded him thoughtfully during the meal, which I could tell he sensed. For the first time in years, though, a festive atmosphere reigned over our house. It would be the last time that I would be with my family.

We left home next morning, and I bade my father farewell. As I hugged my brother, who now seemed somewhat dejected, he put something in my hand. I didn't look at what he'd given me, but put it straight into my pocket. I wanted to cry, but somehow I was unable to. Mary saw me and said softly, "You are such a brave girl. You know so much and carry it with such love. I promise I'll look after you as well as and for as long as I can. But, you know, God always has His eye on you and will look after you. You really don't have to worry." After I hugged my father for the last time, a wonderful green–golden light flowed out from his heart and enveloped my brother and me. Then Mary decided it was time to go. On that day, I left the house of my ancestors, and it was only very much later in my life that I was to see it again.

Our guide, Jahor, whom I already knew, was awaiting us, and I was happy to see him again; I had always felt safe in his company. Mary said we really should go quickly, fearing that there could be all sorts of problems on the way. "It would be better," she explained, "if we took a relatively unknown route. We don't want to be at the mercy of vagabonds or criminals." With this in mind, we set out. Jahor had brought two donkeys this time, one for me and one for Mary. I was now quite a bit older than I had been on my last journey with him, and had a better sense of time. I could feel more clearly how the day progressed and the position of the sun in the sky. I estimated that it was about midday when we stopped for the first time. Jahor came to us and suggested that we should stop overnight in a friendly village, as he had heard that gangs of thieves preferred to attack travelers at night. So it was decided we would travel by only by day and seek safe haven at night.

We arrived at a house where Mary knew someone, and we were made most welcome. She looked at me and said, "There are Essenes living here too, friends of my husband Joseph, whom you have not yet met. In this house I think we will enjoy a comfortable evening. You and I can spend a bit more time together this evening." I later learned that the Essenes were scattered throughout the whole country. They formed an enormous network of trustworthy friends over the whole of Israel. At such places we would always find a haven with Essenes, even when they didn't even know us. As is the way with our tradition, we were always treated as a member of the family. Our hosts let us have a large, pleasant room, and then the family withdrew and left us alone. We were treated most respectfully. It was a cool evening, and they allowed us to light a fire and brought us warm drinks.

Then Mary asked me to excuse her for her prayers and her daily ritual. I observed her quietly, which did not appear to disturb her. My capacity for perceiving light had waned somewhat, but I still sensed that inwardly she was consumed by her light ceremony and, around her, white light radiated between Heaven and Earth. Her seemingly simple meditation was spiritually transformed by her energy and her pure, clear light. Afterwards she just sunk into silence. When she opened her eyes again, she moved next to me and stoked the fire with more wood. Without any preamble, she began to speak straight out of her innermost self. "You are so grown up inside now, so I know you're going to understand everything I'm about to reveal to you. I also know that you will keep what I tell you to yourself. Deep within you, you carry a shrine in which you safeguard the sacred chronicles. I want to tell you my story now, which you will one day pass on — when the truth has been forgotten, distorted or refuted." Then she began to recount the story of her life. Her narration is still crystal clear in my mindand I will never forget it. I still carry embedded in my memory every word, even today.

She began, "I was born in a village called Nazareth, and in many ways I was much like you. My parents were relatively wealthy and we enjoyed a very comfortable life. Back then we knew nothing of the Essenes, since we were descended from the oldest Jewish tradition, which could be traced right back to our prophet Abraham. That is my origin and that of my family and of my ancestors. We lived obediently observing that tradition.

"One day, when I was about as old as you are, we went to the temple in old Jerusalem. I remember that there was a wonderful light in this temple. My family and I had always made the long journey to visit the temple for our sacred Passover festival.

43

My father called Passover "the sacred days of our tradition," and we celebrated together in Jerusalem. While we were there, my father would always visit Jochebed, one of the high priests. This visit, though, when the high priest saw me, he looked at me and said to my father, "Your daughter is destined for a very important task on this Earth. She is a being of pure light. A masterful soul resides in her, such as I have seldom experienced. It is time to bring her to the school for priestesses, which guards the ancient traditional knowledge of the White Order of Female Conception. Please permit her to begin her education there, to be trained in the sacred knowledge of women."

"I, too, had to leave my parents. I was taken to the part of the temple where pure 'white women,' priestesses in the tradition of the Sacred White Light of Creation, were educated. Following the recommendation of Jochebed, I received intensive training right from the beginning. I was ordained as High Priestess, in the way that the Egyptian Isis had her priestesses. I received the name Mary.

"I was seventeen when Jochebed came to me and said 'Mary, your destiny is not for you to remain a priestess in this temple. From our knowledge of the annals of the stars, we have investigated your destiny, and I have asked God what will be your future. It is not planned for you to remain here as a virgin priestess. Within three phase–changes of the moon, a friend of the Essenes, a man I know well, will come here for you. He will take you to be married to an Essene from the House of David, who has been chosen for you. It is your destiny to ally the ancient line of Abraham to the tradition of the Essenes. You will be able to retain your own traditions and simultaneously to unify your knowledge with that of the Essenes.'"

Mary continued her narration with the story that Jochebed had told her of the Essenes. "This is a very old country. We were a divine people and we were permitted to receive God's greatest prophet on this sacred ground. God has imprinted the very tracks of His divine knowledge upon this land, tracks that are traceable all the way through the ancient prophets back to Abraham. In so doing, God had simultaneously planted seeds from which a great teacher, the Master of the Fire, would appear in this country. He prepared the way for the birth of Essene culture. The Essenes' knowledge derived from the stars and never depended on the development of our culture. Nevertheless, we always lived in divine accordance and in harmony with them. We continued to preserve our old distinct Abramaic culture handed down from the ancient Jewish people. Although our traditions never mixed with one another, we always had a cordial and friendly relationship to the Essenes. Both of us knew in our hearts that we serve the same God, albeit in different ways.

"For the first time, there will be a connecting link between the two peoples. God has chosen you to unite the ancient Abramaic tradition of our ancestors with those of the Essenes by marrying an Essene. You have been chosen to bear a child sent by God, and this child will fulfill His prophesies. The stars have shown this to me. You will teach your child the old ways and the traditions of Abraham and your husband will teach him the ways of the Essenes. By the grace of God and this child, the two peoples will be united and reconciled once again in the future."

Mary paused, and then continued. "After that, my fate was certain. Like you, I did not know what God had in store for me and which path my life would take; in my heart, though, I was sure that I would serve God. So I waited in the temple in Jerusalem until the day when I would travel to Qumran to meet my future husband. My uncle Joseph of Arimathea brought me personally to Qumran and introduced me there. He was by then an Essene, but he had grown up in the tradition of Abraham. Our marriage had already been arranged when I saw my future husband, also named Joseph, for the first time. I knew that he was a friendly and modest man who earned his living as a carpenter. He followed the rituals and traditions of the Essenes, about which I still had to learn. On the day I arrived, not wanting to overwhelm me, Joseph had tactfully withdrawn from the area. My uncle then brought me to another place outside Qumran."

Mary told me that, in Qumran, it is the Essene tradition for the inhabitants to live chaste, ascetic lives. Marriage was permitted but preparations were made outside Qumran, with one retreat for the women and a separate retreat for the men. Here each partner was separately prepared for marriage.

"I remained for some time with the other women there, and then we returned to Qumran for the subsequent rituals. Outside Qumran, where we were being prepared for the obligations of Essene marriage, we lived differently. When I came to the Essenes, an elderly mistress received me. Her name was Miriam. She had trained successive generations of new masters. It was a tradition that there were a total of seven masters incarnated at any one time."

"My first days with the Essenes were spent with Miriam. She introduced me to the history and traditions of the Essenes. It was as if she wanted me to preserve their inheritance. She told me that that the Essenes had been founded by the Master of the Fire, a teacher from the higher worlds, who constantly brings new schools of learning to this world. Miriam said that in India he is known as Agni and is eternally present in the universe as Master of the Light, of Knowledge and Guardian of All Worlds. His brother is Jesus, the second father of our school of learning and tradition, whose arrival the Essenes await and who is known as Jesus Emmanuel. He embodies the Light of Christ that pervades the whole universe. He manifests the infinite love of God. There are twenty–one Masters who carry the Light of Christ that illuminates and guards the universe. They are the forefathers of the Essenes."

Mary went on, "Miriam explained that long ago Agni had initiated our Masters to prepare the Earth to receive the Light of the Anointed One." (The Christ as the Greeks have come to call him.) "He provided the original fire, which originates from him. Jesus has initiated the Light of Christ in us, to keep and cultivate on the Earth in the tradition of the Essenes. We are the light of reconciliation. Agni has shown us where we should sow the seeds of our culture on this Earth, so that one day it will spread over the whole world. This town is still located at the nucleus of Agni's original fire. Here we guard the wisdom of our tradition. For hundreds of years, the twenty–one Masters have alternated time in this world, so that seven are always incarnate on the Earth. I am on my way back to my world," Mary recounted. "Miriam went on to explain that the seven masters who will prepare the way for the Messiah's arrival were already here and that she was schooling them. Miriam said to me, "I bequeath unto you everything that my ancestors have taught me."

Mary paused, and said, "Miriam looked deep into my eyes and told me, 'You have been chosen to bring the Son of God into this world. You are the anointed, whom God has chosen. You are a Mistress of the White Light, pure and untainted. Nothing has been written in your future beyond your destiny of bringing the Son of God, the Messiah, the Lord of Forgiveness to this Earth.'" Mary paused for a moment. I looked at her and her light was wonderful to behold: white, dazzling and full of purity, hovering and unchangeable. For me Mary was always very beautiful, but never more so than now.

"Miriam explained to me," said Mary, taking up the narrative again, "that there was nothing else for me to learn and that I should withdraw to the company of the wise women, where I could prepare myself for the sacrament of marriage. In the meantime, my future husband, Joseph, had also retired to the place where the grooms were being prepared for marriage. She intimated that as a high priestess, I should retain my tradition and my rituals, but that she would be happy if I would also participate in the rituals of the Essenes. She said, 'If you wish we can take you to our sacred underground rooms, to which nobody else has access.'

"I nodded my agreement and said I was willing to do anything to fulfill the task which God had set for me. Then Miriam said, 'Every morning at four o'clock it is our tradition to retire to the underground rooms to meet. Come with us tomorrow morning. We meet in front of the temple. There we light our sacred fire, which we dedicate to Agni, and then we walk together to the underground rooms, chanting, until we reach the Ruby Room, which contains the Light of the Christ.' I retired that night to my room outside Qumran. It was all arranged and furnished lovingly, and I was treated like a queen. I had servants who looked after me and my room, and gave me anything I needed.

"That night I didn't sleep at all — not one bit. Pictures, images all flowed through my soul, and I asked myself time and time again why God had chosen me for this task. I prayed to my God, whom I knew so well, and resolved once more that whatever He should place in my hands, I would accept as His servant. In the morning, I went into the town and was impressed how the people of this Essene community were attuned to one another. When I came to the gates of the town, they opened as if by an unseen hand. I was admitted without words. The townsfolk moved in silence, but were clearly attuned to each others' minds. I went to the temple where I saw the fire lit. It burned brightly and I had the feeling of coming home. The lights of all worlds were united in this ceremony. I followed the villagers silently, listening to their chants, down the steps into the underground rooms. Here they opened a door and we descended a flight of steps until we came to a room, radiant with ruby-colored light reaching into the Earth. As the Masters knelt, I saw them all for the first time. Including Miriam, they were eight in number. They began their prayers and I joined them. We were immersed in the Light of Christ and became united as one. Our prayers melted into one another and permeated all universes, until the universal tongues of flame of the Light of Christ appeared and, eventually, I sensed it for the first time within me.

"At this moment, a glowing being emerged from the flames and approached me. It was he whose coming had been

49

prophesied. Jesus, as he was called, said 'You are appointed to be my mother on Earth. I will prepare myself to leave the eternal light by my Father's side, with which I am united, to come to the Earth. All the preparations you have made during your many lives are now complete. Do not worry. Everything will come to pass as God has planned. Just be ready for the events as they occur.' "It seemed to me as if that night flew by in just a moment," said Mary. "I did not even notice the sunrise, which the Essene Masters sense even under the earth, enabling them to return to the surface when the sun rises. When I returned to the daylight, it was as though I had come back to another world, leaving the eternity of the all–embracing love which had flowed through me underground."

With barely a pause, Mary continued her recollections. "I remained for some time with the Essenes, and every morning I descended with them into the underground room and was allowed to take part in their rituals. I had received no idea when I should see Joseph again.

"One day Miriam called me to her; she was lying on her daybed. She did not appear to be ill, but I sensed that she was preparing to leave her body. She looked at me steadily. Her eyes were shining and from them an unending love flowed; I could tell they were already seeing another world. She said very quietly, 'Mary, my task here is now complete. Now that I am leaving this Earth, I can see everything that will come to be, and our community has a difficult and dangerous path before it. He who is coming to save us will bring our community destruction. Nevertheless, it is a great blessing for us to be permitted just to prepare for the event. I just wanted to say farewell, since I will not return to this Earth for a long time.

I shall return to my world and ascend to the boundless Love of Christ, whose flame I will guard until I return. Then the seeds we have planted will come to fruition, and I will return to continue my task on Earth. Now I must leave you. I am so happy that we have met here. Farewell!'

She closed her eyes and asked her helpers to come to her. 'Call the Masters,' Miriam said in a quiet, calm voice, 'I wish to receive my last anointment so that I can depart from this life. You should stay here too, Mary.' Then holy oils with wonderful scents were brought. Although her body was very weak, she was able to sit up, whereupon the seven Masters entered silently. Miriam mixed the oils and applied them in silence, as she transferred her knowledge to the Essenes kneeling there in silence. Miriam radiated once more in her Light of Christ, one moment fully conscious and the next simply gone. I felt a great reverence for her."

Mary became very reflective. "Miriam looked somehow unreal. Light flowed through her body, but it was not from this world. I could see how she left her body, without suffering, regret or any feeling at all. The Essenes left the room and I saw for the first time how they tend to their dead. They had given no prayers and no mourning chants, as in our tradition. They simply took the body outside the gates of the city and burned it without ceremony. The ashes were mixed with the earth. All this took place in complete silence, as if it were of no great significance.

"When I met the Masters over the following days, I saw no sadness in their eyes — only joy. Nobody mentioned Miriam's departure. They knew no separation. I had little other contact with the Essenes or the other Masters. And I still had no idea what the plans for my future were."

"One day, my uncle, Joseph of Arimathea returned and said, 'When the sun is in the zenith at the winter festival, it will be time for your marriage. Until then there are three half–moon phases. During this time you should become acquainted with your future husband and spend time with him. Will you permit me to marry you in our tradition? Our ancient Jewish rituals and those of the Essenes will be combined in harmony, to unify our peoples. Will you agree to this?' I nodded my agreement, since I knew that it was right.

"And although I had only seen my future husband once I already felt a great love for him. I was extremely happy to be able to see him again. My uncle said, 'I don't think it wise for you to meet in Qumran. Perhaps it would be better for you to return to Nazareth now, and Joseph may visit you so you can become better acquainted with one another.' I agreed and then returned to the town to bid farewell to the Essenes. This time I met the seven Masters, who received me with great friendliness. They were fully informed of my plans. They said, 'Come to us ten days before your wedding, so that we can consecrate your sacred marriage with our divine rituals for seven days and nights. Heaven and Earth shall bless your union.'

"I left Qumran and returned to my parents with my uncle, Joseph. It was a very happy reunion. I was pleased that I could make all the preparations to become a bride in my parents' home, before I left with my husband to start my own family. We had a wonderful time together. I met many of my old friends and acquaintances, but I spent most of my time with my mother. It was as though she had transferred the instinct, the essence, of being a married woman and mother directly to me. My father treated me with great respect. I was no longer his daughter, but a high priestess that he respected. But the deep trust and love which we shared for one another remained."

Still Mary continued with her tale. "One day, my father came to me and explained that Joseph wished to make his official visit, as is our tradition: he would spend an evening with my father, to obtain his permission to marry me. We women were excluded from such meetings, and I couldn't bear having to stay in my room — knowing Joseph was in our house but that I was not permitted to see him before the formal agreement had been made. Later that evening, my father told me that he was proud that his daughter would be marrying a descendent of the House of David, and that Joseph was a fine and honest man for me. He told me that Joseph would come again later at some point, so we could meet. My parents were pretty open-minded, unlike many around us. My father's words were so kind and went straight to my heart and I was able to sleep well that night.

"My parents allowed me to meet Joseph alone on his next visit, so I had the opportunity to get to know him a little. He asked me if I would like to take a stroll with him. We walked around for a bit and then sat under a tree so we could talk more and deepen our acquaintance. He related in his quiet, warm way that he had taken over the carpentry trade from his father. I wasn't to worry about our material future, since his business was doing very well. He had been completely initiated as an Essene and his most devout prayer was for our future. I felt very secure with him and knew that we would be happy together. We didn't discuss the divine assignment we had received, which would later determine our destiny. It was clear to me that the Essene masters had also instructed him about our future, but we just didn't give the matter a thought at that time. We just wanted to get to know and trust one another. He did not rush into anything but was always thoughtful. I could sense his respect for me, and the love in his heart found its expression in his eyes when he looked at me. From that day on my parents permitted us to spend many days together, in which we took long walks and had plenty of time just for one another. On a few occasions he stayed with us for a meal. The love between us grew and was strengthened by the trust we shared and the knowledge that something wonderful would be born between us.

One evening I sat musing under the stars in a quiet corner in front of our house, which I had always loved in my childhood. Suddenly I was torn out of this world: the heavens shook and the stars above me started to move and melt into one another. Everything in the heavens was in motion and suddenly a brilliant light appeared in front of me. From a sea of flames an enormous, white angel appeared and his voice resonated as if it were God's own voice: 'Greetings unto you, Mary. I am Gabriel: I am a messenger of light from the Lord Himself, who has sent me to you. I have come to announce joyful news of what will soon come to be fulfilled. The Lord's own Son has been given into your charge, and all has already been set in motion. Blessed are you, Mary, anointed one, the Lord is with you in body and spirit. I will accompany you, in His Name, since you are in His protection and care. Nothing can harm you, even though worlds are in turbulence. The forces of darkness are gathering to repudiate and to combat that which will come to the Earth through you. I shall accompany the Lord through whatever comes to pass until he arrives at his home in your womb, to be born here. Be assured, nothing will happen to you, though this is a time of persecution and danger. I shall always be with you and will protect you from all adversity.'

"His brilliant light illuminated and enveloped our whole house, so much so that I was afraid that my parents might be awakened. But they too were shrouded in the light of Gabriel, and noticed nothing. I was, as you can imagine, completely unable to sleep. I prayed and meditated until the next morning. God was with me and filled me completely with the light of His love. I expected nothing. I was absolutely empty, prepared and waiting to receive that with which God had entrusted me."

I was very attentive as Mary continued. "Next morning, something very curious happened. Elizabeth, my mother's sister, arrived in a rush to talk to my mother and me. She was deeply disturbed and excited, and said, 'I must tell you what the Lord has communicated to me through the Angel Gabriel.' I listened carefully", said Mary. "Elizabeth had had the same experience as I, although she was quite elderly. The Angel of the Lord appeared to her and to her husband, Zachariah, who served in the temple of Jerusalem, and announced the imminent birth of a son. This angel had said, 'Greetings unto you, Elizabeth. The Lord wishes to tell you, through me, of astonishing news. Blessed are you. You and your husband will have a son, which is His own and will be the reincarnation of the ancient Prophet Elias. He will prepare the way for the Saviour, who will be born unto the daughter of your sister. Keep to your daily prayers and trust the Lord, and your child will be blessed and you will too. The prophesies from ancient times will find their fulfillment through you. I, Gabriel, will always be present. All my Angels will protect you and accompany you through all circumstances. The wonders of the Lord find their form in you. Greetings unto you and blessings for all time.

"Elizabeth finished her story," Mary explained, "and although her husband had had the same experience, she was unable to believe it. She was so old that she should not have been able to bear a child. I took her hand in mine and said, 'Believe it, Elizabeth. It is true. The Angel was also with me, to deliver the same message. Let us pray together. What God wishes us to bear needs trust and protection. Let us retire to silent prayer and meditation, until God's will is fulfilled, as He has planned, and His gifts to the Earth are here.' I sensed that she had become calmer and accepted what had happened and believed it. She then returned home and, three weeks later, she sent us the message that the wonder had in fact occurred. She was with child, and the Angel had already given him a name: John, who was to be born before my son, with all his fire.

"Up until this time, Joseph and I had not discussed the blessing which the Lord had bestowed on us. But now that Elizabeth was pregnant, I took it upon myself to discuss it with him. Joseph also knew that a child was planned for us. He was modest and brave and said, 'I do not know if we will able to fulfill the Lord's expectations, but I trust in God that He will lead us and show us how to obey His word.' The day finally arrived when we were to travel to the Essene community, to complete the ten days of preparation for our marriage. My parents remained at home, accepting that parents were not present at Essene marriage ceremonies. In Qumran, marriage was entered into without any bonds except for those of the husband and wife. There were no family bonds. There were no commitments involved, except for those of the new marriage.

"Upon our departure, my parents gave me a traditional gift from the family: a chest containing the family jewelry from my mother and from her mother, passed on to me as the new generation. My mother Very emotionless." My father treated us with great respect and Joseph gave him a sack full of shekels, according to the old Jewish tradition. In this way, the parents were repaid for supporting and educating their daughter up until her marriage.

"We travelled together to Qumran, and when we arrived, went to our rooms outside the town. After three days in our quarters, the seven days and nights commenced, in which the Essene masters accompanied us in the rituals to release us from worldly connections and to purify and anoint ourselves, to permit us to enter into holy matrimony. Then came the day on which our simple wedding ceremony took place — a silent communion with the Holy Spirit, who appeared above us in flames and bound us together in marriage. This was the first time that my new husband brought me to his house, since it was tradition that a new wife should never see her future home until she is married.

We arrived at his house and I felt at home from the very first moment. This was to be our refuge, a haven in which we would share our lives. Joseph had created and arranged our new home with love and care. It was clean and simple, but was large enough to allow each of us enough space, enabling mutual trust to grow. Some months later, I received the message that

Elizabeth had given birth to a healthy son, and I also found myself pregnant. It was a quiet time in my life, and I was aware of the constant presence of the Angel Gabriel, and everything around us was tranquil and protected by him."

At this point Mary stopped and said, "It is very late. We should retire for the night so that we will be fit for our journey tomorrow." We both completed our Essene ritual washing and Mary helped me to bed, just as my mother used to do, which gave me great pleasure; it had been a long time since I had experienced this sense of care and protection. It was a peaceful night for me, such as I had not had for a long time. The next morning, Mary awakened me and we prepared to continue our travels. Our guides were waiting for us and it seemed that we were taking less–traveled ways on our journey. I was impatient to find a time when Mary could continue her narration, which had completely occupied my thoughts. I was bewitched and the story gave me peace and hope. That day we traveled until well into the night: the sun had disappeared beyond the horizon and the moon and stars illuminated our way as we arrived in Qumran.

We were admitted to the town and Mary said, "Tonight you may sleep at my home and tomorrow we will see where you will be staying. I will look after you and make sure that you have your own room, and do not end up living in the children's communal bedroom. I would like you to find a new home here." Exhausted, I fell asleep immediately, aware of the familiar lights in Qumran. I must have slept a long time, since Mary was no longer in the room when I woke up. I inspected the room carefully: it was simple, bright and calm, filled with loving light and the feeling of the presence of peace.

The next days were mainly spent waiting. Mary came to get me for meals, but it seemed that I had to be patient until my future had been decided. Mary did not speak to me much and it was not permitted for me to go out alone on to the streets, so I had plenty of time to find my own inner peace and tranquility.

Then, one day, Jesus suddenly appeared at my door and asked me if I would like to take a walk outside the town. It was the first time I had seen him on this visit, and I was overjoyed. For him, there were no barriers, wherever he went. I followed him virtually without a word. As we left the gates of Qumran, we didn't meet anyone, and no one appeared to try and stop us. We walked together for a time until Jesus said, "Come and sit down next to me." He looked into the expanse of the desert, and for the first time I noticed that fig trees and palms were blooming around the town. I saw that the fields were being farmed, to provide food for the inhabitants. This would change later. Around Qumran everything was cultivated and green, sustained by the efforts of the Essenes. From high ground, though, I was able to see further into the desert, where the land was dried out and lifeless. Jesus must have read my thoughts, as he said, "Through their love and effort, the Essenes can create new conditions that are not native to the area. Look at the desert out there. It is parched and dry. Essenes have used their ancient store of knowledge to create fertility wherever they wish. Come with me, and I will show you."

He continued to explain, "Whatever happens elsewhere, the Essenes' fruit always grow and ripen to provide us with food — the wonder of their love and devotion." Then he asked.

"Should we stay here for a while?" I was thirsty and he noticed it without my saying a word, asking, "Would you like some water?" Before I could answer, he used his hand to reveal an underground spring and, digging it out a bit, said, "You can drink here. The resources of the Earth are unlimited: You just need to know where to find them."

I collected water in my hands as it bubbled out of the earth. It was the most delicious water I had ever tasted — like honey, blossom, earth and the wine that I had smelled in my parents' house. It quenched my thirst in such a wonderful way. When I had finished, the running water stopped and the earth closed over the source. Jesus smiled and said, "The world is full of wonders, and I am here to awaken them, to bring them to life." He was quiet for a moment and then asked, "Do you know, I have been here in Qumran for some time? The Essenes have communicated all their knowledge to me, but soon I am leaving to travel to foreign lands. I am very happy that you came and that I could see you before I leave, since I will be away for a long time. You should know that you belong to those who will accompany me on my way."

I did not really understand everything he said, but then he added, "I would like you to use your time in Qumran to learn from the Essenes all that you need to know for the future — you will need this knowledge. You are mighty and we have known each other for a long time. Together with many others we have come to the Earth to bring back that which has been forgotten. You can always come to me since I recognize you as one of my first companions. Many others will join us later." Then he stood up and said, "Come! I would like you to meet my dearest friend, John."

I remembered what Mary had told me about John, so I knew it must be the John in our family. We returned through fertile fields where the Essenes were working, diligently farming their land. I followed Jesus through the town's narrow alleys. It was a day when the schools were closed. We arrived at a square where a boy about Jesus' age sat, and I recognized him from my first day in Qumran. My ability to see the energies surrounding individuals had strengthened, and I saw the flames of his aura surrounding John, accentuated by the sunlight. He was more adult than he'd seemed previously. His dark hair and deep-set eyes underlined the fierceness of his temperament. Jesus laughed, and said, "Hello John. Are you cultivating your fire?" John looked at me and smiled. In spite of his temperament and the fire that burned in his eyes, he was a quiet person. There was something familiar about him.

Jesus said to me, "John will also be leaving here soon, since a new assignment has been chosen for him — one for which he will have a new teacher." John looked at me and I wondered whether he really wanted to speak with such a small girl. But he smiled and asked me boldly, "If you want to, you can come with us on our expeditions. Sometimes we creep out of the town secretly to investigate the region. We have discovered some very interesting things." My heart jumped. After the past few boring days I would welcome a change. Jesus and John seemed to be brave and exciting boys who were looking for adventure.

"We have to return to our teaching now," they said. "We will meet up again." Jesus brought me back to my room, and we found Mary was upset. "Where were you all this time? I was really very worried." Jesus replied, "I was in the fields around

Qumran with her, to show her the world outside." It seemed that his words comforted Mary, as she answered, "Alright. But please tell me next time before you leave. I am responsible for her; she has no father and mother here. I am her guardian. Please remember that." Her tone was firm, and Jesus nodded and left.

Then I was alone again. The day drew to a close and Mary was relaxed again as she said to me, "I would like you to come to our evening prayers in the great hall. The Council has agreed upon the details of your future education in Qumran. From now on, you will participate in the life in the town and, tomorrow, we are going before the Council, who will set out all the details for you. I have negotiated some good things for you. You are going to remain in my care, at least for the next months, until we see how matters develop."

She took my hand. "Come. We will go to prayers together." The Essene people were all assembled in the great hall. I joined them in their meditation. By withdrawing into their hearts and meditating on the name "Eli," they developed light of great intensity that radiated into all worlds and unified them. In this quiet moment, I was very happy to have returned to Qumran.

The following morning, I accompanied Mary to the Council of the Seven Masters. The room with the stone tables and benches reawakened memories of the last time I was here with my father. The Council explained that now the time of my apprenticeship and learning in Qumran should commence. Sumaja then spoke to me, explaining that each of the seven Masters and Mistresses in Qumran was responsible for one of the higher schools of Essene learning. The Master or Mistress in charge would teach the children in whom potential talents were recognized.

Sumaja said she would be responsible for the first part of my education. She told me, "Now we must find a suitable name for you. What did your parents call you?" I replied that I only remembered the name "Little Princess" — I had never been called by any other name. Sumaja said, "We must find an Essene name for you. Mary, please find an Essene name for her, since she cannot use her family name here — it would cause difficulties." I only discovered later what she meant.

Mary looked at me and asked, "With what names are you familiar?" I thought for a moment and then said, "Well, just yours." After a pause for reflection, she said, "Then we will call you Miriam, like our late Mistress. This will be your Essene name, which you will bear during your apprenticeship and as long as you are here with us." Then Mary explained to me that she had to return to her husband, but she would spend the last evening with Jesus, John and me. She wanted to tell us the remaining part of her story. She put me at ease by saying that Jesus and John would also like to hear the conclusion of the tale she'd begun telling me, including her wonderful experiences during the birth of Jesus — which were also associated with John. Then she said, "From tomorrow on, Sumaja will look after you. I will show you your room in the Children's corridor." She took me to a small room, which from now on was mine alone. Just for a moment, I was afraid, since in the past I'd always been surrounded by my family, never alone. Mary noticed and said, "Don't be afraid. You will always have everything you need here. We will meet this evening and I will light a fire for us and you will hear the rest of the story that you will store in your heart for the future."

I spent the rest of the day getting acquainted with my room and my surroundings. I found my way to the evening meditation without difficulty. Afterwards, Mary, Jesus and John were waiting for me, and Mary took us to her room. Mary lit a fire the way Essenes do, in a copper bowl, and soon incense and wonderful scents filled the room.

Then Mary began again. "When I was carrying you under my heart, Jesus, I experienced the calmest period in my life with your father, my dear husband, Joseph. Despite the great social disturbances taking place throughout Israel, we had friends who were able to let us know how things were. Nobody knew anything about the child I was carrying in my womb, apart from the family and the Essenes. We were very careful. But one day, the Essene masters reported that Herod, the King of Israel, had been informed by his Magicians, his "Wise Men," that the King of the World would soon be born, that they had read it in the stars. Herod was notorious for his egotism, distrust and for his bad temper and responded to the news with an outburst of uncontrollable anger. Fear of losing his power led him to send agents and spies into the surrounding lands to find the young king and to kill him. Unfortunately for Herod, despite their powers of prediction his sages were unable to name a precise time or birthplace.

"After the departure of the messenger who'd brought us the news, it was obvious that the birth was imminent. Joseph and I considered whether it was safe to give birth anywhere near Nazareth, since Herod's spies were everywhere; no town or village was safe, particularly for families of aristocratic or royal descent. Herod knew that a worldly king would be from royal blood and searched accordingly, which was dangerous for us. We had also received the order to register with the authorities, which Joseph accordingly did.

"Straight after that, we set out immediately for Qumran. We felt that this was the safest place to give birth to our son. My body was swollen and cumbersome as we left our home with our donkey. Nevertheless, we managed to reach the gates of Qumran. "The Master here received us immediately, since the Essenes themselves had recognized from the unusual movement of the stars that the arrival of the Messiah was imminent. However, we were warned that Qumran was not completely safe, since it was one of the first places to which Herod would send his spies and soldiers; he had always viewed the Essenes with distrust and feared that they would attempt to overthrow him. His fear and obsession with power radiated throughout the whole country, so the Essenes decided to send us to a secret place they alone knew. Wise women were to accompany us, to assist with the birth of the Messiah.

"We left the town of Qumran immediately. We were brought to caves in the mountains, known only to the shepherds and the peoples allied to the Essenes who lived there. There were several such unassuming villages, places so small or unknown that they would not draw the attention of Herod's forces. The journey was very difficult for me, since I was already in labour. I prayed to God that that I would hold out until we had found the place, so that I could bear my child under His protection. The Essenes had provided us with sacred plants, healing aids and incense. We came at last to the cave selected for us, and immediately the two wise women hid all signs of our arrival, and we finally felt safe. Then they began to prepare the room for me, to light the incense and the lamps and to perform holy rituals.

"This was the place, Jesus," his mother explained, "where you first saw the light of day, safe, protected by Joseph who stood guard the cave, and swaddled by the wise women. Here we were truly safe — and all in a place where no one would expect a king to be born! They made you a bed out of holy linen sheets and blankets that we had obtained from the Masters in Qumran. I was exhausted but Gabriel and many other angels were present during the birth and I could hear the sounds of heavenly music. The earth opened up and enveloped my body, and gave me strength during the final labour pains.

"The Essenes possess extensive knowledge of healing, so the birth itself was not at all difficult. In fact, I felt as if it had all happened while I was in a trance; we were together between Heaven and Earth and I was one with you. Then," Mary continued, "for the first time I held you, the Messiah, in my arms. The wise women anointed you in the way the Essenes welcome children into the world. One of the wise women — her name was Celia — stayed on to look after me. The other one, Marla, returned to Qumran to inform the Essenes of the birth of the Messiah. We wished to bring the wonderful news to the Essenes who had helped us when we had so needed them. However, we had not noticed until then a magnificent spectacle in the heavens: the stars were moving from their normal positions and indicating that the Messiah had been born.

"When Marla got back to Qumran the news spread so rapidly! Joseph was surprised when three shepherds suddenly appeared in front of the cave, having read the signs of the heavens. Joseph asked them, 'What are you looking for?' The shepherds said, 'We were spending the night with our flocks under the open skies when the heavens gave us the marvelous sign. Many stars combined together to form a single bright star that shone brighter than any star we had ever seen. This light spoke to us and said, "The redeemer has been born! Hurry to welcome him and bring him your gifts." Then angels appeared and told us to follow the bright, wandering star, which would show us the way to this place. We followed the star until it stood still above this cave, where we now stand. Then the star commenced shining more brightly than ever, and we presumed that the Messiah was here, as the stars had shown and prophesied.'

"Then Joseph came in to us and said, 'There are shepherds outside who want to welcome our son on Earth. It appears that God has sent them.' So we let them come in and they were the first people who came to welcome you. A heavenly light radiated from your cradle and filled the room. The Shepherds recognized the light and they fell to their knees and praised God. Then they presented their gifts and to us. They had also brought woolen blankets that they had woven themselves, so we were well provided for. To our surprise the shepherds also volunteered to guard the cave and took up positions outside. They promised us protection from strangers and to shield us from any trouble. Joseph informed them that a woman, a messenger, would shortly return from Qumran and gave them her name, so that she would be allowed to enter.

"I slept that night with the music of the angels ringing in my ears. I was exhausted but content. Joseph remained outside the cave all night with the shepherds. In the early hours of the morning, the messenger from Qumran arrived and told us of what had happened in the town. For the whole night, the heavens had displayed amazing constellations of stars and planets, such as had never been seen before. Hence, the inhabitants of Qumran knew immediately when the Messiah was born. But," Mary had gone on, "everybody knew that they should not make a pilgrimage at this time, to avoid being followed by spies or agents of Herod.

"We stayed there for several days so that I could regain adequate strength from the healing power bestowed by the Essene women. One day, another messenger appeared from Qumran and told us, 'Three high Masters have arrived in the town, apparently mages from foreign lands. They have read the stars and understood God's message that they must travel from their own countries to the Essenes in order to seek the Messiah. They had searched their hearts and saw that they just had to follow God's sign. The Essene people sent me to ask whether you would receive these Magi from the Orient. If you agree, I will return and show them the secret way here.' "

Mary resumed her tale. "We couldn't refuse, since we understood that, God's message had reached people seeking the Messiah. We were just trying to serve you on your path, Jesus. The messenger returned to Qumran, and I rapidly regained my strength, thanks to the wonderful qualities of the Essene healing herbs and ointments. The following evening, the messenger reappeared with the three men, whom Joseph received first. As the men entered, I recognized them as noble men from faraway lands: their clothes were of the noblest material and all three radiated wisdom and majesty. They bowed before me. Then they saw you and fell to their knees before you, Jesus. We received divine presents from them, which I have saved for you.

"One presented you a beautiful bowl filled with wonderful incense, which he had personally prepared in the tradition of his country: here were resins of the Earth, which, when lit, sing in praise of your arrival on Earth, so that all worlds can hear. The second Wise Man brought holy ointment prepared from myrrh, and begged permission to anoint you with it, to which I agreed. The third brought a very old, holy book that had been handed down from one teacher to another.

"He said, 'Look after it well, Mary. The prophecy of the arrival of the Messiah is also foretold in this book. I was never allowed to read the book but my master trained me to recognize that the forgiveness of sin is an important lesson to be learned from it.' Then he gave me the book for me to safeguard on your behalf.

"We learned," Mary told the three of us, "from our noble visitors that they had passed through Jerusalem, and that it was possible that Herod's spies had heard of their inquiries and had possibly investigated further. It became increasingly clear that it was time to leave this place. We sensed that danger was approaching. Joseph spoke to the Magi, whose names were Casper, Melchior and Balthazar, outside the cave, which afforded me a little peace and quiet. They discussed the best way for us to travel, and Joseph realized the prophetic powers and spirituality of the three.

"I fell asleep, but Joseph woke me and said, 'The three Magi have explained that Herod is angrier than ever and has planned drastic and brutal measures to discover and eliminate rivals to his throne. They've advised us to leave Israel as soon as possible, since we are no longer safe here. Our son and John are in great danger. We have to pack up and leave as soon as we can.' The three were willing to accompany us to Egypt, to a people directly descended from Abraham, who would provide a safe haven for us. They lived by our traditions and there were learned teachers and healers amongst them. These descendents of Abraham lived in peace with their neighbors in Egypt and were allowed to live by their own customs. We would remain there in Egypt until the time was right to return to Israel," Mary explained to us. " 'Our son shall return to Israel, but only when the danger had passed,' Joseph had told me. He was going to have to leave us for a while, and conceal any traces of our presence. 'The home of our family is Bethlehem, and it I'm going to need to register our son's birth there,' Joseph explained. 'When I've managed to do that, I'll follow you to Egypt.' The Magi had described the way to him. He would meet us in Egypt as soon as he could. 'You can rest assured that we are safe in God's hands, and that He is protecting us,' Joseph had assured me. Aside from that, the local Essenes had already sent a messenger to Qumran to tell Elizabeth of our plans and prepare for John to travel to Egypt too. For the moment he was safe, but the Essenes would have to find a way to bring him to us in Egypt. It seems the Magi were in some sort of spiritual contact with the Essenes."

Mary was silent for a moment and then she continued, "Joseph said he was so sorry that we had to leave our homeland, but felt it was the safest way, at least for the time being. I had every confidence in him and agreed. The mages decided to leave the majority of their retinue behind and prepared for the journey. They had sufficient supplies, blankets and tents for the journey with us. Under their leadership, we followed secret paths. The two wise women returned to Qumran and, of course, I was very sad when Joseph left us. The three Magi suggested that we leave as soon as possible, so we departed without delay. I carried you in my arms the whole time, Jesus, close to my breast. I prayed to Gabriel, to God and all other powerful beings of light that nothing would harm us. Thus we began our journey to Egypt. Now I was familiar with the story of Abraham's descendents in Egypt. They still lived with deep respect for our ancestors and, in particular, for our founding father. I had already heard a lot about our brothers and sisters in Egypt — our wider family. On the way, I had the impression several times that the Magi were using their hidden powers to protect us. To all outward appearance, we experienced no dangers, but when we sensed intuitively that danger was near our three guides apparently invoked magical powers to protect our journey.

"We had travelled for some days when one of the Magi suddenly said, 'We should seek a protected place to stop on the way. I sense that Joseph has communicated his imminent arrival. We should wait for him, so that he can join us for the rest of the journey.' We set up camp," Mary continued, "and I finally recovered somewhat from my exhaustion. Although the Essene women had supported me in healing and restoring my strength, I was still weak. Two days later, Joseph appeared, and I was so happy to embrace him and to have him near. Joseph told of the gruesome deeds of Herod, in ordering that all newborn babies be murdered. I was sick in my heart, to think that so many innocent souls should have to die to save my son. The country was bathed in innocent blood on your arrival, Jesus. That pained my heart and soul.

"Joseph told us that he had informed the authorities that you were born in Bethlehem. He hoped that it would cover our tracks and avoid trouble for the Essenes who were our friends. Joseph had also warned mothers of young children that they should hide to avoid the danger that would come. But my heart was still sad for the victims of Herod's madness, since I knew it was not yet at an end. When one of the Magi, Melchior, heard what Joseph had relayed, he said, 'Herod's fate is sealed. He shall die a gruesome death, and soon. But his successors will not be better disposed to you: Hence it is better for you to leave Israel at present. Your tracks will remain hidden for some time to come.'

"After some days, we reached the fabled River Nile. Our caravan followed the banks of the river for some time. It seemed to me that the river nursed the country as a mother would her child, and I felt restored by it. At home, Egypt had always been described vaguely and was still shrouded in mystery. I could sense the magic of this land — different from my home in Israel. We crossed the Nile in a boat, and then proceeded further until we reached the edge of a village in the river's fertile valley. The mages who had travelled with us announced that we had reached our journey's end. They said, 'This is the place where you can remain safely hidden. We will accompany you into the village, since we know their initiated holy men. We must reveal to them all the facts about you so that they know who you are and who they are protecting.' We waited at the edge of the village and were able to observe from a distance that the Magi easily gained access to the village, although we sensed that the community was very wary. The Magi returned and said, 'You are welcome here. There are still two high priests and a married couple wise and experienced in the old Abrahmic traditions. They have already read the predictions of your arrival, and are expecting you.'

"We were indeed hospitably welcomed into this community, and for some years we lived happily there. Joseph supported the village with his knowledge as carpenter and I was able to use my healing abilities to help our neighbors. We participated in their rituals and prayers and the general life of the village. One night, an angel appeared to me and said, 'Mary! It is time for your family to leave this place and return to Israel. Go alone. Explain that you are travelers from Egypt, wishing to visit your family in Israel and that you have no other attachment or employment in Israel and hope to start a new life with the support of your relations. Bring Jesus to the Essenes along the concealed routes to Qumran, which is now no longer a dangerous area. It is time for Jesus to be initiated by the Essenes'.

"So, I woke Joseph up," Mary said. "With a pounding heart, I told him of the message from God's angel. Our fate was in His hands, and He protected us all the way back to Israel just as the angel had said. That was the first time that the Essenes and their masters had the chance to get to know you."

Mary was quiet and reflective, and looked out at the stars. It was late and I noted that Jesus and John had listened closely to Mary's tale. After a pause, Mary resumed: "My son. The Essene Masters tell me that you have now learned everything they had to teach you ... Now your time in Qumran is at an end, and you will soon proceed on important journeys. Joseph of Arimathea will take you with him, since he has already visited all the schools of wisdom on this Earth. We will not meet again for a long time. Tomorrow, I'm going to return to my husband Joseph, since I too have fulfilled all my tasks here."

Then she changed her tone and spoke again a mother addressing her charges. "It's late and it's time for bed. There's a magnificently starry Heaven tonight. I think it will receive you and share a part in your own heavens, and I'm going to sink into my little bit of Heaven too." She brought me to my room and kissed me on the forehead. "Sleep well, little Miriam. You won't see me again, at least for a while But rest assured, the Essenes will call me when it is time for you to learn what I have to teach you. After all, you have been appointed to be my successor!" Then she retired and, for the first time, I was alone in my new home. I was astonished to find that I did not feel lonely. I sensed the closeness of the starry heavens and, in the presence of God and His light, I fell asleep.

Sumaja came to get me the following morning, as agreed, and said, "You will begin your education here in my school, and you'll be spending the first day with me. Come and I'll show you the rooms of my school. Tomorrow, there will be other teachers here to educate you." She took me through the various rooms, each of which had its own function and radiated its own light. She said, "I am responsible for the Schools of Healing in Qumran. You will be learning how the Essenes serve. We learn to create unity out of duality, and in this blending we are able to heal according to God's word.

Many Essenes from our school travel through the country, bringing strength and recovery to those whose illnesses result from the duality that plagues them. But we never expect to be paid for this service: that is our rule here."

We entered the classroom and I was astonished at such an unusual sight: the pupils were meditating in a circle and were completely immersed in the silence. As Sumaja entered, all eyes opened. There were children and adults alike in the class: all ages were represented. Sumaja said, "Greetings to you all, healers of the divine light. I would like to introduce a new pupil, who will be joining you for some time." And so began my education with the Essenes.

The pupils of the Qumran School of Healing spent many hours each day in meditation. We were taught to unite the duality of our hearts through love. When she sensed that the pupils had reached this stage, Sumaja would come and instruct us in hand treatments and other techniques. I spent a few months in the school and, every morning, I meditated as Sumaja had taught me: to the sun and moon joined in a fire from Venus, as Sumaja called it. I did not find it at all difficult to immerse myself in the meditation until my heart attained unity. I was completely contented and without material consciousness.

In the few lessons that Sumaja gave, she told us, "When you are fully immersed in the Light of Christ, you no longer need an external method of healing. Other aids are no longer necessary, since the power of the Light is everything you need to heal. It is the pure essence of life. It brings equilibrium to unstable lives. Full immersion in this love enables the dead to be brought to life or the worst illnesses to be removed from the body simply through prayers to God."

When she spoke, her words were accompanied by a celestial light, containing the divine knowledge that she passed on to the students and also to me. Increasingly, I noticed that she always arrived just as I was conscious that everyone in the room had attained the unity of heart. She was always present just as that moment arrived — never before nor after this moment — then she would transmit her knowledge as though it were contained in an envelope of light.

One day she came to me and said, "Now is the time to put your lessons into practice. You can accompany a group visiting villages in the region, to heal the sick. Just believe in the power that has been initiated in you. Everything else is up to God. I cannot give you more advice than that."

The next morning I was permitted to accompany these Essenes, some of whom I already knew, to the neighboring villages. In the first village, not far from Qumran, we were greeted by a welcoming villager, who said, "It's a good thing that you've come. Some of our inhabitants are gravely ill." The healer, Nanea, indicated that I should follow her and said, "Come and help me, Miriam." Now, as previously, I was surprised how the Essenes communicated with one another without words, to know what they have to do. They seemed to organize and distribute themselves intuitively, visiting the people in order to help the village. Nanea and I visited a woman who had a most curious skin condition: her skin was full of blisters and seemed as though it were being eaten away. Nanea said quietly, "We will pray before we start treating her, Miriam. When you notice that the right time has come, we will attend to the woman and speak to her soul. Her spirit will inform us of the degree of healing possible."

Through our meditation, we were in unity with God. I could feel the inner rhythm that existed between Nanea and myself, until I received the impulse and signaled to her. We stood together and placed our hands into the woman's astral body and began to work. I sensed how strong the stream of universal energy was, through my heart straight into my hands. As if in a trance, I felt my prayer to God answered, and I received the message to hold the woman's feet in my hands. She was unconscious and completely quiet until the moment I touched her. Then she awoke and I sensed a jolt run through her body, as if her soul had returned. Nanea looked at me and said, "That was good. Her body and soul had separated and you have united them again. She will heal soon." We prayed and thanked the soul of the woman, as I had learned. At that moment, I was aware of lights, just as I had experienced when my mother healed. They filled the room and placed everything that the woman needed for recovery at her disposal.

From then on, I joined these healing expeditions regularly. When we returned to the village some months later, I learned that the woman I had first healed had fully recovered, and, when she heard that we were there, she invited us to take bread and wine with her. That was the reward for our work. In this way, I continued my learning with the Essene healers for some months. At that time I seldom saw Jesus, and when I did, it was mostly just in passing. Twice I was able to take a walk with him outside Qumran, and the third time he said, "I will be leaving soon. My time is up. It will be a long time until we see each other again." I was sad, since, although I saw him infrequently, I was very happy in his company. His radiance, his divinity and his infinite compassion were very familiar to me. One day, I learned that he had already left. I began to understand that there were no farewells in Qumran. The Essenes did not believe in such gestures — they were so united with their God that they did not encourage such rituals; still, I knew I would not see Jesus for a long time.

My education in Qumran lasted many years — I am uncertain of how many, but it was a long time. After my initiation into the healing practices of the Essenes, I was permitted to work outside the town, on the farm where herbs were grown, herbs from which essences and oils were produced. I was instructed by an elderly Essene named Joshua. He was a wise old man, who made me aware of how the forces of the Earth can be used to encourage plant growth. He taught me the about the ethereal forces that flow through and out of the Earth and into the heavens, and how the healing forces in plants could be harnessed and cultivated, in accordance with the laws of the elements and the rhythm between sun and moon. Sometimes I was permitted to work with him and helpers in his apothecary laboratory, where valuable essences and ointments were produced from herbs, plants and oils. Dried herbs were mixed with resins and then re-dried. I was particularly intrigued to note that, contrary to the way we used to do things in Jerusalem, the Essenes used nothing they had not produced themselves. The Essenes purchased nothing: everything they used was grown by them or given to them as a gift.

The Essenes had a natural rhythm and way of life that gave them all they needed. I loved working for Joshua the apothecary.

Heavy, rich smells came from the thick essences and ointments (which always appeared to me as golden light) that were carefully stored there. The storeroom was inaccessible to anyone but Joshua himself.

Some three or four years later, Sumaja came to me and said, "Your apprenticeship with me is complete and your next phase will be with Mistress Fee. Come to the Council of Masters tomorrow. She will explain what she will be teaching you and how you will be trained."

After the meeting, I went into Fee's classroom and she greeted me cordially. Although she had aged, she had also become more ethereal, even more attractive but also more distant. On this particular day she took me with her into the temple, but before we entered, she explained that Essenes never spoke in the rooms in which they worked. She said, "I am the mistress responsible for fire rituals, aimed to bring the energy of the stars and the cosmic fire to Earth. I work with the Earth currents and the heavenly currents and coordinate them to fill our space with unity. This is a significant part of our responsibility in Qumran. You see, these currents flow in many places on Earth, but they are not in harmony with one another. Universal forces flow into the Earth and these currents mix with the ethereal currents. The job of the initiated is to combine these streams by means of rituals and prayers and to harmonize them with one another."

"With the support of the divine mother and the Brahmins," Fee continued, "I will pass on my knowledge from the time in the past when everything, including the schools, was unified in Agni's fire. These rituals have been retained throughout the years, since mediators still exist who are able unify the colliding forces between Heaven and Earth. This spiritual unity can bring goodwill and happiness to the places in which we live, and I am responsible for bringing this unity to the whole of Qumran. However my being can often extend over the whole world, to harmonise other places, so that those there are also able to accept the divine blessings."

Then she looked at me with her penetrating, flaming eyes and said, "I know that you perceive many different energies and that you are very sensitive to everything that happens around you. Do not be surprised if the rituals I teach cannot permeate into our surrounding region: Israel may not be willing to accept the fire of God's love, but I am still able to supply our town with divine unity and to retain our life forces here. At least, we are able to live within this holy unity here in Qumran. As long as the sacred forces can radiate and illuminate us here, I will continue to spread this knowledge throughout Qumran. But, I fear, soon these energies to which we have become accustomed will not be able to unfold further."

"Sometime in the future," Mistress Fee explained, "I will have to leave this place; I will no longer be needed here. I want you to learn everything I know. I am going to withdraw to a foreign land beyond the mountains in the country known as India. From there, I will be able to continue my work and fulfill my responsibility to the Earth. If I am unable to protect my work here on Earth, I must hide where I cannot be found, to protect the world from any misuse of this energy." She looked at me then continued, "The originator of this discipline is my father. He always used to send me where such cultures of the spirit exist, to ensure that they are established and maintained.

Now he is sending me to another unknown place in need of my help, since I can hold the very Earth in my hands with my fire energy." As she spoke, flames of infinite compassion streamed out of her heart and reached to the outer spheres. For the first time, I looked deep into her eyes, and I thought I recognized her and I told her so. But she hardly answered at all. She was completely untouched by space and time. She had no questions and no answers; she had just her existence.

After that, I was allowed to join Fee and enter the Essene temple: the secret inner place from which all the energies necessary for life in Qumran originated. Fee then cleaned the utensils used for the rituals, and prayed in preparation for the holy service that takes place in the early morning. It was her regular routine to prepare for the next day in this manner. During our time in the temple, we did not speak; I only watched. She ignored my presence until she had finished, when she indicated with a gesture that it was time to leave.

When we were outside, Fee said, "You have perhaps noticed that I lead our devotions in the early hours of each morning. From now on, you too will join us for prayers every morning in the Ruby Room underground. After that, you will come to the temple with me. You are going to learn to perform the rituals that I dedicate to the world every morning. You now have the rest of the day free. Tomorrow morning we'll meet here shortly before four o'clock and you'll follow me in silence. You will simply be present, watching and learning."

After all the time I'd been there, I had access to everywhere in Qumran, and I spent the afternoon wandering through the lanes and alleyways. I realized that there were more schools.

I learned that there was a school for the stars and planets, where astronomy was taught, and another that taught how to recognize the auras and the light from beings. In each, all knowledge was carefully written on the unique Qumran scrolls. That afternoon, I strolled past the schools, wondering about them. I had not attended any of these schools but I had been told that I would not need to. Every Essene master or mistress was responsible for one of these schools, and their exact responsibilities and jobs remained secret. I have never found out what they are.

That afternoon, I met up with my old friend, John. I had not seen him for a long time, since he had gone with Jesus, the two of them sent to a teacher in the mountains. He must have returned a few days earlier, but I had not seen him. He was wilder and livelier than before, and greeted me warmly. He possessed a natural openness and spontaneity, resulting from his closeness to God. He was also more grown-up and wiser than before.

I dared to ask a question that was a bit unusual for Qumran. "Where have you been, John?" He hesitated for a moment, and said, "I am with a teacher now but I come here from time to time for classes with the Essene masters. My teacher is a secret, a hermit in the mountains from the Nazarene school. He set me to my tasks and responsibilities, and is teaching me to be a prophet, which I was in earlier lives. He is reintroducing me to the knowledge of who I am. Sometimes, he accompanies me to the River Jordan, where he initiates me into the secrets of the waters. He says I am a "Baptist" and it will not be long before I am able to fulfill the responsibilities of Baptizing in God's name."

John smiled, and said, "There I get to live so differently than I do here. We live more naturally in the wild and nourish ourselves only with whatever nature presents. You are all so protected here. It is a luxurious world compared to the one I live in now. But truthfully, I feel better there. Houses are strange to me and I have never really known security; the wilderness is my element, my home. Sorry, but I have to go now. I have an errand to complete. Bless you."

John's words, as everything in his life, were simple and straightforward; he never felt the need for embellishment or indulgence. He was always friendly, though, and I liked him just the way he was. It was just that he had neither the habits nor the thoughts that come from civilized society. He was just his own, wild self.

At the evening meditation, it was as if new energies were flowing into me. I was conscious that the time of learning with Fee had really already started and that God had already sent some stream of wisdom that expanded my knowledge. I had learned by now to recognize the streams of energy and to manipulate them. It was as if they were familiar to me. But my most intimate friend from my childhood was God, and my childlike conversations with him had never stopped.

I spoke to him in my meditation that evening, and asked "What are you going to do with this Earth, God? What are your plans for us? Where will you steer us?" But that evening, the Lord was only with me as a presence; I could sense the future but God Himself remained silent. I was only vaguely able to discern the future in my dreams, which he sent through me, without taking on any more concrete form.

Next morning, I awoke and performed my ablutions, which had become ever more extensive as had I grown older. We cleansed body, soul and mind every day. I was at the temple very early and waited until Fee came and I followed her inside in silence. The masters and mistresses were there, together with others who had been chosen for the day. Then the masters and mistresses began to sing and speak in a way I had never heard before. I had heard them every night, but being in the midst of them was very different: it was as though they had stimulated some kind of resonance in the very rubies, during which they were surrounded by a ruby-colored light. After the ceremony, I followed them through their secret passages, and at a well–camouflaged location I was permitted to accompany them underground. For the first time, I saw the room that Mary had described to me years ago with my own eyes. As always, we received no instructions. I followed what was going on only according to what I saw and what my instinct told me. I was deep in a meditation, and all of us were all immersed in the Light of Christ that filled the room.

Suddenly, it was as if I were in contact with Jesus, across the borders of many lands. His image appeared as if he were next to me, and we were able to communicate with one another. He was in a wild, unfamiliar country and I could see that the land was greener and not as dry as my country, but I could also sense that it was colder. Dazzling white surrounded him, as though he were amid dunes of sand made up of tiny crystals that reflected the sunlight. Later I learned that this was snow. He showed me where he was and the vibrations that I received were a voice, saying "I am with the most exalted and wisest teacher on Earth. I will remain here for some time, then I will travel on to other countries." Through the vision, I could see that that he was traveling in foreign lands and in schools of wisdom quite different from those I knew. Then the vision faded and I returned to oneness with the ruby light, until the other Essenes were ready to leave the underground chamber. Intoxicated as if with wine, I followed them out into the gray of the breaking day, and followed Fee back into the temple.

As we re-entered the temple, I shrank back for a moment: a radiant being was waiting for us. It not a human form, but appeared as a being of divine light emerging from a fire. They all bowed down in reverent obedience. The divine being's form subsided in a golden glow, and I could tell it was incredibly powerful. It appeared to radiate into all worlds. Then the Essenes present in the temple completed their rituals, which were also filled with the power of those masters and mistresses — and with the power of God. I couldn't really describe the divine presence in the room; everything was immersed in fire, a fire from God Himself. Fee murmured some words that I did not understand, and, when she had completed the ritual ceremony, we both fell into a trance. Now we were ourselves fire and in complete unity with the divine presence. As the ritual ended, the spiritual being faded away and we returned to consciousness. At a signal from Fee, we left and she guided me to a place behind the temple. Here there were springs in which she performed her morning ablutions, and I followed her example.

After our ritual washing, we ate our communal meal. Fee led me to her private quarters, which I had never seen before, and she lit a fire on her small altar. It seemed to me as though she never slept, and was always wide awake. She said, "This morning in the temple you have met my father, the father of our tradition, our teacher of wisdom. He comes every morning in the form of fire and helps me blend the fires between Heaven and Earth. He has taught me everything I know."

I wanted to ask questions but Fee quickly went on, "To answer your question, he is not with us here. But I have been in contact with him for a long time. He is present somewhere else in human form; he has returned but will not visit us here in that human form. He is here in Israel and has prepared himself for a task he will carry out together with the Messiah. Sometimes he contacts me, but I have never actually met him. He appears every morning in the temple in his spiritual form, and out of the divine fire extracts the living knowledge we need to sustain our teachings."

Fee finished the explanation, saying, "For the rest of the day you can meditate, until you have learned the basic elements of my teaching. From now on, you will not speak until I release you from my schooling." Time spent in silence was not so difficult in Qumran, since many Essenes scarcely talk at all or just wish to be in seclusion. Every night I was with the masters and every morning I returned. They shared their knowledge with me, but the power of their rituals was my real source of insight. I was beginning to comprehend the energy flow between Heaven and Earth. Sometimes I was in foreign lands and observed how the fiery wisdom of the stars combined with the fire from the Earth, and how the knowledge was spread all over the world. As each individual ritual was performed, I picked up a little insight into this secret knowledge but it was all piecemeal. The knowledge seeped from my subconscious into an awareness, even though I did not always know its application at that particular moment. Only later in my life, in a distant country, was I able to use the all that accumulated knowledge.

Later, as I was silently on my way to evening prayers, I suddenly realized that Mary was standing in front of me. We just looked at one another for a time and amazingly she understood immediately my voiceless speech. She infused me with the white light of love from her eyes. She was carrying a little boy. Together, we went silently to evening meditation. Next day, Fee came to me before we entered the temple. It was an extraordinary experience: she spoke to me without opening her mouth or using speech. Her voice came directly from her heart and it said, "Today you will perform the ritual." After all the weeks attending the rituals, I knew just how to go about it. Her silent voice encouraged me: "Find your own way. Only Agni, the Lord himself, can teach you. Don't be surprised to find your rituals are completely different from mine."

I was permitted to perform the morning rituals in the temple for the next twenty–one days. Following each ceremony, we went into a trance, a state we maintained throughout the day. After the twenty–first day, I had returned to my room when I was called to see the masters. Mary was also there. Fee said, "The time has come for you to leave us, Miriam. For the time you remain here, we would like you to continue performing the ceremony as prescribed in the rites of the Essenes. I will also be leaving soon, following predictions and new responsibilities." Then Mary spoke. "Miriam, from now on, I will pass on the knowledge that I have learned as a high priestess." Then she introduced the small boy I'd seen with her. "This is Jacob. Before he left on his travels, Jesus prophesied that one of his companions would become incarnated within me." I looked at the boy — he seemed the embodiment of love, but quite different from Jesus. Nevertheless, he radiated a halo of light and a bright star shone over his head. Later, I would meet many people who carried the same signs, and would learn that they were to accompany Jesus in his various tasks.

Later that day, I was invited to the masters' chamber at sunset. That evening we would not participate as usual in the communal meal. Following the evening meditation, I was permitted for the first time to experience what was seldom celebrated in Qumran, and only in private and on special occasions. The masters ordered a meal and proffered wine. I had heard of the Essene wine, made in Qumran, and knew where it was prepared, but this was the first time that it had been before me on the table. It was a festive meal to which I had been invited. Mary was there, and all the Essene masters, male and female. Although not a word had been spoken, I knew it was a farewell meal for Fee, before she left to pursue her new career. We ate well and drank the wine, which for a moment numbed my senses. I sensed again the ruby–colored light that I experienced in the underground chamber. The wine penetrated me, affecting my awareness of my body and stimulating a buzzing I can only describe as 'audible oscillations.' We were all more cheerful than usual. We laughed and were really boisterous. It was different from the evenings when, as a child, I had celebrated with my parents at home. It was a festival for us all, until Fee stood up. Everyone apart from me apparently knew what would happen next. That evening, I learned about the Essene ritual for departures. Fee brought a basin of water and silently washed our feet. This was done to remove traces of the paths taken together, so that it would be easier to prepare for new paths. Then Mary washed Fee's feet, and hence Fee was free to leave: the paths behind her had been eliminated. The evening was long and the masters drank until late into the night. We all celebrated, intoxicated by joy and by the wine. The next day I found Fee had left without a farewell.

I never again saw Fee in this life. From that day, though, I had an inner contact with her and could follow her lonely way to distant lands. She journeyed a long time, until she arrived in the country beyond the crystal mountains — a land which would come to be known as Tibet. There she resumed her mission. I was often in spiritual contact with her: there was neither time nor space separating us. We were allies, since we had performed the fire ritual together. She also appeared sometimes in my dreams, and reminded me that our connection was older than just this life. It was a friendship from primitive times, an old, unshakable closeness.

Following Fee's departure, I became responsible for the observance of the rituals in the temple, and Agni, the Lord of fire, became increasingly familiar to me. Mary accompanied us, with her son, every morning into the underground Ruby Room. Until that time, I had remained silent, a silence that I had only broken for Fee's farewell celebration. Then, one day, Mary came to me and said, "Now is the time to break your silence. Continue to perform the ritual as before, but you may speak whatever you consider necessary. Tomorrow morning, after the ritual, you should come to the masters' common room."

After the morning ritual, I entered the room where the masters and Mary awaited me. Now I was to learn a new discipline in the Qumran tradition, under the leadership of Master Agnisha. Mary explained, "You will be instructed in an advanced discipline in the Essene tradition. Agnisha is the master who teaches this special knowledge to the most capable students. It will be read into your ‚akasha,' the ethereal library in which is written who you are and whence you come. That will help me to educate you, since I can then choose what I should teach. I myself will initiate you in the tradition of the Diamond Way."

It was all so sudden and surprising. Agnisha sat next to me. In spite of his youth, he was very mature and wise. It surprised me each time we met. He looked at me and filled me with fire. Then he began to speak: "Miriam, you belong to the selected beings with the highest Shakti energy. You originate from that energy and it is part of you, as created by God. The original power of the Shakti wisdom flows through you, and, with it, you prepare the world. You belong to a group of ten women descended from the lineage of female ancestors. Mary is from another line of Shakti, and will be your teacher. Shakti knows Shakti and is eternal."

His words transported me into another world, into the universe filled with light and life, where all my strength resided. Then my spirit slowly returned to my body and I was looking into Agnisha's eyes again. He smiled and said, "Don't be surprised. You have already met my wisdom teacher in the temple — Agni. He is the guardian of the akasha lore and had taught me this. Only a few in Qumran are trained to read into the soul." He had a mischievous and infectiously joyful nature. His style of teaching was incredibly far–reaching, into the very depths of my soul — simple, unaffected and without pathos or drama.

Then Sumaja spoke to me. "I think you need some peace and quiet now, because soul–reading has made a deep impression on you and you may need some time to reflect. Now you should take a rest." Then she looked at Mary and said, "In three days Miriam will be ready to continue." I was accompanied to my room, where food had been prepared and washing facilities provided for me.

For three days and nights, I fell into a state between a trance and sleep, which seemed to go on forever. Light shone through me, combining visions and new insights with my fire–activated spirit existence, my own elemental force and my inner world. Images from my life appeared to me, although I could not understand them. Only after returning to full consciousness was I finally able to leave my room. I made my way to the temple, and although I had not performed the ritual for three days, the energy from the temple did not appear in any way diminished. I met Agnisha again and plucked up courage to ask, "Agnisha, what is Shakti?" I think he was expecting the question, and he said, "Come here and sit down next to me on the steps." We settled onto the steps between the Essene quarters and the temple. Agnisha was very patient. "In many schools of wisdom the same elemental force is described. In our elemental sources, called 'Veda,' this inspirational force is called 'Shakti,' a word with similar origin to the Greek 'Sofia.' It is the female, creative force, born out of the Wisdom of the worlds. I cannot tell you more. This force is experienced as the source of knowledge, which you must decipher yourself from your own spiritual experience."

I thanked him for his friendly and generous support. He was more open and communicative than many of the Essene masters, who were sometimes very closed off, aloof and unwilling to communicate their knowledge. Agnisha was the opposite and his openness was very good for me. I went to the temple after that and cleaned the utensils, to prepare myself for the rituals and to return to my daily routine again.

I had still not quite returned completely to Earth, but I felt more firmly anchored in my body. I also performed a ritual, which I had learned from the Essenes, to connect my spirit more firmly to the Earth. For the first time, I understood the reason for this ritual: when the spirit takes off and leaves the body in a flight of the soul or spiritual experience, one needs a ritual to draw the spirit back into the body, anchored again in the Earth. Then the spirit will not be torn apart in other worlds.

As I was leaving the temple next morning, Mary was waiting for me. She said, "Come with me. I want to show you a new place, where I can give you some special knowledge." We left Qumran in a direction I usually avoided, the side of the town towards the Dead Sea. I always recalled the unpleasant feelings that my first sight of that sea aroused in me. After that, I tried to steer clear of such places. But Mary was determined and I had to follow her. We left the inner walls of Qumran and descended down steps to a spot that I didn't know at all. There stood a temple. I was astonished that this temple radiated a pure white light and was apparently not affected by the energy of the neighboring Dead Sea. It seemed as if this temple must have an even stronger ability than that of Qumran itself to pacify the sea. We walked towards the temple, and the nearer we approached, the stronger I sensed that a primeval fire burned and radiated its elemental energy to us.

When we arrived I saw that priestesses lived here. Mary explained, "This is a holy place for feminine spiritual energy. Since primeval times the white flame of women's creative power has burned here. The priestesses have also been here from time immemorial, and serve the flame. They nourish it and the flame nourishes them! Fundamentally, this is the central source of the Light of Christ."

"Long ago the Qumran community was spread much further afield," Mary explained, "and extended further than today. The Essene community has been in existence for a very long time and has a checkered history. But then there was a war. Not all Essenes were unaffected by the temptations of duality in this world. Originally, there was no desert here, only fertile land. But, some generations ago, after their initiation, several groups of Essenes became involved in magic, and thus their ways divided. We do not speak about it much in our community, and the masters remain silent on the subject. But you can sense what is hidden under this sea. The Essenes remember it every day in their prayers. It is the power of darkness, the shadows of the material world that were born in their own community. They attempt to maintain the pure light, but the force below is the dark force of the Earth — the force of materialism that summons the darkness. Some Essenes divided the community because they believed that as a group they were not worldly enough, since the Essenes neglected the material side of life. Hence a polarisation occurred, which continues to affect the community today. The events are reported in the old chronicles, the story of Sodom and Gomorrah.

"Splinter groups, and others descended from our forefathers, who have left the old Essene tradition created their own communities, and in fact still exist in Israel. But the Essenes you know in Qumran refuse to contact them. I feel this to be a split in Qumran's heart. This temple was actually the center of motherly spiritual energy, which the Essenes had previously nurtured. Jesus has re-awakened this energy, and one day he asked me to accompany him here. He extracted flames out of the earth and said, 'Here is the primeval flame, Mother, which disappeared into the earth. It is the motherly flame that feeds the Light of Christ, the white Shakti-force. In your capacity as White Priestess I beg you to carry it and protect it.'

"I went to the Essenes of Qumran," Mary continued, "with Jesus' request and begged them to give me initiated priestesses who would dedicate themselves to the observance of the sacrament of the flame. The Essene community and the masters agreed. Since that time, I have felt myself to be responsible for this temple and its surroundings. It has again become a temple for initiation. Whenever I come here, I guide the energy of the motherly spirit out over this sea — the sea that seems to scare you. Jesus has taught me these things. He showed me that forces of darkness may not be negated, and that the dark forces that exist under the sea can only be counteracted by accepting them: this is symbolic of the limited consciousness of the strength which humanity and the Earth possess.

"Jesus taught me how to obtain access to these forces and how I can fill them with compassion, so that they can be rede-emed. It needs a strong spirit of forgiveness — which was lacking over long periods in Essene history. The effects of this will soon be noticed here too. Until that time, I wish to initiate you in the flame, just as Jesus initiated me. The fire ritual every morning will support your initiation here. The fire is a transforming force that will sustain you here. After you celebrate your usual observances in the temple you should come here with me and I will instruct you in the elemental Shakti–force and the feminine creativity."

Mary entered the temple and started to perform rituals that appeared to be of a very much older form than that of the Essenes I knew. Three white flames representing the wisdom of all worlds blazed out of the coals. It seemed to me that the flames were diverted over the Dead Sea. I heard souls below the surface calling, crying out for deliverance and mercy. Mary performed the ritual in silence and she spoke only as we left the temple. "The feminine Shakti force is usually able to contact the unredeemed souls that wander between the worlds. This force returns the souls and brings them deliverance and redemption. I think you have experienced enough for today. It probably disturbs you somewhat, since you never hear about these things in Qumran: it is not in their nature to accept these facts. It is Jesus' special wish that we accept these forces in us, since this is a part of our earthly spiritual contact."

I did not sleep at all well that night and I was glad when I could immerse myself in the Light of Christ at four o'clock the next morning. It was perhaps the first time that I was fully pulled out of my own body. I contacted Jesus in prayer, who said, "Listen, Miriam. I move through all worlds and know this darkness that forms the world and it was I who brought you into contact with the compassion of my mother yesterday. Humanity has brought suffering and guilt on its elf, and I will need your help and the help of many others to liberate it from this legacy. I have seen very much worse situations on my journeys, compared to your experience yesterday. Submerge yourself in the Light of Christ that brings redemption. I am that light that fills the room, so accept this responsibility for the task. It is yours! The voices of our fathers and forefathers cry out for salvation." Then Jesus faded and was gone.

I attempted to remain in the Light of Christ, but at the beginning it was difficult. I had seen something that I should not have seen. I asked God why he had trusted me with the vision but, after a while, I again found consolation and peace in the Light of Christ. We left the basement room and I performed the fire ceremonies. I now understood Mary's explanation, that the fire would give me strength to perform these tasks.

The next nights were very disturbing. I dreamed vividly and tossed and turned in my sleep. By day, Mary accompanied me to the white fire, and let me observe how she kindled and charged it and evoked the white flames with her compassion. I found support in the rituals in the temples of Agni.

Dark shadows appeared and I did not know whether they drifted into my soul or stayed outside. I was aware that two or three Essene masters possessed visionary powers. However, I had no training or experience with visions, and so I did not know the origin of the shadows that haunted me at night. I could not remember experiencing such inner disquiet before. The more Mary raised the flames of the fire, the more disturbed was my soul. One day it was so bad that I was in despair and I asked her about it. She looked deep into my eyes and said, "Please have patience."

That same afternoon Joseph arrived. It was the first time I had met him. He seemed somewhat older than Mary and had a compassionate bright light around him. It was only a short meeting on my way to the temple, while he and Mary were on their way to the masters' room. But in that short time I observed his enraptured glow, such as I had lonely seen from someone on his way into the next world. I pushed the idea to one side.

From then on, it was very difficult for me to find peace of mind, and my soul was very troubled. One morning, Sumaja was waiting for me after the fire ritual and asked me to go with her. She invited me to her room, which was more modest than most I had seen. The walls were covered with strange symbols. First she sat at her altar, which is customary among devout Essenes, and began to speak: "I have sensed your heavy heart for some time now, Miriam. It saddens my heart too. My visions are also increasingly dark. Something threatening is growing above us. I don't know why your young soul is so affected by it. The other masters have either not seen the threat or do not want to! But the images that came to me in recent nights were also dismal and dark."

"I don't think our community will exist much longer. I pray to all the heavens and to Jesus that he returns before the prophecy about our community is fulfilled. I can tell that you are receiving such images at night, although I cannot actually receive the same ones myself. I'll ask Mary to let you stay three days with me, since I think I ought to initiate you in everything to do with the gift of visions. You certainly have the gift for receiving God's visions. I have to confess, the images I see are beginning to be a bit blurred."

I was deeply moved and I fell on my knees before her. "Sumaja, I don't know how this is happening to me." She answered, "I don't know either, Miriam. But it feels as if something is coming to an end. The only thing that lightens my heart somewhat is that the Messiah has appeared at this time. So we have at least fulfilled our task, which we have been promising to complete since the time of Atlantis." This was the first time I had heard the name, but I didn't dare to ask any more about it at that moment. Nevertheless, the word resonated in my soul. My instinct told me that the visions of darkness that I'd been getting had something to do with that time.

The next days were chaotic. I did not see Mary at all but I learned that Joseph was there in the Essene community to which he belonged; it had to be because he sensed that his worldly life was leaving him. He wanted to spend the remaining time he had with his family. Each time I saw him, I could feel his hope that Jesus would return before he left his body. Meanwhile, it felt as though all of Qumran suffered increasingly from severe depression.

For the next few days, I dedicated myself to the fire rituals. I spent the nights in deep meditation and in Sumaja's chamber. We immersed ourselves in something indescribable, something that opened doorways for us. I walked along paths in other worlds, until I reached the very gate of God Himself. The gateway between Heaven and Earth opened and pictures appeared without any instigation from me. Suddenly, on the third night with Sumaja, I received visions in which the images were crystal clear. God showed me the future and gave me His advice. Then I knew that I had to tell Sumaja and the other Essenes what I had experienced.

When I opened my eyes next morning, the flood of images had melted away, but I could not shake off their significance. What I had experienced lay heavily on my heart. Sumaja looked at me and said, "Please ... you have to communicate your visions to the Council, since you are obviously the conduit through which they are being transmitted. I will call them all together after the fire ritual, and I can't urge you strongly enough to communicate God's plans to us. I can see that he is sending them to us straight through your heart." As for me, I prayed to Agni in the fire ceremony and begged him to give me energy and courage. My soul was badly shaken: God's visions were difficult to bear. I remembered Fee. She could abandon her own self completely; I prayed for that strength for my soul. In fact, I indeed did come to experience an invisible strength in me.

I entered the masters' chamber at the appointed time, and they were all there waiting for me. They had lit a divine fire to which herbs had been added. The room was quiet and began to grow dark. Sumaja fell on her knees before me and said, "I beg you: tell us about your visions. They show us the future, and we must understand so we can act accordingly. I sense that we have not much time."

That moved me deeply. I described the visions, all the images I had seen one after another. The Essene community around me was in danger of attack. The successor to King Herod had won over the splinter groups of dissident Essenes as allies. The masters in these groups had developed into pagan magicians, and had left the path of the divine light. This alliance was preparing to destroy Qumran. These allies of Herod had become advisers bent on revenge.

I had been deep in a trance, so much so that I had no way of telling what was going on in the room. All the Essene masters who were present came over to me and begged me to share with them the visions from God. They wanted to know what they should do and what actions they should take. One after another, they laid their heads on my knee, and I was able to give each master a vision to take with them. I could see each whole life in front of them, right up to the moment when they would leave their bodies. After all that, I needed a full three days and three nights to recover.

Sumaja came to me, to look after me while I was recuperating. She gave me healing drinks and, gradually, I recovered from the flood of visions and pictures in my mind, which had severely shaken me. Sumaja was very supportive of me, and I was very grateful to her. But, it was clear that the gratitude from her side was even more profound, and I could see it when I looked into her eyes. After all my recent experiences, her strength was very important for me given my young age.

The community was suddenly hurtling itself into action: the Essenes of Qumran called a meeting in which Sumaja explained that they could no longer offer everyone protection. Dark shadows had gathered over the region and threatened our existence. We were all free to leave the town and to commence an unremarkable, secular, worldly existence, for the sake of protecting our lives. She could not guarantee that life within the town walls was safe anymore. With a determined voice she said, "I shall remain here, but the ways of the Lord have revealed that the Masters will leave Qumran. I will be the only one remaining here. I can offer no protection to you, apart from my prayers. Every one of you must choose which path you will take. You may wish to disappear into the culture of the worldly life, without repudiating your faith and traditions. In public, you will have to deny your beliefs, or you will be persecuted. Those who wish to avenge some imagined past slight have distorted the mind of the king. You will be outlaws if you admit you are an Essene." There was absolute silence after her words. At that precise moment the light of Jesus appeared to us and filled our hearts. Throughout the whole gathering only one sentence was audible, starting quietly and rising to a crescendo: "Lord, thy will be done on Earth, as it is in heaven."

Mary came to me later and said, "Miriam, I had hoped that there would be enough time for me to initiate you fully in the ritual of the white flame, the mother of all creation and the healer of the world. But we only have a few hours before I have to go. Come with me and I will do all that I can to transfer my most important knowledge to you. You'll have to then discover the rest for yourself, in the course of your life." I followed her into the Shakti–temple with the white flames. She meditated and contacted Jesus, immersing herself in his light. Then she laid her hand on my head. I was just fourteen years of age when I was initiated in the ways of that discipline and charged with all its knowledge. I had no idea then how I could use it.

When she had removed her hands from my head, she looked into my eyes, and I saw tears in hers. She said, "Have faith and trust only in God! All paths shall be uncertain from now on." She bid me farewell, and said, "My family and I have decided to return home with Joseph. He will feel more secure there, when his time comes. We are hoping that Jesus will return before his father departs from this life." She kissed me on the forehead and I cried in her loving arms. Then she left Qumran with little Jacob and Joseph.

I continued with my ritual acts, and in particular I served the white flames of Shakti. Many of the local Essenes had decided to leave the town and the community. One day, when I was leaving the temple after the ritual service, Agnisha was waiting for me to bid me farewell. He thanked me for my vision, which showed him that he should depart. It was difficult for him, but he had received the vision to go to Aquitania, where he would be able to continue spreading the tradition of the Essenes in safety. That made him optimistic. He said goodbye and left Qumran on his way to a new life. The visions I had passed on in my trance had also shown the way to all the others. Sumaja was the only Master that remained in the town. It was very lonely, but we continued with our rituals. Every morning we went to the Ruby chamber, where I performed the fire ritual.

One day, Sumaja stood in front of me saying, "Miriam, I'm going to send you back home now. You cannot stay here any longer. I have to tell you that your father has been killed in a fight and your brother has taken over the house. I have sent a messenger to relay the news that you will be returning home. Your mother's sister is there, looking after the house. I see that you really have to go, since you have duties to complete there. Can you remember when we could not find a name for you? Your parents deliberately gave you no name, since the origin of your family is the royal house of Solomon. In the old tradition, names indicated origin. Your parents, though, decided to conceal your name in these dangerous times. They knew that Herod sought to destroy all the ambitious or successful people of royal lineage. That's why they changed your name — and they never really officially gave you a name at all.

"And now you must leave," the mistress told me. "You have always been a good pupil, and though you don't originate from us, we have always respected and honored you. Your path in the world has been determined while mine ends here. I'm going to support all those who have decided to remain here. I plan to ensure that the role of Qumran is recorded and hidden in the caves. "I am so happy that we received the visions early enough to permit the images and words to be recorded before it it is to late. Even if they fall into the wrong hands, no one will know what they mean. This will be my last task and then ... Miriam, I don't know if we shall ever meet again — in this life, anyhow," she smiled. "But perhaps in one that is yet to come when the prophecies of the Messiah will be fulfilled on Earth! Now go and pack. You must go straight away."

I packed my things. In all the time I had been there, I had never truly become an Essene, but I cried that I had to leave nevertheless. Then my old friend, Jahor, picked me up. I had not seen him in all the time since he first brought me to Qumran. He was grayer than before, and had brought a donkey for me. Sumaja also came to bid me goodbye. We fell into each other's arms and gave the traditional Essene farewell: "Shalom, and may your path be blessed."

I had mixed feelings on my journey back to Jerusalem. After so many years, I was returning to my parents' home. We travelled in silence. My guide and friend gave me the feeling of security: while I was with him nothing could happen to me. Behind me lay the experience of Qumran and ahead of me uncertainty and the unexpected. I did not know what it would be like to return home, after all those years and everything that had occurred. I wondered whether life in Jerusalem had changed. We were constantly receiving news of trouble in the region, so I knew better than to expect a peaceful return to my old home. I rode on my donkey into an uncertain future. What I loved remained behind me. My heart ached when I thought about Sumaja's fate. Although the Essenes do not believe in farewells, I was very sad that I would not see Sumaja again. I buried the memory as much as I could and left the future to fate and put my trust in God. In His infinite wisdom, He would know how to determine our fate. We were silent a long time, but one day my guide said, "The news is going around that the Messiah has returned from his travels." Then he was silent. For one moment, I was very happy, but then the joyful feeling gave way to doubt, since I was deeply occupied with my experiences and what I would encounter in future.

By night, we found accommodation with friendly Essenes. I learned to value the network that the true Essenes had established. In every house where we stayed, the feeling of uncertainty was present despite the welcome we received. The homes we stayed in were full of the signs of intimidation and the fear of being exposed. This fear was in tune with my own feelings, and intensified them. Then a few days later, we first saw the walls of Jerusalem. It was no great pleasure to return, at least at the beginning. That all changed when my guide knocked on the door of my parents' house, and a servant opened it. My old nanny broke into tears when she saw me.

Immediately, the whole house was in an uproar and they called for my brother.

I was heartily received by my brother, who was now grown up. I sensed immediately that he was the master in the house and had accepted the role without difficulty. He introduced the sister of my mother, Martha. I could not remember her, but she was very similar to my mother. Her modest, affectionate character made me feel at ease with her from the first moment. My reception back home was also full of love, which quieted my otherwise disturbed soul. I was given my old room, which I had had as a child. My brother told me that it had remained just as it was when I left it. Nobody had been allowed to stay in it. When my father was still alive he had kept the room free for me, as if I was still in the house. But I blocked any conversation about my father. It was painful for me that he had departed from this life while I was away. I did not want to hear any more about it.

After my return home, I spent a couple of quiet days alone and tried to find myself again. I followed my ritual observance, but I missed the temple in Qumran and the spiritual inspiration of our prayers. Inside myself, my daily routine still remained the same. My brother travelled a lot, and I gathered that he was strongly integrated into society and life in Jerusalem. I realized only then that we were a very prosperous and highly regarded family, and my brother upheld this tradition. I asked myself what I sensed in his aura, since I knew that he had too received mystical training.

We had not yet had any very deep discussions, for which I was grateful. I was, in fact, very thankful that he allowed me time to collect myself and to come to terms with my inner world. We ate together and sometimes we exchanged our views and impressions or talked about small things, but always with restraint. We were hesitant and tactful in touching on the other's world. I was very happy that our meals were taken in the Essene tradition of my parents. One day at the evening meal, my brother said, "We are invited to visit a Roman family tomorrow. They are my friends and they would like to meet you." I agreed, but said nothing else on the subject. I could not remember ever having had contact with any Romans. It was certainly a whole new experience for me.

I resolved to leave my lonely life behind and to accept the visit as a first step toward integrating into life in Jerusalem, and enjoying it. Next evening, we were collected in a Roman carriage, accompanied by slaves, as Roman servants were. It was a kind of chariot with two wheels, pulled by the slaves. I had already sensed that our hosts were rich and influential, and that feeling was confirmed when I saw that they could send a chariot with slaves to bring us to their house.

It was the first time since my childhood that I travelled on the streets of Jerusalem. Our house was located outside the city and so we had to travel through the city gates to arrive at our host's house.

The gates were opened to us but still I refused to let the atmosphere of Jerusalem encroach on my awareness. I found the streets and alleys of Jerusalem were darker and less friendly than those in Qumran. We stopped at a house built in the Roman style, and were led inside and received in a sort of hall or atrium.

An elderly lady, clad so differently than I in my customary Jewish clothing, approached me. She wore a long white dress and her hair was artistically arranged. She radiated wonderful warmth, and emitted a golden light from her heart. I was very happy to discover a friendly person amongst the Romans. Her name was Irisa. I admired her beauty: she was tall, had fair hair and was more strongly built than we Jews, who are generally small, dark–haired and delicately built. She said, "Simon, welcome to my home. I am so happy that you have brought your sister with you. You are heartily welcome. I heard that you were away for a long time, although Simon did not tell me where you were for so long, away from your family."

Over the course of the evening meal, I learned that Irisa was a rich, Roman woman and a generous, compassionate widow who had come to Jerusalem with her Roman husband and had, since his death, remained in the city. She led a comfortable and sheltered life. She was very friendly to us, and told us that since she had come to Jerusalem she had had more and more contact with the traditional Jewish ways, and this had appealed to her more than a whole atrium full of Roman gods — which she found to be idolatry in any case. In particular, the simplicity of a monotheistic belief appealed to her. For some time, she had been following the rumors that the Messiah had already arrived amongst us. She said, "I have heard that he has been journeying and has now returned to Israel. My heart longs to meet him, he who is even called 'the Son of God' in some circles." She knew a lot and had many contacts.

I was silent and did not mention my connection to Jesus. That was the evening I learned that John was now known as "John the Baptist." He had started on the banks of the River

Jordan, making prophetic speeches and baptising those who came to listen. This was all widely known in Jerusalem and the news had spread rapidly throughout Israel.

She said, "Opinions are divided on the subject. Some go along in enthusiastic crowds to him, just drawn by his speeches, and others maintain that he is the reincarnation of Elias — I think you call him the prophet Elijah. Sometimes his speeches scarcely conceal his attacks on the royal house. On the other hand, some just label him as a heretic. He doesn't just have friends in the country so the king and his supporters have had an eye on him from the beginning." I learned much about the stories circulating Jerusalem from Irisa, which I digested and tucked away for the future. It was clear to me that my life was about to change.

Getting home that evening, I was sure of two things: that Jesus had returned and that my brother had chosen good friends. I was sure that Jesus would appear in the next few days, so I began increasingly to adapt myself to a new way of life. I went out into the streets and purchased what we needed from the market and helped around the house. Slowly, I got the impression that I was becoming the lady of the house. I also heard a rumor spreading rapidly through the markets and on the streets that the Messiah had returned and was travelling through Israel. The people were already saying that he was performing miracles and that he was a remarkable person. The murmurings on the street always ended up posing the question of whether this was truly the Messiah.

I remember I had the impression that by now Jesus must be a full-grown man. I wondered too how Mary and Joseph were, and then reflected that it was fairly certain that Joseph was already on his way into the next world. I suppose I now had time for such thoughts. One day, we received a message from Irisa. She informed us that she had heard from friends that Jesus was on his way to Jerusalem. She had sent two slaves to Jesus, with an invitation to live at her house. He had agreed, although he did not even know her. She had also invited other people during his visit, since she was convinced that he was truly the Messiah, and she invited us to come too. Jesus had sent word to her that he expected to arrive within the next three days. As soon as she knew more details, she would have us picked up and brought to her house. The messenger reported this to my brother, and I was very happy when he let me know.

I had listened to all the news from the messenger, and spoke to my brother about my eagerness. He answered impatiently, "What are you saying? A new Messiah? Do you really believe that?" I looked at him imploringly and begged him, "Please, Simon. You know that I can't leave this house alone. Please do me this one favor. I met him in Qumran and got to know him. Believe me; whoever he is, he has something very special, something I have never in my life seen before. Please! Let's go to Irisa's when he comes. I have not seen him for a long time and I'm so eager to see what he's brought with him from his travels. I'm begging you, please ... as a favor?" I noticed his hesitation, but I did not stop begging him until he had agreed to grant my request. We had by that time developed a very affectionate relationship between us, as a brother and sister who value and respect one another.

One evening, when the sun was setting and the house was settling down for a quiet night, there was wild knocking at our door. It was one of Irisa's slaves,. "The master has arrived. I am instructed to ask you to come quickly. I have to bring you to the villa." I wrapped myself in my warm cloak as fast as I could and shook my brother, looked him in the eyes and said, "Come on. You promised me." Then Martha stood up and said decisively, "I'm coming too. I want to see him."

Escorted by the slaves, we were brought to the home of Irisa. I had not anticipated that so many people would have come to see Jesus. The news had spread far and wide. There was an enormous crowd, but we made it! A servant guided us through the throng until we reached the entrance hallway of the house, which was also full of visitors. We were unable to move forward, and there was a tense silence there in the atrium. Although Jesus was not there, my heart started to beat frantically. I could scarcely stand due to my excitement. I began to feel sick and hardly knew how much longer I could bear it when Jesus appeared from a side room.

The people made a path for him wherever he went. Through the gaps between the people I was able to get a glimpse of him now and again. He had grown older and was much more mature. His hair fell down to his shoulders and he had grown a beard. The light in his eyes was even stronger than before. His infinite radiance filled the whole atrium. My ability to perceive energies and auras was not as strong as it had been before, but, that evening, his dazzling light was clearly visible. I had first seen it in our childhood many years ago, but it had become even stronger. He radiated infinite compassion.

I could scarcely breathe. At every opportunity, I just kept trying to catch a glimpse of him. He just stood there and spread his love and compassion throughout the room. All was quiet, so quiet one could have heard a pin drop, as if those present wished to hear his very heartbeat. Not a sound came from the mass of people. He radiated love and peace. Irisa followed him out of the room, and her eyes shone with joy at the sight of the Messiah. Even from a distance I could see it.

Suddenly a voice out of the crowd asked, "Are you the awaited Messiah now returned to us, for whom the people have waited so long?" I could sense that the waves emanating from Jesus changed. He replied softly, "Your love has called to me. Here I am to answer you." I saw how those near to him fell on their knees. As if in a daze, they reached out to touch him. Then a wave of energy came from him; he seemed to be holding the people back. It was an energy filled with compassion, patient and understanding. "I have not come for you to kneel before me: I am here that you would fall on your knees to yourselves. I am here so that you may recognize that you yourselves are this love and compassion. You do not need to touch me. Reach out and touch one another."

Those near to him in the crowd moved back and suddenly a woman came to him and said, "Jesus, many people whom you have healed on your way here were my neighbors. I have a sick child, here wrapped in my coat. I know that only you can help my child." Jesus was silent for a moment, as if he were praying, asking God if he should incite a possible disturbance amongst the people there by fulfilling the mother's request. Behind me the crowd began to murmur and ask what he was going to do. Then his face changed and his look was full of fire. "If you want me to stay amongst you, do not regard me with greed and material wishes. There are some here who seek to do us ill." With that, he paused, sunk deep into prayer. He glanced at the woman and said, "Take your child home." He looked at Irisa and asked her to have her servants make a path for the woman through the crowd. It seemed to me as if he wanted to avoid a commotion.

Suddenly we heard a scream outside and the voice of the mother cried out, "My child! The Lord! He is truly the Messiah! He has healed my child. My little daughter is well again." And at that moment, I noticed that Jesus had quietly disappeared. Some of those present then fell on their knees. Others were visibly agitated, others still left quietly. It was an incredible atmosphere. Those on their knees were in quiet prayer, praising the Lord.

It was just then that somebody tugged at my cloak. It was my brother. He said, "Come on. Let's go. I think it is unsafe in here." He had to pull me a couple of times. I did not want to leave. But he held my arm and pulled me firmly outside and said, "Don't do that again with me. What you were up to here is dangerous. You know how the situation in Jerusalem is. When it gets around what went on here tonight, we could be in danger." He pulled me to our chariot, and on the way home I was in a daze. Martha sat next to me. She was as intoxicated from the experience as I was, and had a happy smile on her face. I smiled briefly at her: she had understood me.

During that sleepless night I tossed and turned but found no peace. The sun was near its peak in the sky the next day when there was a pounding on our front door. I went to our inner courtyard to await our unexpected visitor, while one of our servants opened the door. I cried for happiness: it was Mary.

112

I rushed towards her and we hugged each other tenderly for some minutes. After we had released one another, she said, "Well, at least it's not improper that I visit you. Your father and mother were very close friends of our family, so officially I am paying you a visit!"

I invited her to stay and gave her something to eat and drink. I was dying of curiosity, and asked, "Mary, how have you been? Have you news from Qumran? I have not heard any news for a long time. Please tell me." She recounted that she had returned home with Joseph and Jacob, and as they had arrived, Jesus was already standing at the door, like an apparition. She was extremely happy to see him. While abroad, he had become aware of the inner voice of Mary that his father would soon be departing from this life, so he had come to him. Jesus was there with by Joseph of Arimathea, who then bid us farewell and returned to Jerusalem.

I learned later that Joseph of Arimathea went with Jesus on his journeys in foreign lands. He and Jesus shared some inner link with one another. Joseph knew many places from his extensive business trips, and returned frequently to Israel for his business, which included political matters. For years they had travelled together, frequently in distant lands. This time he had accompanied Jesus here. Mary told me that Jesus intended to remain, since her husband Joseph was visibly weakening, and in the last days, Jesus was with him day and night. She was deeply moved by how Jesus remained with him until he passed on from this life. Then she observed the customary period of mourning. After long years, she once again had time just for her son. When the days of mourning were over, Jesus said to Mary, "Now I have fulfilled my responsibility to the family. I have done my duty and honored the world's rules. Mother, I would like you and your small son to come with me; my brother, Jacob, will grow to be my companion. Now is the time for me to begin my mission here in the land of my fathers." Mary explained: "You know, Miriam, as always, he didn't make any demands: he left me free to choose. That night, I decided to leave the life I had been leading, and all the security I had enjoyed, and to go with him. We travelled from one place to another. In the beginning, we visited Essenes and stayed with them. Increasingly, I experienced how my son, whom I had nursed as a small boy, could stop unexpectedly and just start preaching to a crowd. We didn't know from one moment to another what he had planned. I never knew what was going to happen the next day but that is the way of life I chose." I listened to her words, spellbound, and then I asked, "Mary, I scarcely dare to ask, but do you know what happened in Qumran? I've heard worrying rumors that it was attacked and razed to the ground. I'm so scared, I don't know if I want to know what has happened, particularly to everyone I know and love there."

Mary was silent and inwardly shed tears straight from her heart and was quite still. Then she said, "I have good and bad news for you. Many Essenes lost their lives in a very cowardly and unnecessarily brutal attack. Now, as I tour through the countryside with Jesus, I have to say that I just do not believe in coincidence any more. One day, when we were near Qumran, Jesus suddenly informed me that he would leave us for a day or two. Two days later, he returned — bringing Sumaja with him. He had seen what had gone on in Qumran and persuaded her, almost against her will, to leave. He had made her understand that her task on Earth had not ended. Later she went to stay with a travelling sales-man — an employee of Joseph of Arithmea. They have ships that often sail between ports around here and the coast of Occitania. They helped her with arranging passage on a ship and also helped her enter the country where Agnisha now lives. That is the good news."

"We don't know for sure where she is, but we do know that she is safe and well. Believe me, she did not want to leave, and was prepared to sacrifice herself for Qumran. But Jesus was adamant. He had almost had to command her, and then he'd said, 'You cannot change the fate of others, but you must fulfill your own destiny; otherwise you will be taking on the guilt of others as part of your own fate.' So, finally, she did follow him. Two days later Qumran was completely destroyed. We made a long detour to avoid Qumran, since all the turmoil and destruction would have put us in danger too."

I listened intently as she recounted what happened next. "We did not hide the fact that we were Essenes; it was a miracle that we managed to travel through the country without danger or hindrance. It was like Jesus was invisibly protecting anyone who had listened to him. Wherever we appeared, we were safe and undisturbed. Finally we got to Jerusalem after a lot of stops, and the rest of the story you know." Finally, she added, "One day, a couple of messengers came to us with an invitation from an unknown Roman lady, to be guest in her house, to which Jesus has agreed."

I was glad that my brother Simon did not disturb us. We could be alone, and my old friendship with Mary was renewed and did me good. Her motherly spirit quieted my troubled heart.

I felt relieved and I sensed Mary did too. Then she bid me fetch my brother and Martha, whom she knew from the friendship between our families.

Mary then spoke to my brother. "Simon, you are the man of the house. I have come on my son's behalf to ask if you would extend an invitation to him; he'd like to visit you. Joseph of Arimathea is also with us at the moment and it would be nice if you would welcome us to your home." I was astonished at Simon's answer. "The friendship that you enjoyed with my father and mother is the key to a new friendship. I'm going away on important business but I would be pleased to invite you as my guests in two days. However, I have to ask you, please keep your coming and going secret, since Jesus has been in the middle of more than a bit of commotion. Is that possible?"

Mary laughed and replied, "It has become a part of our life, moving around invisibly, remaining undetected and keeping from being followed. Rest assured, no one will see us arriving or departing from this house." Then Mary and Martha left us and I could only hug my brother and thank him. For a moment, we were like children again. I said, "You really are my big brother." I realized that, somehow, something had changed in him. His fear of acting against the norms and risking our standing in Jerusalem society had softened and given way to something more positive. That made us allies!

I had time to think and reflect on events in the following two days. The question that increasingly occupied my mind was, what was Simon's political business? I had never asked him. As he was away again for two days, I began to be interested in what he did when he was out of the house. I sensed that it must be quite delicate business. He had connections to influential people, and even to the royal family. I was not permitted to be present when he had visitors on business, and he and his guests always retired discreetly to discuss matters. Their business seemed to spell trouble, but I did not know how.

I did not have a chance to speak to my brother about such matters. Martha and I followed our daily routine in the house, and prepared for Jesus' visit. That evening I could hardly contain my excitement. I calmed myself by lighting the oil lamps and placing holy water where guests could wash themselves on arrival, as I had learned from the Essenes. Martha sent me out of the kitchen, since she said I was unbearable at present. Simon returned in the afternoon and he seemed to be thinking deeply about something — but I was in no mood to discuss such matters with him. Suddenly there was a knock on our door and, although it was not customary as a woman, I opened the door myself.

There they were, Jesus, Mary and Joseph of Arimathea standing in the doorway. It was Jesus who advanced into the house first and after such a long absence, we spent the first few moments just looking at each other. The boy I had known years ago had grown into the Messiah. I had a great respect for him, and kept my distance. Now he was Jesus, Son of God. Despite my reticence he came straight to me and gave me a big hug, saying, "It is good to see you again, Miriam. I give thanks for the welcome to your home." I noted that Simon was irritated behind me: I had broken the rules of the man of the house. He greeted the guests, and then they washed, as was our habit, before sitting at table. The atmosphere became very relaxed and familiar, more so than I had experienced for a long time in our house. The conversations were light and friendly, and even Simon seemed to enjoy it. Mary and I joked with one another and Jacob had grown into a mischievous, intelligent boy. I could not wait for Jesus to tell us where he had been for such a long time. But I did not mention the subject at table, uncertain as to whether he would speak freely when Simon and Martha were present. Suddenly Jesus said, "Simon, would you permit me to speak to Miriam alone?"

I noted for the first time how little Jesus observed the conventions of society. He did as he liked. He did not bother about society's demands. Simon swallowed hard next to me, and I hoped that he would agree. I knew that it would be a serious conversation with Jesus, one not suitable for the dinner table. Mary and Joseph said nothing and then Simon said, "We've got a small courtyard at the back of the house, with a little garden. I wouldn't like you to be seen from outside. If you ever want to speak to my sister alone, you can do so within the walls of this house." Simon himself brought us into the garden, which I had often used when I wanted to be alone. I was terribly excited. We sat on a stone bench from which we could view the landscape. Jesus was silent for a while, until in my curiosity I broke the silence. "I am impatient to hear where you were, what you have experienced and what these years have done to you. I can't imagine where you were in the world." He smiled and said, "I think these matters would be interesting to all of you. Joseph of Arimathea does not know them all either. When your family permits I would like to tell all of you all about it — especially you. I know my mother has told you all about my youth. What you don't know is that the story of my life will be engraved in your heart, so that one day, sometime in the distant future, the story will see the light of day again."

Before I could formulate any question he continued: "The story which is now unfolding will be changed and distorted by those who hate us. You will retain the true version. You should know every step that I have taken, to enable the true story to be told. There has never been a story such as this. Beings from throughout all the heavens have accompanied me to Earth. The most powerful of all masters, goddesses, angels and those who are my companions on my mission are here, concealed in the form of inconspicuous humans. We are assembled here to enable God's kingdom to exist on Earth for a short time." I didn't know exactly what he was telling me. It was so incredible. I felt very honored that he trusted me with his story. His visions allowed him to read God's plan.

"You should know, Miriam, I am going to share my experiences on my journeys with all of you, since I want to prevent any of this knowledge being lost or eradicated. It should all be conserved, since the travels were important. They formed me. I will now entrust to you alone just one of these stories: after I had visited schools of wisdom in Egypt and Greece, I travelled to Asia, to India and Tibet. Through connections of my uncle's, who is also a high master, I had contact with the best schools that exist outside the land of Israel. In each of these schools, I was a student myself until my understanding was great enough. From Tibet, I started the long journey home, and finally I met him, the one whom I had sought so long. I saw him face to face, the master of all masters. In India, they call him the great Baba, a name meaning 'father'. I had wandered alone through the snowy mountains when he suddenly appeared before me. Baba just said, 'There you are, at last.'

"I stayed a long time with him, until other masters appeared one after the other and we shared the visions for the Earth. Masters we will meet here on Earth were there in their spiritual bodies. The great Baba initiated us. In his presence, I recognized myself on Earth again. Everything I sought in human existence was perfected in his presence, to be integrated into my everlasting being. Later he explained to me that I did not have to be initiated, since I was and always shall be initiated. Nevertheless it was an important schooling. I am telling you this because he also confided something very important in the course of his tutoring me. He showed me that I will have companions for myself and for my mission, whom I must — and will — find in Israel. Some of them were there with us in their spiritual bodies. Now I have to find those in human form. He also showed me that he sent you to support me. You actually come from him. You shall accompany every step that I make, from that moment when the events of my vision begin. You will gather the story within yourself, so that it is stored for posterity — it could otherwise be forgotten, distorted or negated. The story which begins now will live again one day."

I could hardly believe what Jesus was telling me. I was so astonished I could have fallen almost off my seat. A thousand questions raced through my head. "Jesus, how do you imagine something like that is going to happen? You travel everywhere around the country. How could I possibly accompany you? Don't you see who I am? I am a woman; I can't just wander everywhere with you and write your story. How do you propose to solve that problem?" He said simply, "I will ask your brother whether you can go with me." I could not imagine how Jesus' idea could be realized. We lived in Israel, after all. A woman who is not his mother may not travel together with a man. She would only gain a very bad reputation in any towns or villages that she visited. I knew exactly what people would think; after all, we were old–fashioned Hebrew Jews. I would simply be labeled as a whore.

Yet again, I recognized that Jesus obeyed no conventions, no rules. Such things simply did not interest him. A wild idea came into my head: there was nothing I would rather do than win this freedom and accompany him. But I had no idea how it could be arranged. It appeared impossible to me. Then he said, "It is time to return to the dinner table." We returned and sat down with the others. I did not know how to process my thoughts out that evening. I would have liked to return to my room, since I could not look at my brother this evening. I was very disturbed and my heart beat faster. But Mary seemed to know it all already. For her it was easy: she was a widow and Jesus was her son ... but, for me, it was completely different. I did not find peace that evening. Later, Simon became relaxed and jolly. He placed the best wine from his cellar at our disposal. Jesus seemed to like wine, and we drank and were happy.

Suddenly Jesus looked at Simon and said, "From now onward you will no longer called Simon. Your name is Lazarus. You belong to a group of one hundred and eight who accompany me. Simon, who is now Lazarus, I do not like your daring underground profession. I do not approve of your political ambitions; nevertheless you belong to me. I will not attempt to stop you. Just rest assured that I know what you do. And, because you belong to me, you should help me find the others." Then he was silent. The shock was visible in my brother's eyes. He was short of breath and clearly disturbed. Nevertheless, from this moment on a strong bond of friendship grew between the two of them. Although they had radically different opinions on many matters, they were joined by a kinship that nobody else could fathom. I was happy that Jesus did not repeat the holy story at table that night; it could have shocked my brother to death. When our visitors were departing Jesus said, "I am going to be in Jerusalem for some time. Many families have invited me. I will contact you again sometime soon."

This was the time when Jesus began to appear in public. My decision was made: if God wished it, I would accompany Jesus, in order to get the full the story. He would know how to overcome the obstacles that troubled me ... At the same time, though, I couldn't help feeling that I was somehow defying God. Why had he brought me into this world as a woman? Would it not have been simpler if I had been born a man? Within myself, I could not avoid complaining to God, questioning what he meant by it. I watched my brother with amusement in the following days. He was confused and disturbed. My God, what had Jesus stirred up in our society? He was not only Messiah; he was also rebel. He broke all the traditional rules as we knew them, that much was clear to me and I approved of it! Anyhow, the conventions of Jewish life were too narrow and conservative for me.

The next day, we were unexpectedly collected by one of Irisa's servants. By now, we were learning to accept Jesus' spontaneity.

Martha, 'Lazarus' and I were cordially welcomed into her house, the house of a Roman woman who had helped us with her contacts, knowledge and respect in society. I was beginning to develop a close friendship with her. That evening, Jesus, Mary and Jacob were there too — they had been living there. Joseph of Arimathea was also there, and a couple of others I did not know.

Jesus offered us all wine, and began telling his tale, which lasted for several evenings. He shared the story of his journeys and experiences with us. Whatever Jesus left out was filled in by Joseph of Arimathea, who had often been with him. We were happy and light-hearted, and we consumed much excellent wine. We were all very contented. Then Jesus commenced the story of his travels, which had lasted many years, until his vision for Israel was imminent, and caused him to return.

"I left Qumran because I had received the inner call from masters in distant lands. Joseph accompanied me and we first travelled toward Egypt. This country had been the home of the sun–cult for a very long time. I realized immediately that the spirit of my Father was turbulent within me: the distortion of the creation, of the mind and of the spirit was so extreme here. As we travelled in the valley of the River Nile, I really did not know whether we would find traces of the Holy Spirit. But, eventually, we did come to a place near to the Alexandria of ancient times, where we found an old spiritual school in the original spirit of Egypt that, in turn, was connected to the era of Atlantis. It was a school, a discipline in its original, unmodified form, unimpaired by the worldly might of the Pharaohs, who had corrupted the teachings. There is a library in Alexandria, and my arrival had been expected.

"There were three masters remaining in the school who had heard about me from Casper, Melchior and Balthazar, and who knew all about this place. The masters begged me to instruct them, but I had to tell them that I was there to learn from this earthly school, as a scholar and not as teacher. They said that there was nothing they could teach me that I did not already know. For some time, I studied their manuscripts and rediscovered their knowledge, which God had long ago embedded in the earth.

"When I had absorbed this knowledge I dreamed one night that God spoke to me and said, 'My son, knowledge comes and goes on Earth. Inform them of My will. They should sink all their books in the sea; the time of Egyptian knowledge has passed. That country has carried out My will up to today, but shall do so no longer. It will follow a path in which the lights of the holy initiation will be extinguished. You have raised the knowledge you possess to a living wisdom. I am not served by the transmission of lifeless knowledge.' I informed the masters of my dream next day. I do not believe they liked God's will, but they followed it and left the school with me. We left no trace of our presence. Thus we followed my Father's will and the primeval knowledge of Egypt was extinguished and sunk in the sea."

Jesus went on to tell us what happened after they left Egypt. "We travelled by ship to Greece. During the journey, Joseph of Arimathea told us that there are very old schools of wisdom and enlightened masters there. Some of the masters still radiate this divine consciousness. But the more we travelled through Greece, the more I sensed the source of my love dry up. As we disembarked, I looked at Joseph and said, 'Joseph, the knowledge here could be enormous, but it is without love. I do not wish to visit another school of wisdom that has not love at its roots. What does knowledge alone contribute when it has become independent from compassion? Please do not suggest such ideas, especially since I know that what you really want comes through me. Whatever we do must lead to divine equilibrium; it was not a good decision to come here — I should not be getting involved in the kind of thinking that go on here. Let's travel on further. There is nothing here for us.'

"So, then we travelled in a quite different direction," Jesus explained. "I was attracted to an ancient land, of which I had heard from the Essenes — the land of our ancestors, from the lines of Brahma, of Vishnu and of Shiva. That was my goal. On the way there, we visited various schools of spiritual wisdom, which had established themselves on Earth. But my goal was to get to India. After a journey lasting months we finally arrived at the country of my choice. We visited various divine places, still filled with life. But I did not find a place that touched my soul. I have had much contact with old wisdom and with the initiated who have carried it, but nothing touched my heart. The spirit of my Father began to speak through me. I was recognized as the prophet who brings back the living word, and although I had spent a long time in many schools I did not want to stay. It was important for me to read in the books of the ancient Veda the story of humanity, between the lines of which God would speak. Nevertheless I found no trace of the school of compassion, only dispossessed knowledge that had nothing to do with God's love.

"One day I said to Joseph that I was old enough and would continue my travels without him: 'Joseph, you can return home now. I would like to continue my journey alone. I will keep in inner communication with you, so you may know when you should return to me. I cannot say when, but trust me and remain in contact. Then we will return to Israel together, and visit several places. God is with me and will guide me. My Father is so strong in me now that I know the path of my primeval initiations.

"I travelled alone now and always found people who would give me food and a place to stay. I usually remained anonymous, and was just a traveler. I had received the call from a distant land beyond the snowy mountains of the Himalayas, from a country called Tibet. When I arrived, I encountered a holy culture, quite isolated from the outside world. I discovered the place of a very ancient monastery, in which I met wise guardians, whose age was very difficult to guess. As it always is when masters meet, they knew who they had before them, so they accepted me immediately and invited me to stay. A high master, who radiated a golden light of love and wisdom, said, 'You are here to exhume our buried Shambala. We have guarded the markers that will unlock our ancient city since time immemorial. I recognize you: you are the key to open the doors to Shambala. Our consciousness has been awakened by your arrival.'"

Jesus continued to relate his experiences, which lasted for several evenings. When the next sunset came round, he started telling us about Shambala: "From this monastery, I started opening doors and finding ways as in a dream. Sometimes, I wandered through the mountains, sometimes I made my way only in my dreams. I knew all the time that I must find the key to something that was locked up beyond the worlds. My earthly consciousness had to reach the higher levels of my spiritual consciousness. I alone held the key. Then, one night, the flames of God's love reached me, and I sent a messenger of fire on a path through all worlds. That sea of flames dispersed the fog of illusion and next thing I was standing in front of a door. Beyond the door was Shambala. I had found it.

"I entered the town, which was full of life. I had returned as ruler. My human and superhuman consciousnesses were no longer separate. So I had returned to Shambala. The wisdom of Shambala is very old, and I would like you to become acquainted with it. It is a primeval place, in which the highest spiritual masters from all universes, those that we name avatars, including God himself, have their seat. It is the spiritual hierarchy, the universal consciousness that has its place on Earth here and rules the whole universe with compassion. I accepted my role as ruler, beside another four. When I arrived we renewed the alliance of the avatars for the Earth. Avatars are higher beings, about whom you have not yet learned. They represent the meeting of energies from all worlds, which appear from time to time on Earth. I blended my consciousness with that of the other avatars."

"I found myself in union with one avatar, who is at my side beyond the dimension of time — and that means for all time. All worlds and universes know his name: Agni. We rediscovered our old brotherhood, the spiritual consciousness of all worlds. In Shambala we formed a new alliance for the Earth, the consciousness of the Light of Christ. They were cosmic unions. Bonds between the divine light and the avatars were unified in me. We travelled through all worlds together. The Earth received a new beginning, after a long period of darkness. We renewed the bond of forgiveness and conciliation, and I accepted this vision for myself. Resurrected from the human body, belonging to the avatars and immersed in the Light of Christ from my Father, I accepted this mission for the Earth. The forgiveness of sins should be manifested through my compassion. This we agreed together, and founded a new heavenly sign. The harmony of the Earth was restored. We were unified in the combination of all worlds, which we wish to teach those who fill the Earth with their spiritual consciousness."

Jesus paused at this point and then said, "Perhaps you do not understand everything I am telling you. But it is the primeval bond with my Father that we have renewed. From now on the consciousness of the divine light will again penetrate the Earth. And I am the first messenger, to stimulate this consciousness with the flame of the Light of Christ. The avatars come to Earth from time to time. My task is to prepare for the subsequent arrival of avatars in the age of Aquarius, to renew the real alliance for the Earth. I have preceded some avatars, but one has come to the Earth with me, in whom I can plant my seed. He is always with me and we work side–by–side. The master of fire, Agni — my everlasting friend and my everlasting brother."

That ended his narration for the evening. We were numbed and drunk from the experiences from so many worlds. With his consciousness he changed ours. The message on this evening was meant for all Israel. He sought everyone who was willing to unite with him. The room shook and vibrated. Through his words we entered a world that had long ago disappeared from this Earth. That night I dreamed endless visions of God's kingdom, and I did not know how to recapture my wandering soul. I was sure that Jesus had a good reason for telling us his story. We were following him into the higher planes, other spheres, as if he wished to bring back a piece of the eternal heaven.

We had to experience these things before choosing to accept the challenge of his mission for the Earth. It seemed to me that each of us had consciously decided. We acted in the name of many who would join us later. We were from that time bound to the task: an inner circle had closed! We knew the knowledge we gained was important, that we pass it on to others. That night I lay in flaming fire. My consciousness extended over many levels of light. I recognized the all–powerful existence of God, completely different from that which I found on Earth. I saw that we are beings who accompany greater beings who will come to Earth. One of these is Jesus Christ, the Messiah. This promise originated in primeval times. Compassion and the consciousness of God are our home. Whatever the future might bring, we were prepared to accept the challenge.

On the following evening we were invited to Irisa's house. When the three of us arrived the house was festively illuminated. She had invited with great hospitality, and it was to a further exhilarating evening, in which Jesus served us wine which intoxicated our souls. He continued his account: "When I had reached agreement with the other avatars in Shambala, and we had united the seal of the new age within us, united for the Earth, I realized that it was time to leave Shambala. I embody the Light of Christ, which was confirmed within me. I determined again to give this Light to the world, in order to break its karmic cycle and bring forgiveness and salvation. I consciously chose the material way and embarked on a pilgrim's journey. "When the gates of Shambala had closed behind me, I tramped through broad valleys of snow, quite alone. I needed no supplies, since all that I needed materialised in front of me. I was neither cold nor was I hungry. Even the wild animals were my friends, and did me no harm. I made my way back to the monastery in which I had previously met the High Master, and expressed my thanks to them. It became clear to me that they were responsible for guiding me back to Shambala. Out of gratitude, I presented them with the gift of everlasting prayer.

"I then travelled further into Tibet, where I spent a few years, teaching those whose thirst for living knowledge was waiting to be quenched. I immersed myself in the ancient culture of Tibet, which will survive long into the future, in the Christian Consciousness. They taught me and I taught them. I brought back the Prayer to God for them. Then it was time for me to leave Tibet, and once again I journeyed through the snowy valleys and then home. Israel was already in my inner consciousness. Then one day a man stood in front of me, his eyes full of fire, and I recognized him immediately. He spoke to me: 'Are you going my way, Son of God?'

"We were able to see one another through the eyes of the other," Jesus went on. "Through his eyes, I recognized him as the great Maha Baba Babaji. He wanders eternally through the holy mountains of the Himalayas and rules and awakens the consciousness of the people there. He is the great teacher of the worlds, who in eternal youth retains the awareness of God. Through my inner vision I recognized instantly his knowledge and experience. Then he asked me, "Will you stay in order to perfect yourself? I am the Master of all lives. Your life path will be shaped by me." So I remained seven years with Maha Baba. For those seven years, I was one with Maha Baba and he prepared me for my path. During this time I encountered all beings that I would later meet on Earth. Together we dreamed common dreams for the future.

"He and I were united as one," Jesus explained about the Maha Baba. "We trained each other and reached perfection through the other. One day he brought me to a cave, and through his mantras and his signs blessed and confirmed the knowledge I was to take with me. Then he looked at me and said, 'Now is the time for you to depart. We have been together long enough that you can now return to the world. The path that has been predetermined for you is prepared.' I drew great strength from Maha Baba's recognition and support, so that I was prepared to start the next stage of my journey. I left Maha Baba and commenced my return to Israel. I sent an inner message to Joseph of Arimathea, and he met me in a town in India. We travelled through various countries, including Afghanistan and Persia and visited various schools of wisdom there.

"From then on I was the teacher. Each of these schools of spiritual consciousness is part of the Wheel of Knowledge, and I was able to set God's flame and the seed of Christian Consciousness, so that wisdom and love were finally united with one another." With that, Jesus began to wrap up the story of his travels. "After a long journey, we made it back to Israel. In this forgotten land of God, my mission begins and I begin to collect my chosen companions, those Heaven has sent me."

Jesus then ceased his narration, and we celebrated long into the night and drank good wine. It was as if we had established a united nucleus, which was to expand and contact others. Then in the early hours Jesus spoke briefly: "Twelve companions will join me, to form the inner circle, including three women, one of whom will accompany me in some of my travels. A further 108 companions shall constitute the outer circle, to support my mission." After a short pause he murmured, "All this will appear at the appropriate time." Then he was finally silent, apparently deep in his inner world, into which nobody could follow.

We all returned home in silence that evening. Lazarus and Martha were lost in thought, deep in their souls. We had arrived at a turning point, defining our way for the future. This night was quiet and without images or messages. But it was clear to me that the future had commenced, in accordance with God's word. I determined only to trust this future course, with all of my body, my soul and my intellect.

In the following days, it became increasingly evident that the word of Jesus' healing powers had spread in Jerusalem. Jesus requested that Irisa receive and coordinate the large number of people who wanted to visit him. She had a wonderful ability to organize. Everybody wanted to go to him, since his divine healing powers had become known. I kept myself increasingly withdrawn, to collect myself together. I was determined to continue my studies and to devote myself to learning. My brother, Lazarus, agreed that my previous teacher could visit me again. So I spent my days with my books, learning various languages. I had missed my studies, and was happy to be able to recommence them. I was greedy for new knowledge, since it extended my horizons and distracted me from daily life. Every now and again I visited Irisa at home, where I was most affectionately received, as a sister. We became deeply attached to one another.

Jesus no longer had much time for us. Sick, despairing and helpless individuals came to Him, or just inquisitive persons, curious to see whether he was truly God's son. He received them all. Now and again he appeared in the inner courtyard of the house. I observed him and was astonished by the patience and devotion with which he received all his visitors. Everyone was admitted and many were healed. Hopeless people departed filled with hope and the flame of his love, ready to receive what life offered. It was very touching to see how his light and love spread into the room and filled each and every soul who came to him. All his visitors left with his love shining in their eyes.

I withdrew as far as possible into the house, in order to avoid the turbulence of so many people and to regain my inner peace. One day, I visited Irisa's house; Jesus saw me arrive and said, "Miriam, come to me." I made my way through the crowd, which had already assembled.

A woman stood in front of him and he said, "I need your help. Now you can show your powers of healing. I think you can help more than I can." I was naturally irritated, since I had not practiced my Essene healing for a very long time. But the look in his eyes fired my heart and all my healing powers returned. I knelt before the woman who had begged for Jesus' help, and looked at her and saw a dark creature: a demon was living within her. I sought help in Jesus' eyes but he said,

"Only you can conquer this demon, since it originates from within her family. You possess this knowledge." It was as if I only had to hear Him and all the old healing powers returned to me, and enabled me through my prayers to fulfill God's will and heal the soul of this woman. I approached the woman and embraced her. Suddenly I trembled all over and experienced a divine prayer in me. I was able to release the demon in her and to return it to the world in which it belonged. The woman collapsed in my arms and was unconscious. As I returned out of the trance, I saw that one of Irisa's servants was looking after the woman.

I knelt down and emptied her of the thoughts, worries and feelings that had filled her — as I had learned from the Essenes. With the healing power from her own divine soul, she was filled with her own pure self again. She awoke and radiated light and joy from her eyes. I then bowed to her and wanted to withdraw, but she knelt before me and began to cry. I helped her to her feet and said, "You should not thank me, but the Messiah, who gave me the strength — who gives everyone the strength. He restores God's light to all of us." I do not know whence these words came; they seemed to speak for themselves without any thought from me, as if he gave them to me. Then I glanced up to Jesus and the love streamed out of his heart directly to me: the feeling of pure Love, flowing from him to me, transfixed me. Nothing else mattered. I was enveloped in his limitless love. The moment seemed to last forever — I lost all track of time.

Then Jesus returned to his visitors and I withdrew again into the inner part of the house. I had to gather myself together after such a spiritual experience. I did not know immediately what this love signified for me. It disturbed my inner being and touched my soul. It was not a love of this material world. I sensed that my love for him was limitless and uncontrollable. I resolved to return home, although it was difficult for me to find my way through all the masses of people waiting to see Jesus. Eventually, I reached the street and made my way home. I was deeply troubled; it was difficult for me, so young and inexperienced, to cope with my intense love for him. I fled from Irisa's house and tried to find peace in my soul in my own home.

When I visited Irisa the next day, I heard a servant say, "Jesus has departed on a journey." I went into the house and found Irisa. Before I could ask, she said, "Jesus decided to go this morning. He didn't say where. He just said, 'The desert calls. I must go. I cannot say when I will return.'" Our eyes met and it was as if we had secretly agreed to keep watch for him. We sat in silence. But we had no idea where he had gone. The days passed, and it gradually became quieter in Jerusalem. We heard nothing from Jesus and received no news. Nobody had any idea where he had gone or why. I tried to concentrate on my books and learning, and gradually began to enjoy the studies of the Greek and Latin languages again. I visited Irisa daily and began to see the fear growing in her eyes, worrying about Jesus. Even Mary hadn't been informed of Jesus' whereabouts, so she decided to return home, to Nazareth, taking her youngest son with her.

It was quiet and we were increasingly worried. But we received no news of Jesus; I began to count the days that he was away. Then on the thirty-ninth night I awakened with a load scream: I saw him in the desert. He called me. He needed me. I did not understand how I received the message, but I was sure that he had sent me an inner message. I awakened my brother and asked him, "Bring me to Irisa's house. Jesus needs us. He has called for our help."

We stumbled to Irisa's house in the darkness and after a short while she let us in. She recognized immediately that the situation was serious, and looked at us worriedly. I told her of my vision of Jesus in the desert, and that we must find him to bring him help. Irisa asked, "How do you intend to find him? We have no idea in which direction he went when he left the house." But I insisted that we must search for him, since I knew he needed us. Lazarus decided to accompany me and I said to him, "I don't know where he is, but I will trust my inner voice to lead me to him. Please let me have a couple of servants to accompany me. We must find him. Something inexplicable has happened to him and he needs our help."

We left Jerusalem in the direction of the desert. Lazarus kept looking at me incredulously, as if I were slightly mad: how could I imagine finding Jesus in this endless desert, where no human can exist alone? We walked for a while, but I do not know how long — I had lost all sense of time. All I knew was that we must continue. Then suddenly we saw a man sitting in our path. He wore a white robe and had blonde hair. A bright light radiated from the man, as if he was from another world. He asked, "Are you looking for Jesus?" I knew he would bring us to him. He wordlessly indicated the way, and I knew we could trust him. He had suddenly appeared from nowhere and showed us the way. After a day travelling in the desert he indicated a cave in which we found Jesus. My heart almost stopped beating when I saw him: he was scarcely alive.

He was pale, thin and emaciated. The stranger went over to Jesus, made a mark on his forehead and held his hand there for some time. It appeared as if the stranger and Jesus communicated with one another. I saw it as if I was in a trance. Lazarus and I were in despair and afraid that Jesus would not survive. Then the stranger looked up at us and said, "Now you can bring him back to life. Miriam, you can now help him to recover." I wondered how the stranger knew my name, but at that moment it did not matter. Then the stranger left us and disappeared into the desert.

The servants had brought a stretcher with them, upon which we laid Jesus. I offered him some water, and he drank a little and then opened his eyes slightly. Although he was exhausted a wonderful light radiated through his half–closed lids, as if the divine love and compassion was even deeper and greater than before. Then Jesus spoke, so softly that I had to put my ear to his mouth: "Now you can bring me back, Miriam. I am so grateful that you had heard me in the night. The Lord of Darkness met me in the desert with his worldly temptations. But God in me finally triumphed." We carried him home, which seemed like a short journey now that we had found him. The time passed so quickly. We carried Jesus discreetly and stealthily to Irisa's house, to avoid being observed. I applied all my Essene strength and knowledge to reviving Jesus. I remembered the healing herbs of the Essenes, which I still possessed and could use. After two days Jesus awakened to full consciousness for the first time. Irisa had prayed for him watched over him day and night, and never lifted her eyes from him. When we finally saw him awaken I said, "Oh Lord, I thank Heaven and all the angels that you have returned to us."

Jesus sat up and said, "I fought with the darkness of the Earth for forty days and nights. I accepted the darkness of humanity, of the Earth within me, with all evils and temptations, until the Lord of Darkness himself appeared. In a three–day battle we fought until the light and love in me triumphed over the temptations of darkness. He was reinforced by evils of humanity, but the light in me eventually succeeded." He smiled and seemed to regain all his old strength. Jesus took my hand and kissed it, saying, "I thank you, Miriam." Then he took Irisa's hand and said, "You too, Irisa. Your support, and that of Miriam, has helped me to clean away the traces of evil that cost me so much strength and almost sapped my body of its life. You have brought me back."

As Jesus spoke, I recalled images from the past — the Dead Sea, Sodom and Gomorrah, and all the old recollections of Qumran. However, Jesus appeared to have emerged from the battle in the desert stronger than before, and his light radiated more brilliantly. After only a few hours his recovery seemed to be complete: he was his old self. Irisa gave him food and he ate it without a word, but with a smile on his lips. I said to him, "Jesus, who was the man we met in the desert who led us to you?" He smiled broadly and then answered, "I have told you about my brother, Agni. That was he." Then he was quiet again and continued eating. After a pause Jesus said, "Now it is time for me to visit John." He looked at Irisa and me: "I want you two and Lazarus to come with me. The Baptist makes fire from water. It is time for me to visit him."

John the Baptist's feats were renowned throughout Jerusalem. One could sense that the atmosphere was tense and that political disturbances occurred. Opinions were divided as to

John's deeds. Irisa was afraid and asked Jesus to let her stay at home. "You know, Lord, that there are wagging tongues here that are angry that I invited you to live here. Of course I invite you to stay here whenever and for as long as you wish. We have friends among the Romans who are somewhat reticent but are as yet positively disposed to you. John's call is somewhat more strident and could be offensive to both Romans and Jews. Hence I beg you to let me stay here, so that I can support you discreetly from home."

Jesus nodded agreement. "Miriam, tell your brother and Martha: we leave tomorrow morning." I returned home and gradually realized that the activities of Jesus and John the Baptist were destined to bring opposition and enmity. On one hand, I knew that I should follow Jesus unconditionally. On the other hand, I recognized the dangers. I spoke to my brother in a quiet moment and explained that Jesus wished us to accompany him. Our Jewish tradition required that I beg my brother for permission to go, although more recently we women had emancipated ourselves somewhat. Nevertheless, I realized that I should attempt to observe the old traditions. Jewish society, particularly in Jerusalem, was very conservative and unyielding. Failure to observe the traditions and rules of the Rabbis could quickly end in being labeled as sinners, and being ostracised from society. That could take place rapidly and be accepted without a murmur by the general public.

Lazarus was generous as ever, and spoke out of his heart. "We are here to accompany the Lord. I will be your official companion." I knew that he had understood, and was glad. When I was with him I was sure that nothing would happen to me. We planned to leave next morning after meeting at

Irisa's house. When we met him there, Jesus radiated the good health and strength he had shown previous times. He had recovered from his collapse in the desert in an amazing way. In addition, he seemed to have amassed supernatural powers in his body.

We made our way towards the River Jordan. It was a pleasant journey and Jesus was in a good mood. When we travelled with him he was almost always relaxed and I felt safe and was sure that nothing would go wrong. He looked after us all the time. When we tired he always sought an appropriate place to rest. His energy spurred us on. We knew that we had to follow him if we were to reach our destination. I do not know how long we travelled on our way to our meeting with John. I remember that Jesus had long conversations with Lazarus. I withdrew from such discussions, since so much had happened that I needed the solitude to recover my peace of mind. I was grateful for the quietness of my soul.

The nearer we approached where John was, the denser the stream of pilgrims became. Now we began to understand his attraction, and how John inspired the people. His magical appeal drew humanity from all directions, and we found ourselves in the middle of this turbulence. Since Jesus had not been seen very much in Israel outside Jerusalem, we were scarcely noticed. This was very agreeable to us, somewhat different from the situation in Jerusalem, where Jesus would be surrounded by masses of people.

That time of year, the nights were pleasantly warm and after a quiet night sleeping peacefully under the stars, we arrived early in the morning at the River Jordan. Hundreds of people sat and waited. John was nowhere to be seen. A curious gray mist enveloped the region, spreading a mood of depression, as if the light did not dare to shine.

Suddenly, a man emerged from the mist: it could only be John the Baptist. As he approached us, his appearance became increasingly astonishing. I scarcely recognized the young man I had met in Qumram years ago: he looked almost like a wild animal with his long unruly hair. He was only dressed in skins and carried a large stick in his hand. With each step he struck his stick forcefully on the ground. He approached us along the path by the river, and his step shook the Earth. It was clear to me that he spent his night in prayers and meditation before returning to the sacred River Jordan in the morning. He seemed to ignore the mass of people waiting. We were on the opposite side of the river from him, where we had selected a place somewhat isolated from the masses. I glanced at Jesus, who was completely relaxed and at ease. I was surprised at how little he seemed to be affected by the sight of his old companion: no excitement or joy at seeing John again appeared on his face, only the acceptance of the situation and the prospects — whatever they may be.

John entered the river from his side. It was apparent that he knew where the shallows and deep water were, and how the river currents flowed. He was already standing in the water up to his waist. Despite the crowd that regarded him in silence, John proceeded to wash himself as if there were no person present — as if he were alone in the Divine Presence.

He took his time and calmly completed his ritual, ignoring all around him. At this time of year the Jordan was not very deep. Then the spectators started to advance hesitantly toward him, but they dared not approach too close and stopped at a reasonable distance. John strode through the water unimpressed by the mass of people, until he reached a large stone, on to which he climbed.

At that moment, the sun broke through the mist and a brilliant sunlight covered the river and the surroundings with its fire. It was noticeable for all present. John struck the stone with his stick and I saw a tongue of fire rise from the place where he had struck and disperse in the atmosphere. I was not sure if everybody saw it, but I certainly did. So John had become fire! And now I understood Jesus when he said the John had become a mixture of fire and water. He was the flame that appeared above the water. Then John raised his voice, which had become strong and forceful. It echoed throughout the whole valley. His untamed character found words that moved the masses deep in their hearts.

John said, "Hear God's word. Don't hear me, because I am just the river out of God's fire to announce the coming of someone greater than me. I prepare the way for him and call for him every day. He is the Son of God who can forgive all your sins and bring God's Kingdom to the Earth. Hold communion with yourself: your souls are darkened and marked with the suffering of the world and your own greed. Subdue your own wishes and convert to God's way. Confess your sins; see how your burdens have increased and how your karmas are loaded. I will prepare the way back for whoever comes to me. I baptize you with fire and water: both are God. The elements are the expression of the Holy Spirit. When you honor the elements they will bless you and wash your souls clean."

"Come to me, since I am here to serve you and to serve God as His prophet — which I am today and always will be. Come to me and let me baptize you, since this is a gift from the Holy Spirit which God has given me."

I shuddered as I heard John speaking. My spirit saw evil snakes rise and entwine everything he said. But the fire in him held them in check. I tried hard to get rid of the vision, since I found it horrible. Then, as John was up to his hips in the water he was ready to receive the mass of people, who came to him one by one. He baptized them with the words, "I baptize you in the in the name of he who will come and in the fire of the Holy Spirit." Hundreds streamed to him. Indefatigably, he plunged them one after another into the waters and lifted them out again, during which a gentleness and compassion came over him and the fire in his eyes was benevolence and love.

Jesus had watched all this from a distance and said, "We will leave this place for the night and I will return tomorrow. Some pilgrims have told me that there is a small village nearby. We'll go there for the night. I will spend a night alone with God." We travelled a short distance until we found a small village behind a hill. The inhabitants were prepared for the many pilgrims. They sold water, bread and wine. And we found peace for the night.

It was a long wait. Jesus withdrew into his world, which for us was intangible. He was completely enclosed in his thoughts, but it was apparent he was completely at peace with himself. I spent the time in silence with Lazarus and Martha. I observed how an increasing number of people appeared, attracted by John the Baptist. It was astonishing to see the fascination that John engendered. He overwhelmed the people with his news of God's message in a land of hopelessness such as Israel. How great was the need for someone who can speak with God's voice, which had been so long locked in their hearts! How long the people had prayed for a saviour! How long had they been enslaved by their own kings, who were increasingly allied to the occupying Romans! In open hearts was the search for truth, independence and an identity of their own. They have hoped to find this yearning fulfilled by John. It was fascinating for me to observe people, to read their faces, their expressions and hear their stories. From the conversations I heard it was apparent that John withdrew in the evenings, so that the majority came to the village at night. There were big crowds and everywhere fires were burning, where people warmed themselves.

Jesus was away for some time, wanting to be alone. He returned in the evening, and I saw how he went to a group and sat down with them at a fire. He sat among a group of men, as if he knew them — and they accepted him. He spoke to them for a long time, while I observed from a distance. There was a clear, starry sky above, spreading its cloak over us. On the Earth, the fires burned and the starry fire returned the compliment. Eventually, Jesus sent somebody to fetch us.

We followed his request and joined the group. Next to Jesus were two men. Jesus said, "This is Simon and his brother Andrew. I found them right here at this fire." We were somewhat surprised, but we sat down where it was warm. In the quiet of the night, Jesus suddenly addressed Simon: "Simon, recognize who I am. I have followed your call, to find you. Leave your past life and follow me." Simon answered, "Who are you, that I should follow you?" Jesus replied, "Just wait. Tomorrow you will recognize me." Then he said to Andrew, "Prepare yourself, Andrew. You shall also leave the last traces of your past behind you, and eliminate them from your memory. You are here to follow me." A third man asked, irritated, "Who is that, saying such things?" Andrew hesitated a moment then asked, "You, sitting down here with us by the fire. Are you the Messiah everybody's talking about? Are you Jesus?" Jesus replied quietly, "Yes, I am he!"

Andrew stood up and then knelt before Jesus. "If you are the Lord, as prophesied, then I will follow you. I will give up everything I own. Everything belongs to you. I know in my heart that you are he." Behind him Simon asked angrily, "How do you know who he is?" Andrew quietly replied, "I know because my whole being says so. You should also recognize him." It was very late, so I decided to withdraw and to seek a quiet place for the night, away from all those people. I awoke at daybreak, disturbed by the movement of crowds towards the riverbank. They wanted to ensure they got a good place when John reappeared.

Jesus sat down beside me. He said, "I know how difficult it must be for you. I admire your attitude, not asking me any questions. Would you follow me to the river? I wish to meet John the Baptist again." He went to Simon and Andrew, and to a third man who appeared to be their friend. Jesus said, "Would you like to follow me?" He avoided saying where or for how long, saying only, "Follow me!" Without waiting for an answer he turned and led the way to the bank of the river. The show of the preceding day was repeated: John delivered his inspiring speech and the people listened enthusiastically. Then Jesus stood with those who wished to be baptized. I was near to the bank, so I could see clearly what occurred. I leant my head on Lazarus, who had appeared beside me. He was there! My brother had overcome all his fears and had found a deep inner connection to Jesus. Both of them had developed a very strong affinity for one another. An invisible bond held them together in an intimate friendship.

Jesus stood in front of John the Baptist, who was gazing at the water as if in a trance. He appeared to be intoning magic words of divine salvation to the water. Suddenly he raised his head, saw Jesus and asked in astonishment, "You? Coming to me? Should I not be baptized by you?" Jesus replied, "No, John; you should baptize me." From that moment on, they never spoke again. Some have reported that they did speak further to one another, but it is not true. Maybe those people just heard the different inner voices of the two. I, for one, certainly did not hear them.

Jesus let John baptize him in the water, and then emerged, looked at John once and silently walked out of the water to the bank of the river. He just left without a word. The crowd had observed the scene and waited with high expectations, hoping to hear what the meaning of it all was. I looked in the direction Jesus had taken as he nearly disappeared on the horizon. We did not know whether we should follow him or remain where we were: he had said nothing.

John interrupted our thoughts. He stood on a stone and began with his strong, resonant voice, "He who came to me today is far greater than I. He is the man for whom I prepare the way. You should not follow me; you should follow him! He is the Son of God, the all–praised Messiah, who has been promised to us. I am only his prophet and act in his name."

Then I knew. I said to my companions, "Come with me. We're going to Jesus." In the distance, we could just see the three men from the previous evening who had stood before him and then fallen on their knees to him. They were from then on the first three followers, who would not leave his side: Simon, Andrew and Philip. They had recognized him on the banks of the Jordan. When we were far away from the crowd Jesus came towards us and told us, "You should go ahead, back to Jerusalem. I will come to you in a few days."

In Jerusalem, I immediatcly sought out Irisa and told her the story of our experiences. She was really worried, and said, "My God, what has Jesus planned? He's officially paid a visit to John the Baptist, and his speeches echo all the way to Jerusalem. Doesn't he do enough to attract the people away from the synagogues and the Hebrew Temple itself? John's speeches attack the king. What bad times will come to us?" I remained for a time with her, and tried to quiet her fears. Then I decided to return home.

I began to reflect on what was happening to us. I was no longer in control of my life. I was empty. I was not sure where this would lead. I felt as though I were drugged, and I did not know how to free myself from my lethargy. Lazarus, Martha and I avoided speaking to one another. It was a feeling of uncertainty, in which all our feelings were disoriented. I cannot say I was comfortable. Jesus had eradicated the past for us. We were all in a no–man's–land. None of us knew whence we came and where we were going. I felt neither compassion nor optimism. I neither heard God's word nor did I sense the everyday worldly life. No external task seemed to have a meaning. My history had disappeared from my soul. A few days before I could have said what I sensed, what I liked, what I hoped. All that had disappeared. That would continue until Jesus returned to Jerusalem.

Some days later, Jesus reappeared with his companions: my brother had invited them to be our guests. As they arrived and I greeted Jesus, I noticed he had changed. He was no longer distant and unapproachable, but was affectionate, familiar and joyful. His three companions also stayed at our home.

We all met for the evening meal, and for the first time I scrutinised his three companions. They were all three strong personalities, with great spiritual content. As I regarded them, I knew that Jesus must have awakened much in them that had lain buried below the surface.

Still, I did notice that the eldest, Simon, cast a skeptical glance during the conversation. It seemed to me that he was not accustomed to being so free in the presence of women. As a result, there was a bit of tension in the atmosphere in the beginning — there were still some very conservative attitudes towards women in Israel's society, where they had their traditional roles and little freedom. Jesus had in the last few months taught me, a young woman, freedom and equality with men. I was able to express my opinion and move around freely, just like any man. I saw in Simon's eyes that he did not approve.

148

Jesus was extremely relaxed. Then all of a sudden he once again took up the subject he'd begun days before about his mission. "My first three companions are now with me. One day, it will be twelve." It was evident that they had experienced a lot with Jesus in the last days. They began to grow together. Jesus had the ability of radiating a warm familiarity from the first moment he met someone. He attracted people like a magnet, and drew them into his field of compassion. Although I sensed the conflict in his heart, Simon was a true and loyal follower: his conventional world and the revolutionary Jesus were at odds. Hence Simon was very thoughtful, attempting to reconcile these two attitudes.

I found the other two less complicated. They behaved in a relaxed manner, and were very friendly to our household, particularly Andrew, who sometimes came into the kitchen as we were preparing meals. He joked with Martha and me and offered to help. The prohibitions and limitations of society did not worry him, and he had a refreshing honesty and directness. We could joke and discuss without offending or shocking him. We remained the whole evening with Jesus and his three followers. It was clear that they would remain with Jesus, and accompany him wherever he went. They were the first three of the twelve, who would constitute his inner circle. Simon would play a very important role in Jesus' life: many layers of convention would fall away until his compassionate heart was finally free. For him a long journey had commenced.

The next day Jesus contacted Irisa, and he and his three companions spent the evening in Irisa's house. I decided to remain at home. The news had spread like wildfire that Jesus was again in Jerusalem. The size of the crowd had multiplied, as had the number who wished to speak to him. One evening, I was over at Irisa's, where we were always welcome. We were always safe here, since Irisa enjoyed respect and influence in Jerusalem. We had just relaxed after dinner when there was a frantic knock at the front door. In the doorway was a young woman with black curly hair and wild eyes. She immediately shut the door behind her and said, "Nobody should see me here. I want to speak to Jesus." Irisa brought her into the room where we were all assembled. As she saw Jesus she fell on her knees in front of him: and said, "Jesus, please, please don't give me away, don't tell anyone that I've come to see you. My position doesn't allow me to be in your presence, not for one moment. But I have heard of you and I couldn't help wanting to see you."

She was Salome, daughter of the King Herod, Antipas. Nobody knew why she wished to meet Jesus. She was a beautiful, untamed woman, and black fire burnt in her eyes. She said, "Accept me, Jesus. I want to belong to your supporters, and not to the sinful mob that exists in the court where King Herod and my mother reign." Jesus looked into her eyes and replied, "It is not yet time for you. You have an important task in the palace. I cannot accept you into this circle until the fate of the royal family is determined." We were shocked. King Herod had spread so many terrible stories about Jesus; how could the daughter of such a man come to him? If this were to be known it would be treated as betrayal. Happily she was able to slip out of the palace without being noticed.

From then on, Salome would take every opportunity to visit Irisa. She would also come to see us, but she preferred to be in the presence of Jesus. She used to disguise herself and slip out of the palace. I talked to her, a warm–hearted woman, a passionate being. We liked each other immediately, but we did not back then foresee how our fates would later be entwined with one another. Through my talks with Salome, I started to understand Herod and his dealings for the first time. I learned that she had used his absence on a journey to escape from the palace. I perceived a black fire surrounding Salome, and I sensed that the royal family was destined to meet a terrible fate. Nevertheless she was one of us. Some of Jesus' followers were destined for worldly downfall. I began to appreciate that there were people with positions in the material world who came to him, but did not let slip their allegiance to Jesus. Salome was the first person I had known who displayed this secret loyalty. Her fiery temperament fascinated me.

Jesus spent some weeks in Jerusalem, and began to renew his contact with Joseph of Arimathea, who was a member of the Jewish Council of Elders, the Sanhedrin. At one point there was a confidential meeting held with influential persons in the city, one of whom was Nicodemus, a friend of Joseph. After the meeting, Jesus decided only to be available for consultation on certain days. Nevertheless people continued to come to him — from all classes and professions. He was well known and his time was constantly in demand.

We were with Jesus and his companions frequently, and these disciples now spent all of their time with Jesus. As for me, however, I spent more time at home, which gave me peace and security. I began to rediscover my own life. The unexpected events of the previous weeks that Jesus had introduced into our lives were gradually brought into perspective at home.

Even so, we still enjoyed the invitations to Irisa's house. At the same time a relaxed relationship grew between me, my brother and the apostles. They began to accept that Jesus had no time for society's conventions. Men and women were equal for him, and he saw souls rather than positions in society. I learned that one of Jesus' apostles, Peter, formerly Simon, had a wife and family at home, but had decided to go with Jesus. He was just waiting for an opportunity to return home and tell his wife.

It was a quiet time. I had little to do with the contacts of Jesus. The previous weeks had thrown me into emptiness, where I no longer recognized myself. Now I was feeling better, though, and the days passed pleasantly.

One day when I was at Irisa's house, I found that one of her guests was the blonde man who had waited for us in the desert. I immediately recalled the pictures of the desert, and recognized his composure and how he led us to Jesus. This time, he was dressed differently, and he and Jesus retired into another room and were absent for the rest of the night. The next day, the apostles reported that Jesus had not mentioned the man's name or who he was: that remained a mystery. But the two treated each other as old friends. No one was permitted to be present during their conversations, and, just as the man had appeared on the previous evening, he disappeared next morning. Nobody knew where he came from nor how Jesus knew him.

Naturally Irisa, Martha and I puzzled over who he was, since we were surely the closest and most trusted friends that Jesus had. But I restrained myself and did not relate that I had already met the man in the desert, as we were seeking Jesus. I knew that he was an unusual being. His charisma was somehow familiar to me and I was reminded of the Essene light, which I had begun to miss. Even though Jesus was not far away, the outside world was incomprehensible, rough and filled with dark energy. We were happy that at least there was no gossip about us. It was a relief that we heard no grumbling in the city while Jesus was away. It was a harmonious time, and we began to develop close friendships and trust between one another.

Mary returned and she and Jacob stayed with us. Jacob had now developed into a lively and intelligent boy. I relished the time with Mary and was happy that she had returned. She was a second mother and a friend to me, and we spent many quiet hours together in conversation. Some evenings we met the others, but often we were alone together and simply enjoyed each other's company. It seemed as if we might develop our group in harmony, but that was unfortunately short-lived: for a brief period all was peaceful, until the next bit of trouble arrived.

One evening, we were all together when there was a frantic knock at Irisa's front door. We opened it and John the Baptist stood on the threshold. Wild as ever, he took over the room. Without looking at us he went immediately to Jesus, who only said, "I have been expecting you, John." John and Jesus withdrew into another room. After a short time John left, as rapidly as he had come. Jesus returned to us, apparently very worried. Unusually for him he began immediately: "John has decided to accept his difficult fate. He came to shatter the foundations of the ancient throne of the king. He has set himself the task of challenging every King of Israel who rules from a false oath. He is willing to risk his life for this mission."

That night, Jesus explained that, long ago, God's enlightened kings ruled this holy land. The country was led by initiated men and women who understood how to support the spiritual and material needs of the people. The stories of Abraham, Moses, Elias and all other prophets came much later. Israel was one of the springs where God had planted his own people, a golden land, which radiated peace over the Earth. But then things started happening that would determine the fate of Israel. He said, "The spirit of this ancient land was destined to disappear, as every culture at the height of its prosperity. Harmony was exchanged for duality."

Jesus continued, explaining that certain persons began to attack the power of the God–appointed throne. Consequently, the divine rulers withdrew, leaving the rebels in power. But God loved the ancient seed of his people, which had always been true to him. He sent loyal prophets to lead his people back to him. But God also permitted those who renounced him a part of the power. Jesus closed with the words, "John is the redeemer. His prophecy, as Elias, was that he would behead the false gods and kings of Israel when he returned to Earth, during the time when the Messiah was here. John was ready to sacrifice himself in order to destroy the evil 'snakes-heads' who ruled Israel and endangered peace in the world, with words and deeds — if necessary with his own life."

Jesus left the room, and I heard, scarcely audible, that he was weeping, shedding tears for his friend. He had already seen John's fate. His silent tears penetrated through to me from the next room. He was trying to accept John's awful destiny. I had frequently seen how Jesus cried over the fates of others whom he loved – it was as if he took over a part of this destiny so that those who would suffer the fate might not suffocate in it. Inside myself, I cried with Jesus: I experienced at that moment everything that he felt. From that moment on I began increasingly to sense every feeling in him. I sensed everything that occurred in his world, and lived it with him. Only when he locked himself in his world, in order to be alone with God, was he inaccessible.

In spite of all many events that occurred around that time that would shape the future, it was a peaceful time. Nevertheless, following John's visit, we knew that a black star was in ascendance, and would take its course.

Around that time, Jesus was not well known to the religious leaders. We would remember fondly the previous weeks and days, since in that period we were closest to Jesus and were his most intimate friends. Since the day of John's visit, however, it was as if we stood before a closed gate. That was when we just did not know in which direction we were going. Jesus was much sequestered over the next few days. Nobody came to him: there were no further official visits. Whoever wished to come to see him was not permitted. He withdrew into Irisa's house and remained there. We too saw him very seldom.

Since my return from Qumran, events had radically changed my life. We followed Jesus without thinking or asking questions. It was like an uncontrollable euphoria whenever one came into contact with him. Life became so concentrated in his presence. Jesus had withdrawn from us for the time being, which gave us a moment to catch our breaths and to enjoy the quiet of everyday life.

At last, I had the opportunity to get into more extensive conversations with my brother, since I really knew so little about his life. I wanted to finally get to know him as he really was. I only knew fragments from my family and even less about him. One evening the opportunity to talk to him occurred. Up to this day I had not been confronted with the political situation in Israel. The Essenes had shielded me as I was growing up. Now, back in my parents' home, I really did not know where I lived. My conversation with Lazarus would change all of that.

It was my brother who began, saying, "Miriam, you don't know much about our family. I have kept these matters to myself up to now. On his deathbed our father trusted me to take over the family affairs and businesses. You know he sent me to the School of the Ancient Magicians. I don't really want to speak about this time of separation from the family but, believe me, I was confronted with things in Jerusalem which gave me much to think about. I was not quite so protected as you."

"As you know, we live under the rule of the Roman Empire. But we are an ancient race. We Jews originate from a people governed by great kings, great prophets and great leaders, and a deep respect and affection for God's laws — which have guided us since time immemorial. I don't want to go into great detail, Miriam, I only want you to understand what I am involved in, and about the family's heritage." I learned from Lazarus that the School of Magicians was concealed from the Romans, and, in secret, taught the tradition of Solomon's temples, a tradition which still exists. The initiated are only the chosen sons of the Jewish people, and had to pass very difficult examinations. No Roman knew about these schools.

Lazarus continued, "The School of Magicians was a legacy of Jewish mysticism. The leaders of the school represented the Jewish people, their ancient connections and their heritage. The School was critical of the loss of the people's realm, of their royalty and of their rights. I am convinced that we Jews should rebel. I have joined with others who work underground and are known as 'Zealots.' We believe that one day we can break the grip of the Roman occupation and reinstate our own king. You know that Jesus comes from the House of David. The Zealots have their eyes on him; all share the hope that he will be our worldly king."

I looked at my brother for a moment and said, "Do you really think that Jesus is here to sit on the worldly throne of the Jewish people?" He replied, "That is our hope. When the time is ripe I want to offer Jesus a revolt of the Jewish people in his name. The powers that have ruled us must be removed to return the historical inheritance to the Jewish people. The divine people of Israel will then be ruled by a truly spiritual king."

He continued, excited, "Even the priests in the temple of Jerusalem and the council of wise elders are traitors, including Joseph of Arimathea and Nicodemus. They are servants of the Roman occupiers and do not represent the interests of our people. I have secret connections, of which you have no idea. We hope that one day our plans will be fulfilled."

My feelings and my mind were in turmoil: "Lazarus, I will not hear any more. How can you believe this idea? Don't you see what Jesus is really doing? Everyone he meets receives peace, compassion, reconciliation and healing from him. How can you believe that this plan that you foresee for him can ever be realized? I detect an unhealthy agitation in your heart. I am reminded of the evening when Jesus said that your political convictions had not pleased him. I beg you, forget such ideas! Follow Jesus, as he has offered you. Please set aside such revolutionary ideas. We both know that he is the Messiah. He will renew the unity of our people, but not with rebellion and war. Please break the political connections: I want nothing to do with them. Give them up!" But I sensed that I had not convinced him.

He replied, "You know that I am devoted to Jesus, and am his friend. But let us drop the subject, since you have no idea what is going on in the hearts and minds of the Jewish public. Our ancient and wealthy family always protected you from the outside world. These matters have not affected you, and you went away too soon to learn about these things. But now is the time to tell you more about our family. We are not only rich, but we also can trace our lineage back to King Solomon. Our father was not only an Essene; that was his secret world. He was also a high priest in the Temple in Jerusalem. We are very wealthy and we have property over the whole country. It is important for you to know this, and know that you will never have material worries. You can have everything that you need. Father entrusted me with the administration of the estate. This property, our house in Jerusalem, is only a small part of our inheritance. You are provided for until you die."

"I've realized that Jesus wishes you to accompany him wherever his plans may take him, even when we don't know them. This is your decision, Miriam. Although you are a woman, with no rights to inherit the family wealth, I would not force you to enter a religious order, as was the tradition of our family. You must decide what you will do with your life and I will support you with everything you need. You are now seventeen years old and can go your own way without material worries. The power and the inheritance of our family give me the right and the duty to protect and support your decisions. We are a free family, which is unusual in Israel. But consider, when you get to know the life in Jerusalem and the Hebrew society, you will constantly be confronted with women who are not as free as yourself. They are tied down and have no rights. There are few families who permit them inheritance."

I learned much about my brother that evening. The freedom that I had gained, to be a woman who makes her own decisions, was a wonderful gift from him — and I thanked him from deep in my heart. It was now getting late, but before we retired to bed we embraced one another as allies and companions, out of friendship and heartfelt affection.

The next day was peaceful for us. Martha and I looked after the house and enjoyed each other's company. We began to develop a deep friendship, and were becoming close companions. I recognized her generous and loving heart, and her affection for me. One day, in the kitchen, as we were preparing the meal, she looked at me and said, "You know that I am your mother's sister, but what you do not know is that we are related on the maternal side to Mary, Jesus' mother. We descend from the same line and one of my grandmothers, who you never met, was also the grandmother of Mary." I looked at her and said, "I never knew that Mary was connected to us through the female side of the family, nor that we were even related to her." She only said, "Miriam, we keep these things secret, because we belong to an ancient alliance of women who come from a select circle of initiated persons. We must keep this completely confidential. Your mother protected you by excluding you from these circles, but I was initiated with your mother. I believe it is the wish of the Great Mother, whom we serve, that you are finally informed of these matters. Please do not ask me more. But I felt it was my duty to tell you how we are connected to one another and that there are things you should learn when the time is ripe. It is very difficult for me to discuss such matters: I have lain awake at night turning the matter over in my mind."

"You see, the line from which we originate has long been kept secret. We are labeled as traitors even amongst the Jews. We have no right to exist. We are even open to persecution. Mary was placed under the protection of the Essenes, as was your mother. I was schooled and served in the ancient Order of Ephesus. That is why you have never recognized me before. I never wear the traditional clothing of the Order for fear of being recognized, insulted and perhaps even stoned by the angry citizens. We are outlawed. But believe me, where I was schooled we were the holiest women and the high priests who rule the city fear that which we have learned. They fight against us with all the means at their disposal. There is another secret in my family, one day I can tell you more. Just give me time." I was in suspense, wondering what she would tell me. I asked, "Why do you tell me all this?" She said, "Because Jesus requested it."

I had time to myself the next morning, and enjoyed the relaxation. Now I had time to reflect alone. Deep inside me I was conscious of the fact that I knew little of what goes on in Jerusalem. Our house was on the edge of the Jerusalem, outside the city walls, and even when we heard rumors of what was happening within the walls, we could not imagine it: crowds of people of different origins and cultures, perpetual struggles for power and leadership. The disturbances did not reach our front door — inside the walls it was different. I was occupied with my thoughts when there was an urgent knocking on our door. It was Irisa. She said, "Come quickly! Jesus left the house this morning, to speak to the most senior high priests."

I quickly fetched my scarf and collected Lazarus and Martha. Irisa's chariot was drawn by horses, and took us near to the city center. Irisa said, "We must dismount here and go on foot the rest of the way. I hope the news has not yet spread in Jerusalem. Jesus went alone and nobody else was informed. He told me where he was going. Follow me!" We pushed our way through the crowded streets. For the first time in many years I saw the city again from within — the narrow alleys, the stores, the splendid buildings on the way to the top of the hill.

As we arrived at the temple forecourt, some people were assembled. Irisa shouted, "Come with me!" She was determined to be as near as possible to the place where the priests were sitting. We pushed our way through the crowd and into a large room with a stone floor. The priests sat on a raised gallery — I recognized Joseph of Arimathea among them. The high priests wore distinct headwear, and some of them behaved as if they were God himself.

Jesus was there and we arrived in the middle of a discussion. One of the priests repeatedly demanded of Jesus, "The news that you are a son of David has excited the population. They are beginning to rebel and to demand a new king. Are you the king they are waiting for?" The tone of his question was very unfriendly, and every word was aggressively expressed. He was obviously afraid of losing his power and authority. I sensed with every breath that this room ruled the Jewish people, whether or not they agreed. Here were men who pretended to rule in God's name, but in fact they were only interested in their personal power.

Jesus stood there quietly. His dazzling golden light filled the room with compassion and peace. The citizens present sensed the light, but it did not penetrate to the high priests — it broke into a thousand pieces and turned to dust at their feet. Only Joseph of Arimathea and Nicodemus, who were secretly in contact with Jesus, were immersed in his light. Jesus patiently heard the questions and after a pause softly replied, "That is true. I am he." The priest asked angrily, "Are you the new king of Israel?" Jesus radiated his peace and compassion again and replied quietly, "The king you are waiting for stands in front of you. But my realm is not this world. And I will not claim a worldly throne, apart from what the Father gives me."

The voices of the priests grew louder: "Who is your Father? To which Father are you referring? Through whom do you obtain the power with which you stand before us today?" Once again Jesus radiated his light of peace and compassion, and in the quiet that followed, Jesus laid his words on a ray of golden light. "My Father is the same as him you call your Father. But I hear his voice, and serve it, whereas you do not hear it." I had not noticed that many people had entered the room during the proceedings. The crowd began to murmur, "The son of David. Our King! The prophecy stands before us. He has come to save us. His coming has been proclaimed in our scriptures."

As if moved by the voice of the spectators, Jesus turned to them and his compassion spread with a golden light over them all. He said, "Place me not on a worldly throne. That is not why I have come to you." He turned again to the priests and said, "It is nevertheless true that the scriptures prophesy my coming as the Son of God. I am here to free the people of Israel. I have not brought the weapons that you know but, unarmed, I bring freedom and peace. There is no war, no revolution in my heart, but I bring the power of the Lord, who watches over us all. I announce this in his name." Then there was complete silence. The priests were stunned by his words. Without waiting for an answer, Jesus turned to depart, and left the room. The crowd moved respectfully to one side to let him pass, but the murmur became louder. "Messiah, our king! King of the Jews, free us!" Jesus did not heed these words — it was as if he had not heard them. He had already disappeared.

We hastened out of the temple building, which was ostentatious and filled with ornate pillars. As I left, I turned and thought to myself, "This place should be the throne of God, ruling Israel?" The building radiated only worldly power. There was nowhere a sign of spiritual leadership, as I had learned with the Essenes. There was no trace of the bright divine light, only stone pillars and stone hearts. We forced our way through the excited crowd, to the forecourt of the temple. I was shocked to see a company of armed Roman soldiers, prepared to suppress any disturbance — if necessary with force of arms. We had not noticed them inside the building. Irisa said, "The Zealots! They have used this opportunity. There are many uncontrollable forces in Jerusalem just waiting for the chance to start a revolt. You must bring your brother to reason, Miriam." I suddenly noticed that Lazarus had disappeared. My heart stood still for a moment. I was terrified by the thought that perhaps he was taking part in a Zealot uprising. Irisa said, "Come on! Let us try to get out of the city as soon as possible. This is not a good place for us." She knew the streets of Jerusalem well, so we left the city center the fastest way possible. Everywhere were crowds, mostly streaming toward the center. We could almost smell the insurrection. But the Roman soldiers were ready for all signs of violence or revolt, prepared to nip it even before it could develop. The eyes of the soldiers were as hard and steely as their weapons. An intimidating sight!

I was happy to leave the place — it was so depressing. We were glad to mount the chariot and to hear the beat of horses' hooves taking us out back to Irisa's villa. Jesus was not there, just Peter and Andrew. Peter was friendly but he was obviously disturbed by the events in the city center, the news of which had already spread to the outer regions of the city. There was fear in his eyes, since Jesus had not returned. This time I recognized his fatherly qualities. We calmed him down and told him that, even if the city was in an uproar he should not worry: Jesus was safe.

Jesus in fact did not reappear for good two weeks. Andrew became more relaxed, but Peter visibly carried his worries in his heart. He would have to learn to accept it when Jesus did not want to say whether he was going and why. What his intentions were remained a mystery. We all had to learn always to be ready, every moment, when the spiritual energy of God's chosen son unfolded and drew us into his irresistible attraction.

During this time of uncertainty, Peter received the news that his wife was very ill. A messenger from Lake Gennesaret, the Sea of Galilee, informed him that he should return home as fast as possible. I sensed the conflict in his heart as to whether he should return home to his wife or wait until Jesus returned. The following day, Irisa and I said to him, "Peter, you should go home and look after your wife. Jesus will understand. Don't worry; you don't need to be concerned about Jesus. This is the call of your wife: follow it! That is the path that Jesus would recommend." Irisa provided him with a wagon and a guide, so that he could reach home rapidly. She promised to contact him when Jesus returned.

The news reached us that Jesus was on the banks of the River Jordan. We had become used to the delays in obtaining news of Jesus; the rumors and gossip reached us much faster! Since his appearance in the temple and the invitation from the High Council of Jerusalem, news of him spread like a wildfire over the whole country. We followed the rumors. It seemed as if the people of Israel increasingly hoped for a king with worldly power who would release them from the yoke of oppression. Simultaneously, the Romans strengthened their military presence. Jesus was well advised to leave the city, to let the excitement subside and the tempers cool. Then one day, we received the news, confirmed by neighbors, that Jesus was on his way to Jerusalem. He returned to Irisa's house and had two new companions. Martha, Lazarus and I waited for the invitation to visit him. Not much later we were picked up by Irisa's wagon. We then met Phillip and Nathaniel, two men who said nothing about themselves or their origin. I learned that Jesus found them with John. Up until that time they had been John's followers, but Jesus only needed to look at them and then said, "Follow me. Come with me. From now on I will lead you." I could feel from the beginning that they were men with quiet clarity who radiated their honesty and compassion. It was clear that they had recognized Jesus' message and followed him.

Peter had not yet returned and we learned that his wife was dying. Our hearts were with him; I too had learned to love him. I thought of Peter and his sadness and difficulties with Jesus' unconventional attitudes. He was very conventional and embodied the ethics of tradition. But Jesus treated men and women alike. Whatever sex and name, all were treated alike. Judea had her laws, whereas Jesus had his own, and claimed the right to live according to them. I became increasingly aware of the privilege that we enjoyed with Jesus, privilege nobody else would have given us.

The next days were relatively quiet. Andrew, Philip and Nathaniel organized the people who, at set times, came to visit Jesus. He made time for everyone who came to him. Irisa had also begun in his presence to heal and to help. The stream of visitors had reduced somewhat, since some were afraid to be seen with him. It was a relatively quiet time, and in the evenings we were often without visitors. Sometimes Jesus and I were able to talk alone: he was always so affectionate, attentive and delicate. Here he was no longer the Son of God, but a loving, trusted friend. But he never referred to the events in the temple in Jerusalem. He behaved as a dear friend who wanted to share his life with us.

One day Peter returned. The sadness in his eyes told us that his wife had departed from this life. I was in the house as he entered, and I witnessed how Jesus lovingly embraced him, and held him so long and soothed him until his pain was somewhat relieved. Then he looked at Peter and said, "My rock, do not worry. The soul of your wife is in God's realm." From that time on, Peter was always near Jesus and would never leave his side.

A few days later Joseph of Arimathea visited Jesus and spent the evening with him. He and Nicodemus often passed by. I heard from others that Nicodemus was for a long time skeptical. But Jesus had some deep conversations with him and gradually converted him to recognizing Jesus out of his own conviction — and losing his doubts. Nevertheless he remained for some time a slave of the worldly life that he had previously led.

One evening Jesus had us picked up and brought to Irisa's house. Oil lamps were lit throughout the whole house, and there was a festive atmosphere. Peter, Andrew, Nicodemus, Joseph of Arimathea, Philip, Nathaniel and Irisa were there and we three joined them. Jesus said, "Come, sit near to me." He began, "Our time begins now. The glory of God's will start to shine in heaven. It is visible on the horizon." Then he looked at Peter and said to him, "Come to me! Kneel down before me!" He looked at him for a long time. It was a divine moment. He took Peter's head in his hands and said, "You do not know who you are. You, father of the worlds, have come with me. You are my first apostle. I initiate you in the name of our Father, you great, old, wise ruler from ancient times. You have no further burden on this Earth, no yoke ties you down. You are free but still you have come to serve me. Under your leadership was peace. You were already in the soul of my Father and have chosen to leave it, to join me. You are a free being, and you have already been accepted in the circle of the Masters. From now on you will always be with me, until our task is completed." A brilliant light shone from Heaven and blessed Peter, a good, wise, loving father, under whose soul all beings find peace.

Next Jesus looked at Philip and said, "Come to me." He looked at him a long time and said, "You were always true to me. In all heavens! Always at my side. You carry God's truth inside you, and you will teach the truth in my name outside. You were initiated in the truth from ancient times; you are the second great soul, which previously ruled in Atlantis. Accompany me now without a throne, to reestablish the rule of the heart on this Earth. You have left your realm and have returned in the cup of love, while God's realm withdraws from the Earth. You have also led the Jewish people. You were with Moses and served him too. You have never made a royal demand on Earth, and you will also not be a king in these times, though you were in the past. But you know all this. You have come here to stand beside my throne and to announce its existence." Then he held Philip's head and said, "Be blessed, Master of Truth." And once again a divine light shone down on him, and he said, "Amongst the holy ones that I shall collect around me I choose you to announce my message."

After that, he looked at Andrew. "Come to me, you forgotten one. The yoke that you carry in your heart, you have carried endlessly for me and for God. You carry the burden of humanity. Now you are at my side to help me carry my load. Therefore I love you, because you, great soul out of the eternal heaven, are willing to carry this burden with me. You will carry my cross, and my load shall be on your shoulders.

But I cannot relieve you of this load, since this is your fate from ancient times. It will be so until the power of the burden on the Earth is redeemed with God's blessing." Then he took his head in his hands and the divine light shone on him.

Then he called for Nathaniel and said, "You prophet from ancient times, you angel with the message of the Lord, you are the incarnation of he who announced my coming, my old friend Gabriel. He will serve next to you and be near me to bring the light from God's kingdom. My angel, who carries my torch, you are with me because you will announce me in Heaven and on Earth." And he held Nathaniel's head. As their eyes met they melted and were united as one.

Finally, he called Lazarus and said, "Come to me. Lazarus, you are the first of the Hundred-and-Eight that I am seeking. Tomorrow I leave Jerusalem, I will visit the temple again and then we will go on our travels, since one hundred and eight have come and we have to capture their souls." Jesus smiled and said, "Lazarus, Lazarus, it will be a long time before you realize that no worldly power can ever announce the heavenly power." And then he let him go.

The atmosphere in the room became transcendent and full of a divine light. Jesus requested wine and offered some to us all. He sank into a trance–like state, separate somehow from time and space. He began to speak to us as if from another world: "From this hour the great era begins. Nothing will be the same as it was. I have come at this time to free you from the slavery of your souls. My Father's love has sent me here, and each of you in this room is as free as the Father Himself. You are here because of God's yearning and His wish to free the Earth from its yoke. The love of our Father, who is Father of all on this Earth, sent us here since he has not banished the children who betrayed him. He sent his own son, born from himself, to proclaim his love, which is greater than anything we can measure."

"Every one of you in this room," he announced, "is a part of this love, and is here to carry this love, with me, to those who have forgotten it. I have not come to bring peace, but to bring a sword. Many hope that I am here to free them. But I carry the most powerful sword the world has ever seen. I have been entrusted with the sword that divides the Earth and separates the grain from the chaff. None of you knows what fate has in store for you. Each of you has accepted this worldly inheritance, to be with me. Only divine love has motivated you to do this. I cannot relieve the load on the Earth, though I want to. It was your wish, as it is my wish and the wish of the Father, that we take the fate of humanity on our shoulders and carry it, in order to redeem it from the sin and suffering, and from spiritual death."

The whole room shook for a moment and he looked at Irisa with loving eyes. "Mother of the healers. If souls could see your healing eyes as I can, there would be no more suffering in the world. Believe me, the souls are blind. But I see you, Mother; I see you and will always see you."

At this moment we were interrupted; Mary had returned. She had been away for some time, but Jesus had called her to return. He looked at his mother and emanated pure love for her, saying, "You are always there at the right time." Mary had Jacob with her and Jesus said, "Come to me, my brother. From now on you will be my apostle. You come from the stars, and your news is from the stars. You will follow my paths and you will fill every step on Earth with my light and love. God, our Father, has decided that you shall accompany me. Your kingdom is, like mine, not of this world. You rule in peace, above in heaven. The star over your head signifies your power. The light I carry also lives in you. The love of Christ is in us." He looked at Mary. "Mother, would you give him to me? Then he will always be with me." Mary approached Jesus and laid her head on his knee. She laid all her worries and burdens at his feet. She said, "I knew from the very first moment that I looked at you it is your will that proclaims the will of God. My service and my being belong to you. I am only here because you are here. All that you wish is my wish. You help me to carry my burden, my son, which I have inherited from our Lord Emmanuel. But please grant me a wish. You know my visions, and they are so dismal. When I am alone at night my visions are gloomy, depressing and gray. Please relieve me of them, my son."

Jesus stroked her head and said, "Look at me, Mother. The great time that we proclaim will not be a gift, neither to you nor to me. The Lord, my Father, has a plan that is still indefinite. Let us commence our work, without questions or expectations. Each one who is touched by the Father's spirit can enter into the kingdom of Heaven to eternity. But do not expect happiness on Earth. Not in this epoch. Not at this hour." He took the wine and gave it to Mary. "Drink," he said, "out of the goblet of life, wise woman. You come from the Great Mother and you will return to her. Drink from my goblet. Drink from my love: Every drop of my blood soothes your suffering, since the pain of my birth was yours."

A ruby–red flame appeared above us, and a dazzling light pulsed between Jesus and Mary, such as I knew from the Essenes: the pure Light of Christ, pure compassion, which radiated from other worlds over both of them. Mary was for this moment elevated into the spiritual heaven. I knew her for so many years — an unspoiled being amongst the mortals. She was a noble among nobles. At this moment we saw her entering heaven, the moment when she was ordained. From then on she was on Earth without being touched by the pain of the world. She and Jesus fused together in this instant and were united as one.

Jesus spoke for the whole night. Nobody slept. He spoke of the Kingdom of God, but I cannot remember the details. We were together with him in another world, for an eternal moment. Then he looked at me and said, "We are one, and we will always be one." Then the first morning light appeared and he said, "You who are my apostles, you will accompany me with each step on my way. Together we will conquer this land. Do not leave me for even a moment." Without turning around he left the room saying, "Come! And you, Lazarus, also come with me."

We women remained behind. Martha became ill that night; she had a fever and shuddered in her nightmares. We needed all our healing powers to make her well again. Her soul was inflamed in the night and burned for Jesus. She blazed so much for him that her body found no peace amongst the flames. At midday Irisa came to me, although we had not slept at all, and said, "Come. Jesus is in the temple again. The city is in an uproar. We should go and see what occurs." She quickly had us driven to the city gates, so that we could walk to the city center. There were ways into the center that were only open to the Romans, where Jews were prohibited, but she led us along those forbidden alleys and streets, and nobody stopped us before we reached the temple forecourt.

A great crowd had assembled. Jesus had done something incredible: he was preaching to the crowd from the steps of the temple. As we arrived we found he was surrounded by attentive listeners. From a distance we could not hear what he was saying, but the people were transfixed by his words. The gates of the temple were shut behind him, as if the priests in their anger had shut the doors from inside. It was an unbelievable challenge to the power of the temple and those who occupied it, I knew. But there it was, and it was going to stay that way. The teacher, Jesus, received God's word and brought it to God's people, without considering the dangers. When God wished it, He spoke through Jesus. Then a large powerful man approached Jesus, and as he did so the crowd gasped as with one voice: "The damned tax collector dares!"

The man walked towards Jesus as if challenging him, and said, "They call you the Messiah. You speak of God's kingdom.

But how do you see this kingdom on Earth?" And he put his hand in his pocket and presented money to Jesus. He said, "Here is the God they serve, the Romans as well as the Jews. And I can tell you this is a dirty business, collecting duties and taxes every day like I do." It was a challenge. The crowd was agitated. Then Jesus moved to him and said, "Matthew, I know you." The man looked at Jesus quizzically and replied, "How did you know my name?" Jesus replied, "I have always known you. I will always know you."

Irisa and I had pushed forward and were near this scene. Jesus said, "Give me the money you have in your pocket." The crowd was restless, since at that time the money from a revenue official was considered dirty. The Jews never touched the money of the 'unclean ones,' as they called these tax collectors, men who had been appointed by the Romans to collect money from the Jewish citizens, who despised these agents of the Romans. This Matthew was one of Jewish society's castes of despised ones.

Jesus took the money in his hand and said, "With all this money in my hands you could not even buy a small corner in the Kingdom of Heaven. No amount of shekels can open the door for you. In fact, there is no worthy tribute apart from tribute to the Father in heaven. Follow me, Matthew! Leave your business behind you. Forget Mammon. No rich man can pass through the eye of a needle with the load that he carries. The kingdom of Heaven is proclaimed for you, but you can only know it through me."

Jesus threw the coins that Matthew had given him into the crowd. There was wild disorder, since the Jews who had been touched by the coins shrank back as if they had been touched by vermin. Jesus looked at them and said, "You are servants of the wrong father." He turned to go and his apostles followed him. On the way out he turned to Matthew and said, "Are you coming with me?" Matthew replied, "Yes my Lord and King."

And from that day the story was told by all citizens: the customs officer left his house and all his material property to go with Jesus, never to return. But the minds of the people were troubled, wondering how Jesus could accept an unclean one in his number, somebody that was despised by Jewish society. We saw the group disappear. Even when there was a great crowd, Jesus had the ability of escaping into a crowd and vanishing completely, so that nobody could follow him when he so wished.

Irisa and I returned to the house, where Mary was looking after Martha. Mary had adopted the Essene techniques, and with great affection had nursed Martha and soothed her soul. Now we women were alone. It was the first time that we were all together without the men. Irisa invited us all to stay in her house, since Jesus, his followers and Lazarus were not expected to return. We did not dare to leave the house, since Jerusalem was in turmoil, and we did not want to be seen on the streets. So we stayed together and Jesus was not seen for a long time.

That day all four of us looked each other in the eyes. We were to experience something special. We all recognized ourselves in the others, as we blended our knowledge visually. It was an examination, to test our love. Three days and three nights we did not speak to one another. Only silent caring for each other was allowed. Each woman was in her own world. In this time we lost our sense of time and space. There was a special atmosphere as each of us retreated into our own spiritual world; in spite of this retreat, there remained a loose connection between us, until I broke the silence at the evening meal on the fourth day.

I looked at Mary and saw in her eyes that she knew the answer to the question I had in my heart. "Mary, what can you tell me about the tradition of our mothers? Please tell me the secrets of our family." Martha was quite still next to me as Mary began, "The women in our lineage, your mother, Martha's mother and my mother, go back to a great ordained person, our ancestor, Sarah. In the ancient history of our people, Sarah was a pious woman who had received the initiation of fire from God. In the stories of Sarah, there is no record of what she had actually experienced with God, but it is told that one night, the holy fire was present in her and she was ordained in the power of female creation. She became priestess of the red fire. For this reason, she could not bear a child for a long time, since she had dedicated her life and her priesthood to the holy fire. She was initiated and the primeval knowledge of female creation had been passed on to her.

"Ever since that time, the ordained priesthood of the red women is a part of Jewish culture," Mary revealed to me. "Again and again they called the women to them, who passed on the ordination in secret. Our great–great– grandmother belonged to this order and was initiated in the primeval fire of female creation. This knowledge was never available to men, and was treated as sacred. No man was permitted access to this knowledge, but they respected it. Some of these women were even permitted to leave to have families of their own — chosen to pass this power of female creation on to their daughters.

"But in the last few hundred years," Mary said, "our own people have begun to regard this order, the Order of Ephesus, as disreputable and even dangerous. The power of the priestesses was condemned, and society created strong patriarchal structures. The high priests in Jerusalem began persecuting this order, which subsequently withdrew to caves in the mountains. Increasingly the women of the order were outlawed from society. The high priests then started attacking the individuals of the order, saying that they were not loved by God for their work, and labelling them madwomen from a demon world."

"The order had increasingly withdrawn to more secret places, which I will not name. Following her initiation in this tradition, my mother gave me an intact temple in Jerusalem, to protect our children, that they not be hunted or outlawed. The Essenes were also closely connected to this free and holy order of the divine powers. Your mother, Miriam, was never touched by this belief, but Martha was chosen and was passed on to the red Order of Ephesus, to be initiated. I cannot tell you the purpose of this order: it is secret."

"Jerusalem," she said, warming to her subject, "and the high priests worship only Mammon. If the women of Ephesus were found, they would be stoned by the ignorant crowd. The power of the women is condemned today and they are labelled as the agents of Satan. But I know that all members of this lineage are sacred. Only the holiest of women are incarnated in this tradition and possess the power of the

Great Mother and her ordination. Martha was released from this order and brought blindfolded into the house where you live today, so that even she does not know where she is hidden. The women today are nevertheless very powerful. Each of them has the ability to conceal the initiation deep inside her, so that she is completely inconspicuous. Nothing of the order would be revealed, even to protect themselves from arrest or even torture.

"That is why Martha was so ill last night," Mary whispered. "The energy of her initiation burned inside her. Jesus reawakened her with his light and love. Women such as these serve only the primeval divine fire. I don't know where Jesus was informed of the order, but he has spoken several times to me about it – as if he was completely familiar with it. All women in this lineage recognize those who are ordained in this order and reappear.

"Miriam, I see something in your eyes. Above you hovers the characteristic ruby–red light in which all secrets of life and creation lie embedded, to reappear in your initiation. It is no coincidence that you ask me, since your soul has already been prepared for your ordination. But Martha will never return to the order. She carries the information coded inside her and has chosen to serve you and Jesus." Mary was quiet for a while, and then she said, "I am very sorry that I cannot tell you more — even if I wished to, I could not. But I know that it is no coincidence that we have come together. I sense in each of you the divine power of the Holy Mother, to whom we prayed in ancient times. But the force of darkness and the dark authority of the patriarchs have pushed us to one side. The situation deteriorates more and more. Nevertheless, the fire inside us still glows, and within you, Miriam, it blazes. I see it in you and around you.

"I am certain that this order exists secretly in our country. There are many myths and legends about our order, but also malicious stories, in which the women are demonized and labelled as witches, wielders of pagan magic. In earlier times, the women came to the people and served them with their healing skills. Today that's absolutely forbidden. Our people recount the story of how manna materialized in the desert as divine food. But believe me, Miriam; the power to make that happen was only possible for ordained women of the order. They alone are capable of concentrating the power of creation in themselves. They alone could create divine food, and they alone possessed the power of creation within them. They are not witches and not whores. They are truly free women. They are not barbaric. They are a fundamental, primeval force of the universe."

Following Mary's narration, we were speechless. We were captivated by a force that we could sense and were touched by but could not clearly define. Then Mary indicated that we should follow her into the room in which Jesus always stayed, and broke the silence. "I will light a fire for us, and then I will pray — a very old prayer in a language that has been forgotten. My grandmother taught it to me." She lit the fire and added myrrh. Then she smiled and said, "I always carry a few grains of the holy myrrh my grandmother gave me. She told me, in divine moments, to throw a couple of grains on the fire, that the sacred fumes will evolve and hence ensure that our power never dies." Mary recited the prayer in the ancient language consisting only of vowels. The room was filled with a magical energy, imbued with a powerful creative force that captivated us all, embracing us and filling us with joy. We sensed that this energy only lives in us women. As the fire died, we all fell into a trance and we followed the steps through the mists to ordination that was open to us. The next morning we found that we were returned to the world. None of us could remember anything, apart from the knowledge that Jesus had been with us. He was the fire! We remained together for quite a few days, and only ventured to leave the house very occasionally. We were a company of women who loved and cared for one another. We were joined together by the unspoken secret that was locked in our hearts.

Some days later, Andrew turned up. Jesus had sent him. He was able to inform us what had happened after Jesus left the forecourt of the temple in Jerusalem. We were very happy to see him again, and gave him something to eat and drink. He was dirty and covered with dust, and when he had eaten and drunk, he began his description.

Jesus had been preaching in front of the temple three weeks earlier and Andrew told us all about what had occurred in the intervening time. "As soon as Jesus had finished preaching, he was in a hurry to leave and we followed him. We left Jerusalem and began our journey to Nazareth. Jesus was very withdrawn and silent at this time. Although we followed him or were close to him all the time, he did not speak to us at all. We had no idea where he was leading us. At night he always found accommodation for us, but he then withdrew to a quiet place where he could remain undisturbed. We all sensed that he wished to pray alone, and with each successive night the divine energy in him increased. It was as if he needed the nights to come closer to God and integrate his spirit within himself.

"When we arrived in Nazareth, Jesus visited the synagogue alone, and he did not tell us where he was going. Eventually we found him, deep in silent prayer and surrounded by sadness and a peculiar emptiness. We hardly dared to speak to him; although he was in the midst of talking and laughing people, he was unrecognized and completely still. Then he looked up at Lazarus and said, 'Come with me, everyone.' We followed Jesus to a quiet location at the edge of Nazareth, where he gathered us around him. He saw that we were all hungry and had eaten our last bread, and he was clearly full of regret. He began to speak to us and it seemed to me that he was simultaneously speaking to God: 'Lord, they accompany me unconditionally. Those around me have, in Your and my names, sacrificed their homes and comforts to follow me. I beg You to have pity on them: do not let them go hungry. They should be nourished and looked after. They should not suffer hunger or poverty in Your and my presence.'

"Jesus began praying again," Andrew recalled. "He was sinking deeper into himself, as if he was informing God that we had chosen a life of privation in his name. Then he looked over at Philip and said, 'Give me your last piece of bread.' Jesus took the bread and sank into prayer again. Suddenly, before our eyes, there was enough bread to feed us all. He distributed the bread and asked, 'Do any of you have some wine left?' Then he took the remaining wine from an almost empty bottle, and during his prayer a wine jug on the table was filled and all had enough to drink — the jug remained full no matter how much we drank. Our souls were quieted and all wishes, worries and deprivations were forgotten. We were full, nourished and lacked nothing.

"On that day Jesus left again on retreat and got back late in the evening. We then lit a fire and in silence Jesus approached each one of us and traced a sign on our foreheads saying to us, 'Seek those who seek you, and go out into the world and unite those who are waiting to be found.' Visions and pictures of this went flitting through our minds. We recognized that many were searching, waiting to make contact with us. Jesus explained that we should go to the holy monastery near to Qumran. We left that night, unprotected and without provisions. The amazing thing is we suffered neither from hunger nor cold nor from any other hardships on the way.

"So," Andrew continued, remembering all that had happened, "That night, the sky was clear and the stars particularly bright. It was as if the universe itself was making direct contact with our very hearts. I know I felt like a wanderer on Earth, moving without even thinking about it: in fact, the others told me that's how they felt too. We managed to get in touch with the Holy Mother, but we weren't from this world, we were outsiders. I felt like the moon was nourishing us, showing us the way. Jesus was striding out ahead of us, imperturbable and determined as ever, until we reached the gates of the ancient monastery up on a hill — well more than a hill, I guess. We had all heard of this abbey, a holy place of worship, attached to the monastery of Judea. We looked up at the building and the only way I can describe it is it appeared as if thunder and lightning reigned there. The whole sky was lit up by lightning though there was absolutely no cloud in the sky. Jesus found a place for us all to rest at the foot of the hill and said, 'Tomorrow we will find someone who is waiting for us. He will have a recognizable sign, to tell us that he is the first to be found.' So then we fell asleep.

"The sun was coming up as we started climbing the hill, and Jesus told us on the way that there was a very old order of ordained priests that had been established there. I think he said that they'd once been associated with Qumran and the Essenes there, but today the priests live out their holy lives within the walls. The monastery was completely silent when we got there — it's pretty isolated — and, I don't know if it makes any sense but even the walls radiate silence.

"Right, so then we knocked at the door and were admitted, with Jesus going in first," Andrew said, realizing we were wrapped in his every detail. "We were in a holy place, right? There was no sign of trappings or decoration within the monastery. You know what? There was not one sign of the Jewish tradition at all. Jesus begged an audience to speak to the high priests, and we were led into a simple room. There were seven priests who received us. Jesus began to speak. 'You holy men, priests of the thunder and the lightning, I am here to collect him who reigns amongst you. For all of you, your time of isolation is at an end.' He approached one of them, whose devotional presence and humility filled the room. He and Jesus recognized one another. When they faced each other Jesus reached out both his hands to him.

"I remember clearly", Andrew told us, "he said, 'My brother, all of your prophesies are fulfilled. The holy breath of our Father fills this room. John, my companion, leave these silent walls and come with us. From now on you shall always be by my side.' All of a sudden thunder and lightning echoed round the room, and the room shook. He and Jesus held each other's hands, and the mighty energy of the heavens' throne shook the Earth. John stepped forward and knelt before Jesus, saying, 'Son of God, for many nights and in many visions I have received the divine message of your coming. God has announced it to me, and thunder and lightning have described you. I could feel your imminent arrival every moment. I have awaited you. I am prepared to receive what you have for me.'

"Then Jesus said, 'Stand up and you are with me. We were born in the same Heaven of creation. We are one. You should not kneel before me, but rather meet me face to face. John, my brother, you should travel throughout Israel and the Holy Land at my side. Yours and mine are one. You are now initiated and thunder and lightning are your being. Cast off your priesthood here, since you are beyond any high priest here on Earth.' Then Jesus turned to us and said, 'Truly, truly I say unto you, just as I was born out of God's seed, so is John born out of the same seed. We have neither mother nor origin: we are sons of the Father himself.' Jesus and John merged into one light before our very eyes. Then Jesus turned to the remaining priests and said, 'You safeguard here a wonderful chalice, one that has been preserved for hundreds of years.' Then John nodded and gave a sign to one of the priests, who went into a neighboring room and returned with a golden chalice, which he handed to John, saying, 'We have saved this until he comes, he who can fill the chalice.'

Andrew continued, evidently deeply moved. "We all saw that the chalice originated from long ago, and was a very sacred object. John handed the chalice to Jesus, whereupon Jesus sunk into prayer to God. The chalice filled with wine, and Jesus handed it first to John and said, 'Here is the blood of life. Everyone in this room will drink, since I am the chalice of life.' The goblet was passed around until all had drunk from it. Then Jesus and John left the room, and withdrew from us. We were all drunk, intoxicated by God's love. The priests provided us with food and lodging in their modest rooms, so that we could recover from our journey. Jesus and John had disappeared, and then reappeared in the evening. We gathered in the sacred room of the monastery. Jesus placed the chalice on the stone table and said, 'This chalice was not prepared by human hand.'

Andrew continued with shining eyes, "We were all astonished. The chalice spoke and narrated stories from ancient times, and we were all fascinated by the incredible sensation that emanated from it. All of us, save for Jesus, were bewitched by it. He said to John, 'The era of your guardianship of this monastery is finished. Take this chalice and come with me. One day it will find its correct place. Tomorrow morning we leave here.' The priests seemed disturbed by what had preceded, but Jesus clarified the situation and told them, 'The rest of you must leave this place, because tomorrow it will no longer exist! All signs of your presence here will be eliminated. Come with me. We have a long way before us.'

Andrew told us that in the night God's lightning reigned over the monastery, though no thunder echoed in the sky. No one was able to find rest in the night. Jesus explained to the priests again that their function in the monastery was ended and that they should leave without leaving traces of their presence. Although they had been guardians of this place for a very long time, they had all fulfilled their obligations here. The next morning we all breakfasted together. Then Jesus left the monastery with the words: 'It is time to go to Canaan.'

Andrew continued his narration. "We set out in the direction of Canaan. The priests from the monastery were dressed so that they could not be recognized as such. Jesus told us that he had received an invitation to visit a house in Canaan, which he had accepted. When we arrived in the town Jesus led us, single–minded, to a very noble house, which appeared to belong to a very prosperous man. He begged us to wait to one side. The door opened and he was admitted. After a short time he returned, and bade us follow him. 'Come! You are all welcome in the house of my friend.' We entered the house, which displayed all aspects of a very auspicious standard of living. Every one of us had his own room, since the house was very large and was obviously designed for very many guests. Even the priests were catered to. After the hard week behind us, we revelled in this unaccustomed luxury. Jesus informed us that his friend would welcome us during a festive meal that evening. We would meet again for dinner at the hour of sundown. At that time we would be collected by servants and led to the great hall, where the festive table was set.

"Jesus and his friend were waiting for us. His companion seemed familiar to us. He and Jesus were free and easy in their association, but very natural — as if they had known each other forever. His uncommonly light blonde hair was very unusual. His clothing was that of a very prosperous Jewish man. He and Jesus behaved as very old friends, and during the meal the two of them conversed almost continuously. None of us knew how they had met one another, and we puzzled as to how they came together. Jesus' friend was very hospitable, and he himself proffered us his wine.

"He said, 'Each of you is very welcome in my house.' After we had all eaten and drunk plentifully Jesus stood up and said, 'I am in the house of my oldest and most intimate friend. I know him since time immemorial, and have often enjoyed his welcome and his home on my journeys. In this house lives my most powerful companion. His house will always be a place of communion for us.' It was a wonderful evening filled with joy and good hospitality. Every one of us recognized that the closest friend and confidant of Jesus sat at the table: Jesus treated him differently from us. At the end of the table sat two intimate friends. The two of them exchanged ideas and conversation as equals, but what they said to one another remained a mystery, and remained their secret. There was an infinite trust between them.

"We spent three happy days in the house, and every day was a feast for us. On the fourth day Jesus said to me, 'Andrew, go to Jerusalem and bring the women here. We shall celebrate a great festival in seven days.' And to the others he said, 'Go and collect your dear ones and bring them here. Those you love. All of them are invited to this feast. We meet again here in seven days, and celebrate together for seven days and nights. The holiest feast will take place here, a gift from God.'

There Andrew ended his narration, telling us, "I have come to fetch you and to ask you to accompany me to Canaan. Jesus' friend has assured us that you can all live in his house, and extends his most cordial hospitality to you." We were all very enthusiastic, and in a short time had prepared ourselves for the journey. We four women left Jerusalem with Andrew, and made our way to Canaan.

To travel with Irisa was a luxury. On the way to Canaan I had recollections of our wanderings through the desert in earlier times. How different it was in a comfortable Roman chariot with horses. And how quickly the time passed! The dusty streets of Jerusalem were soon behind us: we were on our way to Canaan. Andrew was a good guide. He knew the way and after a journey of several days we arrived at the house of Jesus' friend.

Jesus received us himself, as he was expecting us. He welcomed each of us women with heartfelt warmth. He was very happy and appeared completely relaxed. From the first moment I sensed that he was not a stranger in the house, but was at home here. A few minutes later our host appeared, and I was almost speechless: here was the man I had already twice encountered: the first time under mysterious circumstances in the desert, where he suddenly appeared out of the sand and led us to Jesus, and the second time in Jerusalem, when he came to visit Jesus. And when he introduced his friend this time, he laid his arm across his friend's shoulders and said, laughing, "Yes, Miriam. Don't be surprised. This is the greatest magician in all worlds, though his accomplishments are unknown outside of his house. But we have often had the opportunity to meet in this way and exchange ideas."

We were led into a large room where a luxurious meal had been prepared for us. The hospitality of the house was very impressive and friendly, as Andrew had reported. During the meal my heart went back to my times with the Essenes. I could not recollect having even the possibility of revelling in luxury such as I experienced this evening. But the sight of Jesus' friend jogged my memory and took me back to my time in Qumran, while at the other end of the table he radiated joviality and contentment. I was reminded of something, but could not iput my finger on it. We spent the day joyfully and restfully. We were welcome in this beautiful house and the afternoon was the happiest that we had all experienced for a very long time.

I got to know the sister of our host that afternoon: Helena Salome. She joined our group of women, and in the course of the conversation we learned about her family, about which I was very curious. She told us that her father was from a very rich and noble Israeli family that had business connections with other countries. Her father had travelled widely, including to Greece, where he lived for many years and where he had met his future wife. She was a slave in a Roman household, and originally came from a northern country. He fell in love with this woman with her flowing blonde hair and begged her master to permit him to buy her freedom so that he could marry her. Helena Salome explained that it was very unusual to purchase a slave from another family. But her father had insisted until he was able to purchase the freedom of his beloved. Then he returned as quickly as possible to Israel, to erase the memory of her slavery. According to Jewish customs he could not marry her in our country, so he married under Roman law. They had two children, Helena Salome and her brother.

Helena explained that her brother had extraordinary qualities from birth. He was a radiant, happy being, and already in his childhood he displayed unusual powers that were occasionally visible. Once he was observed as he left the house secretly, speaking to the stars and the heavens, whereupon strokes of lightning from various parts of the sky struck the earth at his feet. Another time he was observed as he sat in the house and kindled a fire with his eyes. Helena's father recognized that his son, then only ten years old, was a very special individual, and he sought the advice of one of the Hebrew magi, who were in hiding but of whose existence we had heard. The father brought the son, whose light blonde hair attracted much attention, to one of these magi in Jerusalem.

Helena explained, "The wise man, whose name was Melchizedek, lived very modestly, a recluse with just the basic necessities: his scriptures and his God. He took the young lad into his holy chamber, and as he saw him he said immediately, 'Your child has extraordinary spiritual gifts.' He told my father that his son, my brother, possessed great powers, and that he was well advised to hide him from the Jewish magicians: they would misuse his powers or perhaps even try to eliminate him. He recognized great magical powers in the boy, a mastery of the elements and an enormous fire of his own. He said, 'I will contact a high priest that I know, ask his advice and try to find a solution for you and your son. Your son is here to cause great things to happen. But I would beg you to live in an as quiet manner as possible. Only let him come into contact with uninitiated persons. I will consult the stars and the councils of the heavens to enable me to give you more information about your son.'" That was where Helena Salome ended what she had to say. The evening drew to a close and the servants began to prepare the house for the night. It was time for us to withdraw to our bedrooms.

I can scarcely describe how happy and optimistic we all were. Although I hardly had a chance to talk to him, I was happy to see Lazarus again and have him near to me. Light heartedness and joy lived in this house. We were protected and safe here. That night I dreamed of my times with the Essenes. After a time I also dreamed of Fee and of the time we were together in the temple. My nightly visions awakened memories, and suddenly I was in the middle of a blazing fire that brought good luck and happiness and enveloped me completely. The master of the house and the master of the fire melted into one person, and then into a brilliant light of divine joy. It was deeply satisfying and uplifting. I gradually recalled the words of Fee: she had known that her Father was outside, somewhere in Israel. I recognized that it was the man who had offered us so much hospitality — the Master of the Fire, who lived unknown under affluent circumstances, but had found his place in Israel quietly, without awakening suspicion. When I awoke all the pictures combined in me to one question. I asked myself repeatedly how he and Jesus had come together, and how the trust and confidence in one another originated.

When I awoke the next morning, I was even more aware of the joy, good fortune and the exhilaration which filled the house. The sun was shining brightly and blessed each and every one of us. We all enjoyed a splendid breakfast we and were royally served. We women sat together and enjoyed the freedom and goodwill of the house. Jesus and the owner of the house were not evident, while the disciples had left on an errand, but would return shortly.

We were naturally very eager to know more from Helena Salome concerning the story of her brother, and we pleaded with her to continue her story, which she did. "After some weeks my father took Simon with him to Jerusalem" — this was the first time I had heard her brother's name mentioned — "to discover what the wise man had read in the stars. As my father arrived another man was present, whose name was Joseph of Arimathea. Melchizedek explained the message from the stars to my father: that his son Simon was very closely connected to the Messiah, whose appearance had already been announced. Joseph is the uncle of him whom the scriptures named as the future Messiah, which is the reason that Melchizedek had invited him to meet my father. The prophecy had already been received in Qumran, but was at present carefully protected.

"Joseph of Arimathea said to my father, 'Please permit me to present Jesus Emmanuel, who we recognize as the Messiah, to your son. I have had good connections to the Essenes for a long time, though I do not publicize that in Jerusalem. I will be going to Qumran soon, since the great masters have read the message in the stars: it is time for Jesus to leave Qumran. I have instructions to travel with him to other countries and to bring him into contact with other schools of wisdom and with ancient schools of mystery, such as I visited in my youth. My fate determined that I should be a trader in foreign lands. On my travels I have met great men and spiritual masters. Even at that time they foresaw that I would one day come with someone even greater, whom they could not teach, but would teach them!'

"Joseph of Arimathea and Melchizedek told my father that the stars had foreseen that Jesus and Simon were destined to be linked together and that their histories were entwined in one another. Joseph offered to take Simon with him when he and Jesus left Israel to visit foreign lands. He said he would be happy to take the two youngsters. Joseph and my father were both in agreement that Simon should leave the country, since his life could be in danger due to his great magical capabilities, so far beyond the normal human consciousness.

"It was well known that King Herod's fears of opposition could lead to the pursuit and persecution of Simon. Everything and everybody that even suggested opposition to the king would be mercilessly and brutally eliminated. Simon's stars had told of his great powers — greater than any known on Earth. My father had quickly learned to trust Joseph of Arimathea. They liked and respected each other and had immediately developed a friendship between them.

"I remember one day, when Joseph and Jesus visited our house when I was a small child and Simon somewhat older. It was very moving to see how the two boys were attracted to one another and instinctively and impulsively embraced one another. They looked into each other's eyes and Jesus declared, 'This is my brother, whom I have found again. I will travel with him to distant countries, as fate has determined for us, to initiate, to collect knowledge and to grow, in order to return to this country. That is God's will.'"

Helena Salome paused and then continued. "Thus Jesus, Simon and Joseph of Arimathea left this house and were away for many years. One day, when I was grown up, Simon stood on the threshold again. He was a man now, and my father embraced him with tears streaming down his cheeks. He welcomed Simon on his return home. But Simon had changed on his travels: he was not the person who had left us years before. Naturally, we asked him what he had experienced with Jesus. But he only replied, 'Jesus and I were on a very long journey, and were always together. We were so far away that you couldn't conceive the distance. But now is not the right time to discuss these things. Father, I beg you to permit me to return to your house. Then this is my place until Jesus and I find each other again.'

"In the meantime my mother had died, but my father accepted Simon with great affection, and in the following year arranged for him to inherit our estate. He introduced Simon to our family wealth, which he would administer. My father sensed that his life was coming to an end, which indeed came to pass a few years later. On the other hand, when my brother returned from his travels he filled the house with prosperity and joy, which you have also sensed here. He is a great master, who distributes his gifts every day."

Then she ended her narration, since Simon and Jesus had entered the room. Both of them looked at us knowingly, and Simon smiled and said, "Now you all know my story and that of my dearest brother." He looked at Mary, Jesus' mother. "It is wonderful to see you again, Mary, after all these years. It was a long time but still a great pleasure." Then Jesus said, "In a few days there a great festival will begin in this house. It will fill the Earth. We will invite people from the whole city, but we will wait until my companions have returned, so that they can also receive the guests. The whole neigh-borhood is prepared to accommodate visitors. I will go into the village today; from now on the people should recognize me."

194

We followed Jesus to the marketplace. The news of his presence had already spread through the region, and many people had assembled to see him. As he arrived I saw a leper waiting, and as he approached Jesus the crowd drew back to let him pass. The leper called to Jesus, "Messiah. I lay my affliction at your feet. Please heal my soul." As he approached the leper Jesus said, "Your belief alone has cured you. Stand up and walk!"

We were astonished by the miracle, as the leper stood up and walked before our very eyes. Then he knelt before Jesus and rejoiced: "The Lord has freed me from my illness. I was a cripple and now I have regained my health." Then Jesus looked at him compassionately and said, "Your trust in God has healed you." Then Jesus stood on the steps and instructed Simon's servants, who had gathered on the marketplace, to distribute bread and wine to all who were assembled there. Everyone received enough to eat and drink.

Jesus announced, "In three days we will celebrate the presence of the Heavenly Father. You are all invited as our guests. My brother Simon and I invite you all. Everybody who hears this invitation is welcome. There is space for everyone. Come in three days at sunset, to Simon's house — which every one of you knows." Then Simon stepped forward. "The doors of my house are open to each and every one of you. He who we have so long awaited is now here. Together we will celebrate the festival of his coming."

On the third day the crowd streamed to Simon's house, which was opened to all. The apostles had returned and had brought their own friends with them. As the sun set Jesus and Simon appeared for the first time and said, "Welcome to the house of our Father." Simon instructed his servants to provide everybody with food and drink. Jesus walked through the rows of people and spoke to them, observing some with an intense searching gaze. It was as if he was fishing in the crowd. He was searching for particular beings.

At midnight Jesus stood in the midst of the crowd and said, "The call of the Lord has reached many of you. I recognize many of you who are here because you have followed me on Earth. Tonight the wine is initiated to bless you. Tomorrow you should return here at midnight, since from now on we will spend the nights together. I am seeking in your number some persons who belong to me. The outer circle of my followers will be completed. The Lord above is happy that you have found your way to me. Many of you don't know who you are, but I will christen you. We will bring the heavenly wine to Earth and the ecstasy of meeting our Father. I will initiate, I will bless and I will connect those who belong together, in my name."

He let the servants bring the wine that Simon had generously provided. He began to pray and blessed the wine. At this moment I was able to see energies and light, as in old times. Flames came from Heaven and spread over the holy wine. Food and wine were distributed to everyone. Jesus and Simon walked between the rows of guests, and spoke to them. They encouraged them with friendly words and welcomed each one individually. I sat together with Irisa and Mary at the table that had been allotted to us. We observed how an intoxicating feast originates. The Messiah and Simon spread their hospitality and good spirits.

Shortly after midnight Jesus announced, "Please go home now. Tomorrow we meet again at this time. God in Heaven will christen our guests. Everything in the realm of the Father is prepared. Together with Simon I will prepare the highest initiation for those who have come to me and have found the way to the Father. God bless you. God be with you. I am with you and thank you." All guests left the house, and we were almost drunk with ecstasy but also with the happiness of going to bed and sleeping.

But before I drifted off I sensed that two were not asleep: Jesus and Simon were wide awake, as if they did not need sleep that night. They were together. Then I slept. Under the roof of this hospitable and joyful house the atmosphere was as if I was at home.

The following day we all cleaned and tidied the house after the festival, and prepared for a new celebration. We were all keyed up and excited. In the atmosphere we could sense that some jealousy had developed between the disciples. The reason was that Jesus seemed increasingly to favor Simon. In the midst of our work Jesus appeared and spoke to his disciples and to us women. "Come to me for a moment." We sat in a circle around him and he looked at us all affectionately. Then he said, "God created the worlds. His love was the same for all beings that he created. He did not distinguish between them. But there are some beings whose origin is nearer to God than others, and who remained nearer to God. Those whose origin is further from God bring their light and love to more distant worlds. I would like you all to understand that I love all beings equally and in their own way, but there are some to whose love I am bound more closely, because we embody God's realm, His power and His magnificence.

"Each of you has come with me to take his place. But in the realm of a king there are some who sit nearer to the throne, and others who have their place further from the king and still happily perform their duties. But the wise king loves each one of them equally, irrespective of his rank or location. None of them is more important than the other, but while some come into contact with the king, some remain in the kitchen, in other services, in the garden, in the stables.

"Do you believe that one is more important than another? Give the king what is his, and give the servant what is his. Give the people what belongs to them. I hope you recognize the blessing, that you all may be so close to me. Believe me: every one of you has suffered these agonies in many lives. But whosoever lives on the Earth but does not have to fight his or her way through the earthly life, such as Simon and I, are naturally close in another manner. Please understand this and do not provoke jealousy or discord. Then I love you all more than you can comprehend." Then he went to each of us and touched our heads with his hand. I was very relieved that Jesus had addressed the problem unflinchingly. I had quickly sensed the disharmony and was content that peace had returned to us.

Simon and his servants were preparing the house for the new festival. We supported them by collecting the wine pitchers and preparing the food for all the guests. As the sun set, we began to light torches throughout the house and to illuminate the entrance. The sacred atmosphere was again present, and as it became dark we withdrew for a rest. Then as midnight approached we all returned to the hall and helped receive the many visitors, to lead them to their places, to care for their needs and to make them feel welcome. Some asked me how I had come to know the Messiah. They were all curious to hear our stories and in this way we got acquainted with many of them — different beings, affectionate, sad, searching, and recognizing. I was very happy to be amongst so many people. Irisa, Mary, Helena Salome, Martha and Lazarus enjoyed it, as did Jesus' disciples.

We looked after the guests, conversed with them and everyone was waiting for the appointed time. There must have been around two hundred people there. Shortly before midnight, Jesus and Simon appeared together. Then the people started singing, "Hallelujah! Hosanna! Hallelujah! Praised and blessed be the Messiah." Then Jesus gave a sign for silence with his hand. He sat in the midst of us and let his love spread over all of us. I sensed for the first time how he and Simon were one. Together they radiated their compassion over the crowd and uplifted them.

Jesus said, "God's promise and His plan, to send His Son to Earth, have been decided for a long time. God's decision is known from primeval times and confirmed in the ancient writings from Atlantis, an epoch of which no one speaks today. Our people have learned of God's wish from the traditions handed down by Noah. God was determined to save and free the human beings who were trapped by worldly forces and were oblivious to Him through their slavery to the material world. Many of you who have come to me today wish to accompany me on my mission, to support me in fulfilling God's promise. I have recognized you. I see you. I am here to collect you and to lead you. My friend and brother beside me, Simon, has also held communion with himself and has decided to serve the cause. But believe me, he is not less important than I. He does not appear in public. For my part I yearn to seek, to find and to elevate you all. My heart is filled with gratitude and joy that I have found you.

"I am here to guide you and strengthen your faith in God, to free you from your sins, to unleash you by my love and to bring you home to God's realm. He who sits next to me is known since the beginning of time. Nevertheless, he does not aspire to power in this world. But believe me, he has the key to the kingdom of Heaven and I am the gate. I need him and he needs me. We two are the guardians of Heaven beneath God's throne, and for that reason we are all assembled here tonight — to celebrate the enlightenment of many of you in heavenly exuberance. At a later date we will edify others. Let me recognize now those of you who have already consented and identified themselves. But when we do not identify you immediately, be not despondent: we are looking until the end of time. We will find you. That is our promise."

Jesus then sought John, and said to him, "Fetch me the chalice, John." And he left the room and returned with the grail. Jesus placed it on the table, where all could see it. All present experienced a cold shiver down the spine: they saw a chalice that emitted a mysterious vibration and touched all of those present. We had all heard the story of the chalice, and I remembered how we shook when Andrew narrated the story to us. Now it stood before us. And I must admit, the chalice had also a magical effect on me.

Jesus started to speak, and I recognized the change immediately. He was the master and the teacher again: "This chalice was forged from God's hand a very long time ago. At that time Simon and I were kings on the Earth, in God's realm. The Father gave us this chalice, as symbol of the unity of spiritual might and light. The grail switched at regular intervals from one earthly realm to the other. It was constantly filled with God's blessing and with His might. And since that time it is known as the Holy Grail, forged by God and given to the Earth. But then the new era arrived. The realms of enlightenment were obliged to reduce the light radiated from the grail, while humanity also dissociated itself from God — and left the power to those who had created a new order on Earth. We withdrew into the realms of light, and relinquished the might on Earth to the new rulers. Not that we wished to abandon you, but because it was the free choice of humanity, who cried out for the freedom to establish their own order and not to obey the authority of the unity of light and love. In accordance with the wish of humanity, we have left the Earth's dominion to others.

"But the promise of each ruler who came to power never materialized or it was completely different from that which humanity had envisaged, or for which it had hoped. The era of enslavement. Evil kings and presumptuous masters appeared and took over the power on Earth. That is the situation today. The people of Earth are governed by those who negate God's will. Please do not understand this as a judgement of those who rule our country. It is not an indictment of the Romans and Jews who oppress you. Those who know not what they do can find neither happiness nor blessing.

"I am not here with the sword to depose the rulers and take over power. I am here with him who sits next to me to unite oil and fire, the divine fire and the oil from the sacred blood. I have come with the might of holy flames. Before the new era it was decided that the chalice should remain on Earth, retained by a sacred priesthood. Since time immemorial they have guarded and watched over it with their prayers and devotions. The Holy Grail has waited a long time for its rebirth."

Jesus looked at the chalice and tears rolled down his cheeks. "But the chalice shall also decide my fate when the time comes — and yours too. Now I will fill the Holy Grail and pass it to each of you, that you can drink from it. Each one that I recognize and Simon recognizes shall be initiated by us. Tonight and in the following nights we will confer the ordination of the sacred blood amongst you. Simon will unlock the gate for everyone of you who is willing, and I will baptize you in the name of my blood!"

Jesus let the chalice be filled and said, "Do not come to me, I will seek each of you who is searching for the chalice." Then he asked John to fetch water in another chalice, to pour scented holy oil into it and to stand near to him. Then Jesus began to pray, and divine lights appeared above the Holy Grail and filled the room. He spoke the words by which I recognized that he unified Christ within Christ. Then he passed the chalice to Simon, who also spoke a prayer. The oil and fire then appeared to mix in the chalice to give wine. Jesus took the wine and passed it first to his apostles. He baptized them first, by sprinkling water from John's chalice and initiating each of them with sacred words from the Holy Spirit.

Then Jesus went along the lines of people awaiting him. First he stopped at a woman with long, dark hair, and gave her the chalice. "Drink from the blood of life." An unusual light appeared to radiate from her, and a great transcendence. Jesus looked at her and baptized her. Her long hair fell over her body as she knelt before him and laid her head on his feet. He said, "Rise up!" Then they looked at one another for a time, and Jesus finally said, "Stay here!"

Next Jesus turned to a strongly built man and gave him the chalice to drink from. He then baptized him and said, "You are Mark. I recognize you again. You belong to the group of my apostles. You should stay here too." The tension in the house increased.

Jesus now approached a large, bulky man and handed him the chalice. As he did so the man said, "No, Lord. I am not worthy to shelter under your roof." Jesus replied, "Thomas, Thomas, believe me, he whom I consider worthy is also worthy for the Father. Stay here too, this night." Then Thomas drank from the chalice and submitted to baptism.

Next Jesus went through the crowd to a woman, whose age was difficult to ascertain. She was well built and had absolutely black hair. He gave her his hand affectionately and said, "Arise! You have heard my call. It has penetrated to you, and you have you have had the courage to come here. You should also stay here tonight, before you return whence you came." Mary sat next to me and I sensed how she shuddered. I asked her, "What is the matter, Mary?" She replied, "Thank heavens nobody has recognized her." When I asked what she meant, she replied, "She is at present the Mother of Ephesus, the secret order of the women. If someone in the room were to recognize her, she would be immediately be persecuted and stoned." I regarded the woman. She had a wonderful presence and a power all could sense, and which I had never seen in another woman. She fell on her knees before Jesus, who kissed her head and said, "Be praised in the name of the Lord, our Father. You should also remain here tonight."

He then approached a woman with reddish, curly hair. He gave her the chalice and baptized her, saying, "Carrier of the key, are you here to find others like yourself?" He held her head for some minutes, and then she fell on her knees and laid her head on his feet. He said, "You should also stay here tonight."

The silence in the room was almost overwhelming. Jesus raised his eyes and went to someone standing right at the back, next to the door. Lazarus was not far from me and I heard him whisper, "No. Not him!" Jesus gave him the chalice, baptized him and said, "Stay here, Judas Iscariot." I sensed the distress of Lazarus, and went over to him and asked what was wrong. He replied, "That man is a high magician from the School of Solomon, in which I was educated. He will bring bad luck." I said, "When Jesus chooses him you should find peace with his decision." But Lazarus could not be consoled: "You don't know him!" Nevertheless, the man named Judas Iscariot remained.

Then Jesus turned and walked through the assembled crowd. He approached a man and said, "Bring your brother tomorrow. I was looking for him. But you can remain this night, to ascertain who we are." He next spoke to a Roman soldier, who had ventured to enter the house in his uniform. Nobody had attempted to hinder him: everyone knew that when Jesus was there the soldier's presence could only be positive. Jesus gave him wine and baptized him. The soldier removed his helmet and knelt before Jesus, who said, "You are a brave Roman soldier and my protection between the two worlds. But I pray you: do not show yourself in our company in the near future. One day you shall protect us, but the time is not ripe for you. I bless you for that which you do for me. But now you must go, and avoid being seen with us at present. Return to your people. The time will come when I will need you." The Roman left the house only observed by those present.

Jesus then went to a well-built, dark-haired man. He gave him wine and after his baptism asked him, "Whence do you come?" and the man answered, "From Damascus." Jesus asked him, "You have come such a long way to find me?" He answered, "I had heard of you and I walked here until I found you." Jesus replied quietly, "Then stay. You have come with a pilgrim's staff: you will hear my words and then spread them around the world." Then Jesus placed the chalice on the table and said, "The celebration is now closed. I beg all who are baptized to remain here. You will spend the night with us. Those who return home are blessed in my name, and I beg you to return tomorrow."

We regarded each of those who had remained. Most of all I was fascinated by the woman Mary had identified as the initiated Ephesus-priestess. She had shared her secret with me. Jesus assembled all around him. He sat down among us and proffered wine. "Welcome in my name and in the name of Simon. I shall offer seven holy wines this night. We will celebrate until dawn, and then each of you will be released to fulfill his or her task."

Wine was given to everyone and we celebrated. It struck me that Simon and Jesus alternately blessed the wine. With each wine the atmosphere in the room became more euphoric and congenial. It was as if we gave up a piece of our earthly life with each sip. With each cup we left a portion of our past life behind us.

Jesus said to the priestess from Ephesus, "Nobody in this room knows the high price you have paid to come here. But I beg you to return in the morning, whence you have come. Let no one recognize you. I know and you know that you possess a dark ring of power within you. Bring the ring back to your home. Believe me; I will help you carry this ring. But you are initiated and also know that this ring will only be redeemed in much later times." He approached and embraced her for some minutes. He said, "The power that you possess is a heavy burden for you. But I am with you to relieve your load. But I cannot have you remain here. You must return home."

I quivered deep within and sensed that I was connected to her energy. It was as if Jesus had relieved each of us of our old burdens. With each wine we drank, we became more relaxed and joyful. Then Jesus went to the woman he had first baptized and I saw her face for the first time. She was not exceptionally beautiful, but she had a wonderful charisma. He asked her, "What is your name?" She looked at him. "Sara." Jesus looked up and regarded Irisa and me. Then he asked the woman from Ephesus for her name. She replied, "MaRa." Then he said to us, "Sara, MaRa, Irisa and Miriam.

Holy women are amongst us, who will help to shape the future. Each of you carries a different seed. Each of you has her own burden to carry.

Jesus asked the four of us to come to him. He laid his hands on our heads, one after the other. "Each of you carries a destiny of womanhood with her, a heavy burden. I am here to release you from this weight. This is my promise today, which will be fufilled at a future time. In this life you must all return to the burdens you have been carrying, since I shoulder the load of the whole Earth, and thus your burdens too." He knelt before MaRa. "Here in this room everyone may hear who you are, black mother from Ephesus. You carry the great sorrow of those women who were once holy and today are outlawed and persecuted. You cannot relinquish the burden you carry at present. But you shall return to your number one day. Then I will release you into a new freedom. But the time is not yet ripe. Nevertheless, I am very happy that you have come to me. For the present you must carry your load and your black coat: I cannot yet free you. There is also someone in this room you will meet again someday."

Jesus looked at the dark–haired man from Damascus and said to MaRa, "When you have fulfilled this task you will return to Damascus with him, freed from you burden — the burden of which you alone are aware. And you shall make your way in the world with him, and be free again — but not yet. What you all do not know is that Sara, MaRa, Irisa and Miriam are all sisters. They originate from the same divine root; all were at various times great mothers and great women from the sacred folk of Judea. You have returned to reclaim the inheritance of your fathers." Then he said to Sara, "From now on you will work together with Miriam. Stay with her, and stay with us. You belong to our number." He reached to Heaven and set a Light of Christ in her heart. The pain in her face was reduced and she began to radiate her inner beauty again.

Jesus turned to Simon, smiled and said, "Nobody knows that we have goddesses among us. Only the Earth and we know their secret." Then all of us drank a cup of wine and left the Earth behind us that night. Heavy with wine we went to our beds. Jesus begged that all who had been chosen remained in the house for the night. From then on those he had chosen became apostles: Judas Iscariot, Thomas and Mark.

I took Sara to my room and Irisa shared her room with MaRa, the priestess from Ephesus. They were our guests. The night was as heavy as the depth of the wine, in which we immersed ourselves. It was no longer the heaviness of the Earth, but the profundity of God Himself in that night.

Next morning everything was different. During the night other people had arrived, people we did not know and whose presence changed the atmosphere. I sensed that they were somehow familiar to me, but that I would need some time to acclimatize myself to them.

We were all engaged in cleaning the house and restoring some order after the previous night, then we lovingly prepared it for the coming night. Simon organized the preparations and looked after us, and sent the men to purchase wine and provisions. I sought MaRa at the earliest opportunity. She had warm, black eyes and wonderful aura, and was somewhat older than I was.

I asked cautiously whether I might speak to her and she nodded assent. I asked, "Would you like to tell me more about what you carry and whence you come?" She raised her hand and stroked my hair affectionately, saying, "I noticed you yesterday. I recognize the mighty women. I and a few other women in the North of Israel continue secretly to maintain the School of Mystery, withdrawn from the public eye. You must surely know that we have to avoid being seen in public. I can only wear our traditional costume, by which we may be recognized, on occasions such as this — but not outside. The might of the women is transferred to us — the primeval mystery of womanhood, which we accommodate and nurture within us. It has become increasingly difficult since society threatens and abuses us; we have enemies in Jerusalem and had contact to the Messiah for a long time, and he has called me. Hence I left my loneliness and my withdrawal from the world to come here. His call showed the way here. I travelled alone, in order not to endanger friends and colleagues."

I asked MaRa, "What secrets do you carry?" She hesitated, and then replied, "I and a few others carry the ring of female potency. I bear the black ring that was initiated within me, and that I constantly protect. You also carry a ring." I looked at her and asked, "Where do we carry this ring?" She replied, hesitantly, "It is inside ourselves. In our abdomens, since time immemorial. During this age in which female potency and authority are not tolerated, we carry the rings within us, in order to preserve them."

MaRa then approached me, took my head in her hands and then suddenly shrank back, saying, "You bear a more potent ring than mine at present, but you must only bear it within you; life will not help you to carry it. I cannot tell you more, since it would arouse powerful processes within you." I did not hear any more; I fainted and fell unconscious to the floor.

When I awoke, Irisa and Helena Salome were next to me. I did not know where I was or whence I came. I had only the intuition that something had happened to me. I was no longer the adolescent that I had previously been; something was born inside me and I did not feel well. MaRa gave me a special drink, which was unknown to me, and murmured something in an unknown language. My head spun and I felt sick. She brought me to my room, where Sara sat. In spite of my semi–consciousness I sensed that her mind was disturbed. But in my condition I could not help her: my body was not under control. Irisa begged Sara to leave my room and go to hers, while MaRa stayed with me and prayed. Towards evening I felt somewhat better. I stood up and said, "I would like to help. I believe all support will be welcome. I believe that even more people will come tonight." I sensed MaRa's searching glance, as to whether I was well enough. Then she said, "All right, I will help too."

Together we lit the oil lamps in the house. On the way to the hall we met Simon. He looked at MaRa and said, "We have not seen each other for a long time. You have hidden from me for all that time!" MaRa was suddenly grave, and said, "Simon, you know I could not do otherwise." He looked at her for some time and replied, "I had nevertheless promised long ago to liberate you." MaRa answered, "The time will come, but not in this era. I have decided to carry the dark ring inside me, and I will bear it until it is redeemed. You know my decision." He smiled and said, "When the time comes I will be there to help you." They looked at one another with mutual respect, and then he disappeared into a room. It was getting dark outside, and I had hoped to see Jesus somewhere, but he did not appear. I resolved to withdraw to my room again, until the crowd of guests had arrived. I was grateful that Sara had not reappeared. As I left my room somewhat later, I noticed that Irisa was still looking after Sara. She held Sara in her arms and I could see that Sara was crying.

I could only go to them and kneel before Sara. I took her hands and asked her gently, "Why are you so sad, dear lady?" She wept bitterly saying, "How can I believe it? Three of my children and my husband are dead and nobody accepted me. I was banned from society. Then I came to Jesus, and he accepted me and says I should remain with you." Irisa took her in her arms and caressed her. "You belong to us. I sense that you have left your previous fate and will find your peace with us."

At this moment I noticed something in Irisa that I had not previously seen: she radiated an unending stream of peace and tranquillity, in which she enveloped Sara. I had liked Sara from the beginning and I recognized her great sadness and suffering. Apart from that, I sensed something deep down inside her that I loved, and I rejoiced in the knowledge that our fates would be coupled together for a long time.

Now the time had arrived. The doors were opened again and we helped the many people to find places. The news had spread that Jesus was choosing his apostles and companions. It was apparent that everyone wished to belong to that number, so that an even greater number had appeared this evening.

The man whom Jesus had asked to bring his brother was there, together with his brother, who had a fine, honest face. I sensed immediately that he would become an apostle. I was absolutely certain that Jesus would take him. This evening Joseph of Arimathea also came to us and brought Jacob, who had been living with him for some time. I was overjoyed, and Mary even more so. Irisa's delight knew no bounds and we embraced each other long and intensively. Joseph had become a loving, fatherly friend and Jacob an attractive boy. Jacob looked very much like Jesus, but had a softer aura, somewhat more reticent but with great clarity and love.

Midnight drew near and the servants began to fill the jugs with wine. Many more jugs had been purchased due to the great number of guests expected. There was also a plentiful supply of fish and bread. Then Jesus and Simon appeared. Simon took over the role of host by greeting the guests with humor and charm. "You are all welcome in my house in this holy night. You are welcome in our hearts. Peace be with everyone of you who brings peace." Jesus was present but sat in the background while Simon led the proceedings. His lighthearted, joyful temperament charmed all of those present. He sat down so that everybody could see him and said, "You all do not know whence you come and where you are going. Nevertheless I am very happy that you are all here. Tonight I will be your host. Actually I prefer to remain in the background but Jesus has asked me to speak to you this time. Jesus knows and has announced that there are key–carriers in this room."

Here he paused and I saw for the first time tears running down his cheeks. "I have guarded Heaven and the Lord who is present since the beginnings of time. The gate to Heaven is my gate. When the gate opens for one or another of you, I am there and lead you through the gate. But you will never see me outside. I have very often had great offices and responsibilities on this Earth, but prefer to remain unknown. I know the guardians of the keys between Heaven and Earth. The Messiah wishes me to identify those of you to whom I will entrust the ancient keys. He who embodies Father and Son in one wishes the kingdom of Heaven to be present above us tonight. At a glance, I recognize twenty-seven of you who carry the key and the three flames in your heart.

"I would like to tell you something about your origins. You are guardians of the gates of heaven, powerful watchmen between Heaven and Earth, derived from the primeval fire. Born out of these flames, vigorous and flaming like the fire from which you come. Wherever you are the fire shall be ignited. And if God wills it, only ashes will remain. Today you receive your guardianship."

Then he stood up and approached Lazarus. "Jesus baptized you with wine and I now baptize you with fire." He raised his hands and — whether the others saw it I cannot say — I observed flames spouting from his hands, with which he baptized Lazarus. He said, "I baptize you but Jesus will take you over and redeem you. Take the first key to the gates of heaven, which will be created above us." Simon removed his hands from Lazarus' head and his eyes indicated clearly that Lazarus should go to Jesus. My brother fell on his knees before Jesus, and Jesus lifted him to his feet and looked at him. There was a peculiar stillness in the room, as if a sacred key appeared above us, bright and mighty — at least that is what I saw.

One after another Simon called the remaining twenty-six key-holders. First he baptized the woman who had been present yesterday and who remained overnight; her name was Hanna, and she also knelt before Jesus and was blessed by him. Then Simon called Thomas, who Jesus had yesterday named as one of his apostles. He also received the baptism of fire and the key. In this manner all twenty-seven were initiated as key-holders.

Then Simon said to the others in the room, "I beg you who were here tonight but have not yet been recognized to return home in peace. Take the message with you and proclaim peace and love, for which we are all here tonight." All were preparing to leave when Jesus stood up and said to the man who he had asked to bring his brother here on the previous day, "I beg you and your brother to remain here." He then approached the younger brother and asked, "What is your name?" The young man, who I had noticed earlier, answered, "I am Luke." Jesus replied, "You are here at last. You carry the fire of my evangelical gospel. Are you aware of that?" Luke nodded and said, "I know, Lord. That is what I was taught." Luke fell on his knees before Jesus and asked, thrilled at the prospect, "May I stay here, Lord?" And Jesus lifted him up and said, "You may stay."

I liked Luke. He had a pure, affectionate nature and radiated great clarity. This evening Jesus did not proffer wine. All of us — the twenty-seven newcomers, Luke, and those who had remained there on the previous day — received wine from Simon. Before he let the wine pitchers be passed round, he held the head of each of us in his hands and blessed us with a prayer. This time we were not intoxicated by the Earth, but with each cup we floated gradually into heaven. We were lighthearted and playful. We were together with one another and celebrated, intoxicated by the ecstasy of our collective joy. Then Jesus stood up, raised his arms and said, "Open up, gates of heaven!" All twenty–seven stood up spontaneously, while flames rose out of each of them, as if the Holy Spirit was escaping from them. At this moment the Earth shook and the heavens shuddered, then it was quiet. Jesus and Simon were calm and collected. But the rest of us were deeply moved by the heavenly occurrence, which had shaken us, body and soul.

I only recollect being in a state that took me into a dreamless sleep. I do not know how long I slept, but I found that many others had also slept. Jesus and Simon were no longer there. As I slowly recovered consciousness, I observed many others still asleep. I sought the way to my room and found Sara already there; she was more peaceful than before and smiled when I entered. I withdrew under my blankets, but sleep did not come to me. I continued to tremble, as if the Earth was still quaking. As I left my room the next morning, I saw Jesus talking to MaRa. I sensed that they did not wish to be disturbed. As he had every morning, Simon had set the table for all of us. I looked for something to eat, since my body was weak and needed strength and nourishment.

I sensed an inner impulse to leave the house and return home. I needed some distance from the events of the previous days. I crept through the door and left the house.

Suddenly Lazarus was beside me and said, "Please do not go alone. I have been outside often in the last days and know what is happening. You know that I am a Zealot, and I know the Zealots. Each time I went outside the house to purchase provisions, it was noticeable that the peace and tranquillity in the house do not exist outside. Watchful eyes are spying on us." I begged Lazarus, "Let us go for a walk in the fresh air. I need to be outside for a time. Will you accompany me?" He agreed. We walked away from the city, and I was happy to be able to separate myself from the confusion of the previous days. I was still in a slight trance, and Lazarus was attentive and thoughtful. We did not talk much, but we shared a quiet optimism.

After a while I asked him, "Do you know what happened?" He replied, "Miriam, I don't really know. But last night I was in contact with God again. I have not had that for a very long time. Now He is there again. After all these years I have hope in my heart again." I leaned against him and said, "So have I, Lazarus." We returned to Simon's house and recommenced our daily tasks. We needed the whole day to clean and tidy the house after the night's celebration. The apostles had been shopping again, bringing provisions and wine. Everyone helped.

I met Sara and looked at her. Without exchanging a word we embraced each other long and tenderly, and I felt that her soul had lightened. She was lighter and brighter than before and I sensed a white light in her and a wonderful flame, which was familiar to me. We were very happy to be together.

That evening MaRa came to me and said, "I think it is time for me to leave this house. More and more people come to the house and I must remain unrecognized. I will return to the mountains, where I remain anonymous." Then she pressed a note into my hand and said, "Please be careful. This is a map to help you find us, in case you wish to visit us." She kissed me on the forehead. I looked at her and had a deep respect for the primeval powers that she radiated. As she was leaving I said, "Please look after yourself." She laughed and said, "When I don't want anyone to find me, I am invisible and nobody can! I am like the Earth: I blend into her and can disappear and reappear when I wish. You don't have to worry about me." Then she left the house without being seen.

I helped in the preparations. Jesus and Simon had withdrawn into a side room, and whenever I passed the room I heard them talking to one another. I did not wish to eavesdrop or understand what they were saying. But when I was near to the room I just enjoyed hearing the sound of their voices. I cannot say why, but I enjoyed the energy of their exchanges. There was a fine feeling in the air, although I could not describe it precisely. We then withdrew for a while to rest before the great multitude arrived. Irisa had offered Sara a place in her room, and I was grateful that Irisa had sensed the importance of my having peace and quiet. I really enjoyed the solitude, a chance to be alone with myself, since the turbulence within me had not completely ceased, though we later learned that Sara had decided on her own to leave without our knowledge.

When I emerged from my room that evening, there was already a crowd present. I was happy that there were enough helpers there, and that I could retire to a quiet corner. Shortly before midnight the room was completely full. I observed the enormous crowd and tried to withdraw into myself. Then Jesus and Simon arrived. Jesus said, "Tonight is the night of the Light of Christ. Each one who comes to me will be blessed by the Light of Christ." This night there were no words between us. We came to him one after the other, and he held our heads in his hands and spoke a prayer. There were hundreds of people and the blessing lasted a very long time. I was more intoxicated from the atmosphere in the room than from the wine. When all had received his blessing, Jesus stood up and said, "I beg each of you who has not been asked to stay in this house, now to return home."

We bade the crowd farewell and accompanied them to the door. We closed the door and breathed a sigh of relief: It must have been three or four o'clock in the morning. Then Jesus called for wine. I had also been blessed by Jesus, and my love for him was greater than anything I could conceive. We were now a smaller group: his apostles, the few women and special friends. All the others had left. He let the wine be poured and then blessed it with the words: "This is my blood. We were born out of this blood." Then we drank wine and celebrated almost in silence until morning. An all–embracing compassion spread above us, and scarcely a word was spoken. From time to time Jesus filled the pitchers again. As dawn was breaking Jesus suddenly came to me and regarded me with his loving eyes. I was leaning against the wall and was almost asleep. For the first time since I had known him, he embraced me — and I fell asleep on his shoulder. My extreme exhaustion finally found relief and peace.

When I awoke the sun was shining, and I withdrew to my room and fell into an even deeper sleep. I did not awaken for the whole day. When I had washed and left my room, everybody was involved in the next preparations. Silence and quiet harmony bound us together, and all were helping. I went through the rooms and consciously regarded the apostles. It then became apparent how different they were from one another. Some of them viewed me with critical glances: they were not used to women moving around freely in their midst. It was not their habit to treat women as their equals, as Jesus did. Some of them spoke to me amicably. Peter sat in a corner and I sat next to him and took his hand. I asked him whether everything was in order and looked at me with friendly eyes and said, "Yes Miriam, everything is in order. I was just considering for a moment the life I left behind me — and how my life with the Lord will be!" I looked at him and sensed how great my love for him was. He continuously radiated fatherly goodwill. We had scarcely completed our preparations when the doors opened. A fire was burning outside that lit up the dark night. This time the crowd was so great that all could not enter the house, but had to remain outside.

I heard a woman outside screaming and rampaging, and she shouted, "I must get into this house. I must get into the house." Two of the apostles held her hands and led her in. She was obsessed and screamed wildly. Jesus appeared, hearing the noise. She threw herself on his feet and he looked at her and commanded, "Demons disappear!" A shudder went through the room and the woman fell unconscious to the floor. Jesus went to her and held her head in his hands. She was clothed completely in black. As she recovered consciousness Jesus looked at her and asked her, "Black witch, what do you want here?" And from deep inside her came the answer: "To find redemption." Then Jesus said, "Dark witch. You have been fighting against my power for a long time, and then you come to me for redemption. Don't you know that my power and my love can destroy you?" She removed her black veil, and I saw that she had pitch-black hair and eyes.

He said, "Go! One day I will find you and then I will redeem you. But first you must find peace with yourself. Only when you have forsaken your magical powers can you come to me." As she left she began to curse, and it seemed that the demons still possessed her. Suddenly she fell to the floor again, and the crowd shrank back. I could not help myself: I went to her to see whether she was ill and if I could help her. I looked briefly at Jesus and he nodded assent. Then my old Essene powers returned to me. Mary also came to me and together we combined all our united healing powers. Finally we conquered the dark powers and demons within her and with a shrill cry the demons were expelled from her and flew to heaven. Then we held her and let our love stream through her. When she returned to full consciousness she looked into my eyes and asked, "Who are you?" I looked into her dark eyes and replied, "A sister, like yourself."

Her gaze had completely changed. Her eyes still glowed, black as the night, but there was gentleness in them. Jesus came to her and said, "You must thank these women and their love, that the dark forces which you have carried around within you have been released. Nevertheless, you cannot remain here at present. Return home and do only good. Spread your love around. From now on I will be with you."

Then Simon went to her and struck her on the chest with his hand. With a loud shout the last remnants of darkness finally left her with an angry roar. Then he looked at her, smiling, and said, "I have looked for you for a long time. You have dared to come here and now you are free from the old forces. Now is the time to return and bless all that you meet. Do good and announce the glad tidings of what has happened, that all whom you meet find redemption." She began to cry, but Jesus and Simon insisted that she must leave.

As she left the room I experienced anguish, as if my sister had been sent away. But I sensed that she must leave, to extinguish the evil in herself that she had previously distributed to others. As she went I saw a white radiance around her, and I thought to myself how many women fall into this darkness because the world had compelled them. But she appeared to be a person who could be liberated from this darkness. After her departure, Jesus wandered round the room speaking to various people. Wine and food were distributed to all present.

Then Jesus crossed the room to a man who was apparently a Jewish high priest, one who served in the different temples all over Israel and was clothed in his traditional dress. The man knelt before Jesus, who laid a hand on his head and said, "Stand up." The man was very tall and well built, and had not the mundane godless aura of most Jewish priests. He was clean and devoid of the vanity of the Jewish priesthood. Jesus said to him, "Leave the priesthood and become one of my apostles. You belong to me. Put the books that guide you to one side. You are clean and noble. Place your hand on the oath of my heart."

Then I saw Simon approach and embrace him, saying, "You are my spiritual son. Serve him in my name, since I shall not always be with him. But you will accompany him in my name."

Jesus requested a bowl of oil to be brought, and baptized the man, whose noble and modest character impressed me very much. Simon offered him a room in his house, and from that time he remained with us. Jesus continued moving amongst the people, speaking to some and blessing some, saying, "This night is for all of you. Bring out more wine in my name. It should be the most wonderful night of all, under the starry sky of the eternal Lord. We will re-create the ancient times tonight, and celebrate the unity of Heaven and Earth."

We all had a wonderful night together. Jesus was very relaxed and social. He went to many of those present and conversed freely. It was a simple night, enjoyed by all, though nothing remarkable occurred. Jesus invited some of those present to return on the following evening, and Simon also circulated amongst the guests and conversed with many. We drank wine and were very joyous. We sang very old songs, some of which I knew from my childhood, Jewish hymns that praise the Lord. It was a very happy evening and a tranquil night, a celebration fit for a king, when Heaven and Earth unite. I had the opportunity of getting to know and speaking to many of those whom Jesus had invited, and learned whence they came and what they did for a living.

In the early hours of the morning I sat next to Irisa and we regarded one another in silence. We were completely happy. Our eyes radiated contentment and bliss. After a while we were both sleepy and withdrew to our bedrooms, but before we separated we embraced and wished each other good night. That night Fee, Sumaja and Agnisha appeared in my dreams. I was able to see where they now lived: it was as if I was together with them for a moment. Although life around them looked quite different, they lived happily in foreign lands. Nevertheless, they were with us in spirit. After such a long time apart, we were able to reconnect again.

I was awake early next morning. I performed my ablutions in the Essene tradition, a habit I had retained since I was in Qumran, but which gave me special pleasure after my Essene recollections in the night. Then I proceeded to the inner courtyard of the house. It seemed to me that all were asleep. Everything was still and withdrawn. I entered the great hall of the house through which I could step out on to the terrace in front of the house. I stood in the warm sun and let the rays penetrate deep into my body and soul. Suddenly I sensed someone behind me — it was Jesus. He joined me at the stone balustrade, and in silence we enjoyed together the warmth of the sun on our faces.

I scarcely dared to speak to him, since his presence had always filled me with great respect. I also knew that he had not slept that night. He was filled with his prayers to God, which illuminated his aura. The whole time we did not exchange a word. I enjoyed the intimacy we had with one another, until I could no longer tolerate the silence and said to him, "I think I will see if anyone is going shopping in town today. I would like to spend some time outside." He looked at me and nodded. I felt that I was running away, because I was unable to be alone with him.

I went into the house and sought those who were preparing to go into town. I was able to accompany the apostles purchasing supplies for the house. I got into conversation with a man Jesus had baptized the day before. He was very friendly and obliging. I asked him his name, which was Jacob. I started to laugh, "How are we going to distinguish between you and the other Jacob, Jesus' brother?" He answered, "Then simply call me 'the older Jacob'." We finished purchasing our provisions, and Simon's servants helped load the great quantities of wine and food on to wheelbarrows, which they transported to the house.

As we returned the house was full of activity. Today Jesus was in charge, and he supervised the proceedings efficiently but with loving tenderness. At midday Simon invited us to a large terrace in the garden, where a wonderful meal awaited us. The fig trees cast their shade to protect us from the sun and fostered a stillness that we enjoyed. We were all very happy. Everything was familiar and intimate, and we all felt safe and protected from the outside world. Jesus was again silent and withdrawn, retired into his inner world, while the rest of us joked and were joyful. Jesus sat at the head of the table in silence, contemplating. After the midday meal, I retired to my bed, since I knew that the night would be long and needed some peace and quiet beforehand.

Leaving my room after my midday rest, I wanted to help the other women in the preparations. I saw that Mary was tired and said, "Go and rest, Mary. We can deal with everything. You should retire and get some sleep." She sat down for a moment and I could sense her exhaustion. I embraced her tenderly and then knelt before her. We remembered our time together with the Essenes, and I told her about my contact with Sumaja, Fee and Agnisha in the night. At the news of the three Mary recovered somewhat, and was very interested. She said, "I trust implicitly your dreams and visions. And I can feel that all three are safe and secure. How much suffering we have to experience in our lives! I have the foreboding that much sorrow is in store for us, Miriam. I don't know if it is a blessing or burden from God. Then he also gave me the powers of vision. I also know the powers that displease Him."

She paused for a moment and I said, "You know, Mary, everything in this life is God's will. And we know that he is always present amongst us. I don't know in which direction His paths lead, but I am sure we have to follow them. We are always in His hands." She looked at me, full of love and compassion. I felt my tiredness creep over me, and laid my head in Mary's lap. We had become real friends, loving companions. The friendship of many years had developed into deep affection and a trust in one another. Nevertheless we resolved to retire to our rooms to rest. I had just entered my room and lay down to sleep when an unusual light appeared in my room. It was dazzling and blue, and filled the whole room. I immersed myself in the light and mounted into a Heaven full of stars. I travelled through other worlds of stars, bathed in many lights, that one can only see very far off from the Earth. It was a wonderful experience, but was interrupted by a knock at my door. Irisa was there and asked, "Don't you want to come?"

I dressed quickly and hurried downstairs. It was already late evening and the great room was slowly filling. I estimated that the multitude would be greater in number than ever before. This evening I resolved to sit as near as possible to the place where Jesus and Simon always sat. Shortly before midnight, they both appeared and Simon welcomed all present. An older woman who had long, gray hair sat next to me. Simon came and spoke to her as if they were well acquainted with one another. He introduced her to Jesus as his father's sister, a well-known healer who lived in Jerusalem. I was sitting next to her and sensed the healing power that radiated from her. I felt very calm next to her.

Jesus said to her, "Come to me." She wanted to kneel before him but he embraced her, and held her for some time. Then he stroked her long gray hair and said, "How long have you prayed for me? How long have you waited for me? Disregard the aging of your body; you are still there to support me. Will you stay this time?" She looked at Jesus and smiled. "Lord, you know that I am here on Earth to accompany you in your hour of glory." I don't know how it happened, but I suddenly had a vision of a time in the future in which this woman sat next to Jesus in a stone tomb and prayed. I did not know how these visions occurred, but I was not surprised when Jesus said, "She gathers all her strength and prays every day to the Lord. She will help me in my darkest hour."

The pictures I envisaged shocked me: I saw myself standing in a stone burial chamber with this woman. I could not classify these visions. They overwhelmed and saddened me so much that I left the room, and resolved not to re-enter it that evening. Inside was a great festival, to which Simon had also invited musicians. The crowd danced and was happy, but I fled to the terrace, to seek peace and quiet. After a while I sensed somebody behind me: it was the healer. She radiated a warm light that I sensed as she sat next to me. I was sad and silent as she began to speak: "I have seen your visions and they are all true. Do not be afraid of that which comes to you. We are here to support him in the fate that he has chosen for himself. Look at me, my frail body is so old, but will not break down until I have fulfilled his wish, to support him with all my healing powers."

She looked at me and said, "I live in Jerusalem. I hear that you also live there. You can visit me if you wish; I would be happy to receive you. God has spoken to me today and said that I should pass some of my healing powers on to you — those that the Messiah will need. I will need your help, as my strength alone will not be adequate." The vision of Jesus lying in a grave reappeared to me. But the woman reassured me, "Do not be shocked by these images. They are premonitions. I know you, and I have for a very long time. We come from the same Heaven and both serve the Lord."

I did not yet return to the festival, although the atmosphere was joyful and relaxed, and despite the dancing and singing. I enjoyed the quiet and the woman's company and sat on the terrace with her while she related her story to me. I loved this woman from the beginning; how could I not love someone with such a compassionate heart? She told me that she grew up in a Jewish family, in which her father read, with great humility, the prophesies of the Messiah from the Holy Scriptures. One day when she was still a small girl she asked her father, "Father, please let me learn from those who have the sacred healing knowledge. When you speak about the Messiah, it seems that he begs me repeatedly to prepare myself for the time when he will need me.

"My father was a very religious man and my mother died early. He brought me to the temples in Jerusalem, in the time when the wise women still taught spiritual healing. They rapidly discovered that my healing powers exceeded theirs, and they began to revere me and gave me space to practice and become known. Since that time, I have healed the sick in the main temple in Jerusalem. Even the high priests respect me, because they see that God's power flows through me." I looked at her and asked, "Can I come with you now? Here my heart is sometimes so heavy that I don't know what to do with myself." She looked at me for a moment and then said, "No, that is not possible at present. But you can visit me any time when I am back in Jerusalem. Mary knows me from earlier times, and where I live." Then she said, "Let's return to the hall."

When we returned, I was astonished to see her walk amidst the dancers and begin to move gracefully to the music. Her age and her frailty had suddenly disappeared and she moved in a divine dance in the middle of the room. All present stopped to witness her magical movements. She danced for Jesus, she danced for God. Light streamed from her hands and her heart, and filled the room, enveloping those present. She went into a trance and began to sing for God. She enchanted everyone with God's presence. Her dedication captivated the hearts of all of us. Jesus observed her with his infinite love. Eventually she stopped and prostrated herself on the floor before Jesus. He said, "Stand up, Magda. You do not need to lie before me. God is within you. You need not seek any more, and you need not find any more. I love you just as you are. In Heaven we are united, most modest and loving of all women." Her dance had bestowed a blessing on all present. Everyone was more joyful and danced with increased pleasure. Magda sat at the table with Jesus and Simon, and they conversed as if they were very old friends. Jesus called me to the table and said, "You belong together. You are out of the same source. Miriam, one day you will be as great as Magda." I remained at the table and we drank wine together. In spite of my astonishment, I perceived the divine spirit among us. My soul went out to this wonderful, wise woman, who gave me the sense of home, peace and contentment.

In the early hours of the morning Simon said to Magda, "You know, my mother's room is available to you. Please stay with us for the next days; your presence will be very important for us." I did not want to separate myself from this woman. It was as if I had found a mother or a grandmother who I could not leave. It pained my heart when she prepared to retire to bed. She noticed my sadness and came to embrace me. She said, "I will be your mother, since you will need a living mother in the times which are coming. Sleep now and find your peace." Then she bid me good night and left the room. I followed, to go to my own room. I can hardly describe what pleasure she had given me: I had found a mother who accompanied and sustained me in my dreams.

I slept deeply and long, and I was awakened by my hunger! After my ablutions I went to the dining room. Everyone was there. The apostles sat on one side of the table and the women on the other side. Jesus and Simon sat at the head of the long tables. As always, the meal was plentiful. As I went to sit with the women, Jesus beckoned me to him, and asked, "Don't you want to come to us?" I scarcely dared to go, since none of the other women sat at their end of the table. Jesus made a space for me, and I sat next to Jesus and Simon. I sensed the glances of the apostles and some of them bowed their heads to avoid looking. Only old Jacob smiled and gave me a friendly look. On the other hand, Jesus behaved as if it was perfectly normal for me to sit there. He passed me bread and other things to eat. I also enjoyed Simon's friendliness, behaving as if I was his equal. Simon had the charming quality of treating everyone as equals. His friendly character accepted all whom he met. He was pleasant and was always willing to joke.

After the meal we all left the tables and helped to prepare the house again. I observed Irisa and Mary conversing with Magda, and I went over to them and Helena Salome followed me. Magda told us, "You do not know what tasks are involved in accompanying the Lord. Believe me; you will only gradually begin to understand what great divine plan you have helped to bring to the world." I sensed her presence and her light again, stimulating and attracting me to her. Hence I determined to make myself useful in the house again and the other women followed my example.

Towards evening I returned to my room; I was tired and needed some sleep. I lay on my bed and was preparing to sleep when there was a knock at the door, and Mary and Irisa entered. Mary said, "Jesus has commissioned us to ask for your help; since you have the knowledge of the Essenes, we beg you to support us in preparing the holy oil."

I remembered the times with the Essenes, in their herbal workshops. I recalled images of their preparation of the holy oils. I agreed to accompany the women in their search for the necessary ingredients. We went to the market and found everything we needed — the most exotic and expensive available — and we used the rest of the day to manufacture the holy oil, as Jesus had requested. When it was ready we filled the oil into a beautiful container, which Mary looked after. We had still some time to rest before the crowd arrived and the commotion re-commenced in the house. Jesus arrived shortly before midnight, and said, "I would like to celebrate Simon's hospitality with you, preferably outside in the fresh air. We will meet in the garden." Jesus then requested that the servants bring the wine to us.

We assembled in the spacious garden under a starry sky. Torches had been lit everywhere, so that we could enjoy the various terraces and plants. Simon had ordered musicians for the night. The sound of music under the starry Heaven was enchanting, as if from another world. I saw from a distance that Jesus held each pitcher of wine in his hands and prayed to heaven before the wine was distributed. Then he passed each pitcher to Simon, who blessed it with a prayer. Then the wine was passed around to the guests. It was surprising that the pitchers were never empty — when they became empty they mysteriously refilled themselves. The supply was unlimited, until everyone had his or her share of wine. There were hundreds of people present, so many that one could not count them. I sat near Irisa, Mary and Magda during the meal. With every cup of wine that Jesus and Simon poured out for us, the enjoyment of the intoxication increased until the feast became completely euphoric. We observed the stars above and with every sip of wine, we drank deeper into the magic of the heavens.

Suddenly Jesus rose and went to a man who was sitting alone in a corner. The man was dark and rather serious, and was sitting under a fig tree. Jesus went to him, put his arm around his shoulder and spoke to the group. "I have found someone who was always the first to announce my arrival. My friend

Thaddeus, it is nice to see you here. You have been the herald of my work since the beginnings of time." Jesus embraced him and kissed him on the forehead. Then he requested olive oil, and under the starry skies he poured the oil over his head and initiated him. "You are my herald in all worlds, and now you can announce my coming on Earth. You have left your realm in order to proceed before me." Jesus took his hands and said, "Now heal in my name, speak in my name and precede me in my name."

Jesus joined the assembled apostles at their table. It was the first time that I had seen Jesus attend to them so intensively. They laughed and were happy together. The inner circle formed around Jesus. Then Simon joined the table and the warmth at this table spread to all parts of the garden, and continued throughout the feast. Jesus offered wine, and asked his apostles to distribute further wine to the other guests. We were all in a mood of joy and gratitude. Happiness radiated from the stars. The earth beneath us was warm and smelled of wild wine, which enveloped our souls. We were euphoric and no longer felt tethered to the Earth.

At one point in the feast, Jesus stood up and asked the majority of the guests to return home: only the inner circle and the houseguests were to remain. Then Jesus begged us to gather round him. Before our eyes he initiated each of his apostles and promoted them to masters. When he came to Judas he hesitated somewhat. Judas then knelt pensively in front of him and began to cry. Jesus took his tears and mixed them with oil; then he initiated him. Jesus then said, "This is the circle around me, the innermost circle which will also herald me. You are the lords and the kings from all heavens, who have accompanied me but have no inheritance on Earth. But you carry the lore of God in your hearts."

I felt that the stars sunk nearer to the Earth and bowed to Jesus. A bright light radiated from the heavens, enveloped us and flowed into our hearts. When I gazed into the heavens Magda was standing next to me. She said, "Do you see the angel? Do you see how the heavens open to let the angels come to worship him?" I did not want this night to end. I sat outside, untiring, and looked into the heavens. It was as if I was looking at God's throne, which He had lovingly lowered to Earth for a moment in time.

Then Simon stood up in the middle of the proceedings and had his servants bring wood. In the middle of the garden a fire was lit. It was stoked and fed more wood, and Jesus poured olive oil into it. Simon asked everyone to come to him; he then he took ash and wiped it on the forehead of each of us, saying, "All your sins are forgiven. The ashes from the fire redeem your sins for all time." Simon initiated us for our tasks, released us from our karmic structures and blessed us with the power of the divine flames. This evening there was also another power present: I saw an enormous being in the flames, who blessed us with his presence. I do not know if the others saw him. I stood next to Magda, and gazed, transfixed, into the fire. Magda said, "Maha Baba is present, he who has always taught us and always will. He blesses by appearing in the fire." The greatest beings were with us! The depth and intensity of this experience was indescribable. The wine that we had drunk did not only intoxicate us, but concentrated us on Earth and prepared us for our divine mission.

I did not get to sleep immediately that night. The fire burned in every cell of my body. I was just a sea of fire and I was not sure whether the blaze tormented or freed me, but the Great Spirit that appeared in Simon's fire was also present. I recognized him as Maha Baba, who transported me through the world and united all aspects in me. Face to face he calls himself Babaji. From his eyes I received the greatest blessing that I had yet experienced. Slowly I became drowsy and fell into a deep sleep, from which I could scarcely awaken next morning. When I was finally fully conscious I saw the Irisa was sitting next to my bed. She said she had often knocked on my door but had received no answer. She stroked my brow lovingly and said, "It is already midday. It is time for you to eat something."

The house was unusually quiet and I moved as if in a trance. Irisa led me into a room where a table had been set for me, with food and drink. Everybody else was away, preparing for the final night, as Jesus and Simon had promised. Having fortified myself with a good meal, Irisa led me back to my room and remained with me until I fell asleep again. It was very peaceful around me, quiet and relaxing. I still sensed the presence of the great Baba, who had been with me the previous night.

Finally I awoke, refreshed, and dressed for the final evening. In the inner courtyard of the house everything was festively prepared. Many guests were already present. I was still in something of a daze, and only half in this world. All were silent as Jesus and Simon went amongst the guests and gave their blessing. I sat next to Mary and Magda, and we were united in a spiritual trinity. For me everything was unreal, and I scarcely recognized the reality of my situation.

When most of those present had received his blessing, I went to Jesus and knelt before him, at his feet. As he held my head in his hands, I was completely immersed in his light. Then I knelt before Simon and experienced the same. I seemed to lose control of my body, and lost my bearings completely. I forgot who I was and was everywhere and still somehow within myself: I was unable to define the boundaries of my being. I vaguely remember that Jesus summoned Mary to him and that they conversed with one another.

Mary said, "But Jesus, all our stock of wine is finished. You have treated our guests for the whole evening, and our reserves have been consumed." Jesus looked at Simon. He said, "We purchased more wine tonight than on any previous evening." Jesus stood up and ordered that all the jugs be filled with water and brought into the room. He let them be placed on the tables and on the floor. Then he raised his hand and said, "Distribute them!"

The crowd was tense with excitement: the jugs were now filled with wine. The miracle was observed by all present and the news was passed round the room and discussed: Jesus had transformed water into wine. Simon brought me a full cup of wine, which I drank slowly due to my weak condition. It was the most exquisite wine I had ever tasted. It was full of love and the mercy of Jesus Christ himself. There were more guests present than ever before and after they had all been provided with wine. Jesus then ordered bread for the multitude. When all were satisfied Jesus spoke: "I would beg all of you who are not houseguests to go now. My blessing is with you and many of you will meet me again on your various paths. You have come to find me, and from now on you will find me a thousand times throughout the ages, until the end of time. The meeting with me will never end, until you are all in the kingdom of heaven."

When the last guest had left, the doors were closed to the outside world, and it was quiet. Jesus offered wine to those who remained and asked Mary to bring the holy oil. She placed it in front of him and Jesus said, "Now you will experience the most sacred moment of the seven nights together. I will choose three holy women to anoint me, as David was anointed years ago." He ordered water to be brought and looked beseechingly at his mother.

Their glances melted into one another and he said, "Kneel down, Mother, blessed amongst women." He began to wash her hair with the water that had been brought, and we all knew that this was the holiest act that we had seen in the seven nights. The light that surrounded us concentrated more and more, until it was a dark blue. This light pervaded us completely. After Jesus had washed her hair in heavenly dedication he said, "Now is your turn. Take the oil and anoint your son."

Mary stood up and anointed Jesus, pouring the oil over his head. Then she knelt in front of him and sank down in humility and dedication at his feet. Jesus then stood up and went through the room, touching some of us on the head. Then he said, "Bring new wine. We want to celebrate the most wonderful of all feasts." As if by a silent command we all began to revel and to dance. What Jesus released in us this night was completely indescribable and penetrated into our souls more than on any of the previous nights. Jesus seemed elevated above us but simultaneously to be our friend. He circulated amongst us, spoke to a few and then said, "Now I will choose the second woman." He went to Magda and once again ordered the water to be brought to him. She knelt before him and her tears fell on his feet. He also washed her hair and then handed her the holy oil and said, "You are also chosen to anoint me. You have accompanied me since time immemorial, on all my paths, with all your devotion and all your love. You are the queen of all hearts in all worlds, and no earthly queen can compare with you." He bowed his head to her and she anointed him. Then she laid her head on his feet. He lifted her face and said, "You are blessed because you carry the great pain in my heart. You are freed to eternity, and you are lifted eternally into the Heaven of your soul."

Then he ordered more wine and we celebrated once more. This wine penetrated even deeper into our souls. Then Jesus asked me to come to him. "Sit down next to me, Miriam." I was not yet completely present, but still wandering between the worlds. Then he said, "You know Miriam, you, I and Simon are all so connected to one another that our worlds melt and blend together." I was so moved I thought my heart would break. Then he said, "Whenever one of us calls the others, we shall all be present. We are indistinguishable from one another." His words penetrated into my being and the light around me was even bluer. A love existed between us, a blending of souls, whereby we were one soul. Jesus proffered wine again and gave me a cup. I bowed before Jesus and Simon, laid my head on their feet and rose as if to leave them. But Jesus said, "No stay here, I beseech you. I wish to name you as the third of the holy women, who will anoint me and Simon."

I don't know any more what happened after that. I was in a trance again and did not know what was happening. I only sensed that Jesus was washing my hair and layers of the past fell away. Then Simon washed my hair and further shadows fell away from my soul. Jesus then handed me the oil and I grew and grew until I was larger than I had ever been. I took the oil and it burned in my hands. It was not I, but God, who anointed the heads of these two kings. God had found resonance in me. Then I collapsed completely. I no longer knew who I was and where I was.

I was carried back to my room and heard the joyful celebration outside. It was no longer a normal celebration; it was as if the tides had combined and the stars had melted into one another. Then the door opened and Jesus entered. He kissed me on the forehead and said, "I am sorry to say this, Miriam, but your time has not yet come. I will speak to my mother tomorrow morning and ask her to accompany you to the women from Ephesus." I did not know if it was real, and whether he really said that. Then he kissed my heart and my forehead again, and I sank into a deep sleep. I now permanently levitated above the Earth. Early the next morning there was a knock on my door and Mary entered. She said, "Pack your things, and I will bring you away from this house. It is time for you to leave. Take the map that MaRa gave you."

She washed me and dressed me, and early that morning we left the house. Simon had given us two donkeys. We left without meeting anyone, and made our way towards the mountains. I was aware that Mary knew the way to the mountains and to the place where MaRa and the holy women lived. Nevertheless, I was happy to have MaRa's directions with me.

I was still in something of a trance, a state that never seemed to end. Mary looked after me like a mother, and gave me food and drink. She supported me spiritually, since I was not myself, and always found a place for us to rest or to sleep. Then one night, somewhere in the mountains where no human beings were to be seen, we stopped. MaRa was standing there when we arrived and said, "I have been expecting you."

I was brought into a special place in a cave, which was filled with purplered light. Here I was nurtured and attended to. I do not know how many days and nights I remained in that state, but I was cared for the whole time. MaRa visited me often. I could hear singing outside and I sensed, little by little, that I was returning to my earthly consciousness. One day I awoke completely from my wanderings in other worlds, while MaRa sat next to me holding my hand. I looked at her and asked, "How long was I away on my semi-conscious journey?" She replied, "You were away for a month." I asked where Mary was, and MaRa replied, "She left some weeks ago, but you will stay with us for now."

I knew that I was with the holy women of Ephesus, but still did not know where I was. It was a mountainous region, and I could only guess that we were North of Jerusalem. For three days I was left alone. There were five women, who appeared and disappeared, although nobody bothered about me. They did not speak to me or to one another. All was silence. Meals were punctual, and were also taken in silence. Although I sat next to MaRa at meal times, we did not exchange a single word; like the others she was completely withdrawn within herself. I sensed, and knew, that this silence could not be broken. I waited until somebody in the community started to talk to me. I was completely left to myself.

I could scarcely identify the women, since they hid their faces behind red cloths. It was all very secretive. I did not know where they came from or how they spent their days. The cave in which I awoke was my bedroom and my home. I let myself fall into the enforced situation. Then one day, perhaps the third or fourth, MaRa came to me and said, "Come with me, if you wish." She led me to the top of a hill in the blazing sun, and we the country around us. She looked into the distance and began to speak. "We have withdrawn to this place, distant from the world below, where we look after mistreated and dishonored women. We always seek new hiding places in these mountains, to avoid discovery. We are determined to guard the knowledge we have and to keep it to ourselves. The world outside does not know how to use such knowledge; we are stamped as magicians, witches and occasionally as prostitutes. We are outlawed in society, in modern Jerusalem.

"But we are none of these things, and never will be. We call ourselves the School of Ephesus, and our origin goes back to the time of Moses and Elias, the fathers of Jewish culture. At that time holy women were respected. We have retained the knowledge from these times, when this sacred land of our people extended up to Greece. The original mothers of these secret mysteries were full of energy and fertility, and were directly connected to God. But more recently our ancient traditions, in which we were the holy prophets of our culture, became buried under the materialist influence and the godlessness of our people. In our Jewish society today you see men without manliness and women without womanliness, without a trace of God's seed within them. We preserve something as old as the primeval seed of the Jewish people. We preserve femininity, the original motherliness. But for several centuries, we withdrew more and more, because the men in our society have adopted patriarchal structures. The initiated seers have increasingly been pushed to one side and discredited. I bear within me the ancient power of the women prophets.

"But those kings who reign today in Jerusalem and Judea do not want us. They do not wish to have spiritual leadership other than their own. They are afraid of our knowledge. They know that we come from God and fear our judgement." She stopped and asked me. "Do you know why Jesus sent you here?" At that moment something inexplicable in me stirred, and I had to sit down. I sat on the warm earth and regarded the landscape in front of me. "No, I don't know." MaRa sat down beside me and was still for a while.

Then she said, "The more our external strength disappears, the weaker my powers become. The women who live here come from ancient families. You know that even your family is attached to us. Your Aunt Martha was with us for a long time, until her time was up and she had to leave. But the women who remain here do not carry the seed in them, the seed that I could initiate. I am no longer young and my powers disappear. I can just manage to connect between Heaven and Earth. I carry the black ring in my lap; the inheritance that we women carry and preserve from these dark ages is slowly poisoning me. I did not know any more what to do about the situation until Mary brought you here, and my hopes for a solution rose. I felt that something positive was going to happen, although I did not know what. I would like you to consider staying here for some time. I am sure that the Messiah will connect us to the divine forces. The message will come to us both, since we are connected to one another. But at the moment I see no signs of the information — and there is nothing that I can predict.

"However, I beg you not to speak to the other women here about such matters, since we must all remain silent. That is our ritual. That is how we live. I initiate the powers in them as much as I can. I am also the only person here with whom you may speak. I alone am permitted to utilize the power of words externally. Tell me, how much time do you need to consider my offer? It is your choice alone. Your will and your spirit are free." I begged MaRa to give me until next morning, and spent a sleepless night on a hill, trying to isolate myself from all other influences while considering the possibility.

I was conscious of the fact that, since I was three years old, I had always been given over to some organization or persons. First the Essenes, then my brother and then Jesus appeared and at that moment I realized I was with the holy women of our ancient people. For the first time I sensed an inner resistance to the prospect, which was not characteristic for me. My ego hesitated, because in the past others had made decisions for me without my explicit assent. It was clear to me that in the past I had received wonderful gifts; now I was grown up and had to decide myself. To do that, I first had to determine my aims and the direction I should take.

It was Jesus who had brought me into his circle of women, but still I found it difficult and hesitated. I was transported from one energy level to another, and my thoughts were confused. Never before had I considered the direction of my life — I had just accepted what came to me. My heart was unconditionally devoted to Jesus, but the consciousness of my adulthood convinced me that it was my decision and mine alone — and had to come from my heart. Something was waiting for me, to enable me to accompany the Messiah in his mission. But which direction would my life take?

I had already understood that the way Jesus had chosen was probably the most difficult way we had to go. The feelings and thoughts of the normal citizens filtered through into my considerations: when they see women working together with Jesus, their minds are full of prejudice. Our culture today no longer acknowledges freedom for women, no longer honors their own decisions for their lives and is unable to allow them power of any kind. But Jesus had never treated us like that, and we never had the feeling he would. The women around him were not treated differently from his apostles or other men.

But society in general thinks differently. If I took the path of the women of Ephesus, it would make matters worse. Women are always dependent on the whims of society. But this phase will not last forever. One day we will return. Pictures and thoughts mixed together to show me the life that ahead of me, when would I serve and follow the course of the Messiah. I would then refuse to follow the path that could give me the blessing and acceptance of conventions, and assure me of the acceptance and of the applause of the community. Jesus was present within me when I was involved in this inner conflict, until I was quite calm and still — then he withdrew.

I searched again for God's word, and begged for an answer, and in this state I fell asleep.

I was awakened by the sun, which was climbing in the sky and was already blazing, and returned to the cave. MaRa sat waiting for me in my room. She looked at me in silence and I said, "I will stay here and face whatever fate has planned for us. I will dedicate myself to the School and remain here until we both know that the time has come for me to return." She nodded and said, "That is good. Now we must leave here. I sense the proximity of people who should not find us. We must move on to another place. Pack your things together, so that we can leave. You come with me for the time being, although normally we all travel individually, so that we are not found together. And if one of us were to be arrested, we would never betray the others, not even under the threat of torture or death. You don't yet know the paths in this hilly countryside, so we will travel together. I will protect our way by magical means."

We left at night. From then on I belonged to the Women of Ephesus. We travelled around and made our camp at many places. I spoke to nobody and nothing notable occurred on the way. I knew that MaRa was waiting until she received the message as to where we were to stop, which she eventually did. Several uneventful months passed. I did not see any of the other women, with the exception of one, who like MaRa, refused to cover her face with a cloth. Whenever we women met together, such as at mealtime, she impudently uncovered her face. From MaRa's expression I concluded that she disapproved of her behavior. I observed this woman with great interest. She seemed to be a mixture of insanity and sanctity.

Her face was very singular and beautiful. I would have liked to find out who she was, but since we were not permitted to speak and MaRa had not informed me, I did not have the opportunity of learning her identity. I did not receive any duties to perform for the Women from Ephesus. Nevertheless I was happy to be with them. I lacked nothing.

The women knew how to live from the bounty of nature. Some of them disappeared and returned with food for all of us. It seemed as if they had contact with people who liked us and provided us with food. We never suffered from hunger, and we were in good spirits. In this time I learned how Earth and Heaven nourished us, without our missing anything. The only one who broke the silence was this woman. One day I was with her, clearing up after the meal, when she suddenly spoke to me. I was startled as she said to me quietly, "Come with me to the river, where we can wash the utensils."

Nobody had noticed, although I hesitated to do something forbidden, and did not know if I was permitted to accompany her. She had an unearthly air, with dark eyes — dark green with darker edges — and long copper–colored hair. Her face was burned red by the sun. I resolved to follow her to the river, which was not far away. She said unashamedly, "I don't know how much longer I can endure this. But I know you, Miriam."

I did not dare to speak to her. She had a powerful voice, and I sensed something dark and obscure in her. But her power fascinated me. Both qualities combined in her voice as she said, "I saw you when you were a small child, before I was brought to these women. I originate from the same line as you do, but my mother died early and I am a distant cousin of yours. I arrived at the Women of Ephesus with your Aunt Martha. She was my friend, the only one I have ever had. MaRa is pitiless with us. I came here as a small child and sometimes it drives me nearly crazy. But I do not submit any more. Dark nights visit me, but I cannot speak to her about them. Demons visit me in my waking dreams, and I don't know how to resist them. When I saw you, Miriam, when you came to us, I knew that you brought hope for me. I want to leave here. I don't want to stay here any longer."

I askedher for her name, and she said, "Mary Magdalene. Our female ancestors are from the same family. I beg you: help me to flee from this place. Lead me away from here. I cannot stay. I cannot tolerate the darkness that lives in these women. I know that you have a message for me. I have sensed it since your arrival, and I hope you will tell me the message soon." Mary Magdalene was in her mid–twenties. Her depth fascinated me. I said, "Mary Magdalene, I beg of you, let us return. I do not want to take risks. I know that MaRa will not approve of my speaking to you. But I think I know what I should bring you. Give me time until I know the right moment to tell you what you want to know."

Suddenly she began to weep and she fell on her knees before me, crying, "Something keeps me here. I know that you have something for me, which will liberate me. I have only the wish to escape, although it grieves my heart that I should not flee." I said, "We must go now. You can be sure of my friend-ship and support. But I beg you not to be so rebellious. What MaRa keeps preserved here is good, even when you cannot understand it. I know that it is important and that it should be continued to its ultimate conclusion. Please do not chal-

246

lenge the group, as you do at the moment. And please do not provoke me."

I resolved to leave the river to return the others. As I arrived MaRa was waiting. First I thought that she was angry with me, but she said, "I am sorry." I was surprised at her reaction and asked, "Why are you sorry?" She replied, "I have heard your conversation from afar. I know the thoughts of my women and can read them. Please come with me. I want to tell you something." We withdrew to a good distance from the others, and she led me to a mysterious and uncanny place, which made me slightly uneasy at first. She said, "Sit down. Your conversation with Mary Magdalene today has taught me something of which I was not conscious. As I have told you, I carry the dark ring of female power in me. But the energies in the Earth start to change. I had not noticed that the inner ring begins to work against us. Instead of maintaining the initiated form of dark energy, which we women have guarded as our secret, it begins to awaken demonic forces in them. Something has become independent and is getting out of control. The forces between Heaven and Earth have changed. When you arrived I had hoped that I could pass the dark ring on to you, the ring that was bequeathed to me from my female antecedents. This is the primeval initiation of us women. But I begin to realize that this ring will not be passed on. I have resolved to disappear with the ring, until the time comes when I can return to redeem it.

"Tonight I will perform my ancient initiation ritual far away from you, in order to know what I have to do. Something approaches; something unfavorable is near. We have no time to lose. I thank you for your loyalty. Most of the women here are elderly and will not return to society. But I can see that the future looks different for you and Mary Magdalene. Please give me a night alone, but support me with your prayers. You have no idea how great my burden has become. Pray that God is with me, since I do not find the worldly energy I need to help me, apart from that of the Messiah and Simon."

That night I followed my impulse. I gathered wood and lit a fire. It reminded me of the rituals that Fee had taught me. I linked the forces between Heaven and Earth with the cosmic fire from the ground. I recalled the prayers of the Essenes and prayed the whole night, until every cell of my whole body was laden with my appeal to God, begging that He might guide us. When the sun appeared above the horizon I extinguished the fire and went to the river to perform the rituals of cleansing, such as I had not done for a long time.

Then I returned to where MaRa was waiting for me. She appeared to have aged ten years during the night. She was deathly pale and looked as if she was very ill. She said, "Come into my cave. I will teach you the initiation rituals you should use in the future." I followed her into her cave, where an unusual light illuminated the surroundings, a light from white, red and black fires combined. She laid her hands on my head and commenced to murmur ancient, holy words that created short phases of trance in me, and imbued me with primeval knowledge. This time I was astonished that I did not fall into a complete trance, as I usually did, but became increasingly alert and concentrated for the whole time. The ancient force of magic, the rituals and traditional initiation invigorated me.

It lasted a day and a night. MaRa prayed, and from time to time she took my head in her hands. Then she suddenly stopped and let go of my head. As I looked up, I saw the she had collapsed. I knew that I could not ask the women for help. So I tried desperately to heal her with all my Essene energy, without success. She was unconscious and had a fever. I sought Mary Magdalene. "Mary Magdalene, MaRa is ill and my Essene powers do not revive her. Do you know some divine herbs for her? Had she initiated you into healing practices?"

Mary Magdalene did not say a word, but left me and returned shortly with some stones, which she heated over the fire while she murmured some words. She then laid the hot stones on MaRa's body, whereupon her fever gradually receded. MaRa began to recover consciousness and opened her eyes. However, she was still weak. I looked after her day and night and stayed with her. Her fever returned now and again and in her feverish dreams spoke words that I did not understand.

The other women had disappeared; they had withdrawn completely and scattered in all directions. But I knew that Mary Magdalene was still there, observing us and always prepared to help when needed. She brought me food and supported me. Then one day something dreadful happened: I had just emerged from the cave where I had nursed MaRa when one of the women appeared. She was disturbed and exhausted, and as the red cloth fell from her face she collapsed completely. As I bent down to her I saw that she was covered in blood, and her body was badly wounded. In a weak voice she was able to tell me her story. "We were attacked by a band of rough men, who killed all the other women. They are still in this region, and we suspected that they were paid by Herod, in order to eliminate us. I was able to escape with my life, but the others did not. We did not tell them where you were, but you must flee as quickly as possible. Bring MaRa to safety. You must save her. I will leave you now, and with my last reserves of strength and my magic I will survive. But they must not find you. And you need not help me."

I asked the woman if I could do something for her and she replied, "Please don't touch me. I am now anointed and I shall make contact with the spirit of my initiation. With my remaining strength I will try to travel as far as possible from you. Please leave now, and only travel at night; the darkness will protect you. God has told me this." When Mary Magdalene reappeared I told her what had happened and urged her to prepare for the journey. I said, "We must leave here as soon as possible." She replied, "I know where there is a donkey we may use to carry us away, the one we always used to bring us supplies. In two or three hours I will return with the donkey. Hence we can transport MaRa. I know many ways out of the mountains, but after that I am not so sure."

Mary Magdalene was suddenly incredibly lucid, and I was pleased when she took the initiative to act, saying, "Our clothing, in particular our red veils, should not be seen. But we have other clothes here." I said, "I still have what I wore when I came here. I can change our clothes, so that we are as unrecognizable as possible. We will travel only by night. I know a house in Jerusalem where we can stay and not be identified. God should be with us and make us invisible to spying eyes. We must start very soon. Please hurry!" Mary Magdalene departed and I waited for her to return, impatiently and somewhat fearful. Nevertheless I knew that that there was something between Heaven and Earth protecting us. MaRa was still not fully conscious, and I could not explain the situation to her. She was having feverish dreams in another world.

After two and a half hours Mary Magdalene returned, and I breathed a sigh of relief. We lifted MaRa onto the donkey as well as we could, so that she could at least travel. Then we changed our clothing. I begged Mary Magdalene to sit on the donkey behind MaRa, to prevent her from falling. Then we started off. The sun had set and Mary Magdalene guided us through mountainous paths until we had left the region. Then she said, "I will find the paths here by my inner navigation sense."

We started on the second part of the journey over unknown terrain. I do not know how we survived the night. I repeatedly left the two of them on the donkey, concealed in a secure hiding place, in order to inquire about the way to Jerusalem from the local inhabitants. The only house that I could imagine where we could safely hide was that of Irisa. I know that God had guided us on our way. We must have travelled for three or four nights before we saw the lights of Jerusalem. Some heavenly agency must have guided us on our journey, and I was sometimes in somewhat of a trance.

As we approached the city Mary Magdalene begged me to seek Irisa's house alone, so that she and MaRa could rest and avoid added danger. I sought Irisa's house, since I was sure that she would offer us refuge. I felt that we could reach her house undetected at night. That would be our first haven.

Finally I reached the house and knocked on the door, until a servant opened it and recognized me. He let me in and closed the door behind me, as if he knew that my arrival should be kept secret. He awakened Irisa, who came down to meet me. She let out a scream when she saw me, dirty and tired. I explained the situation and she said, "We must act quickly. Please let us go and bring the two women to your house from the outskirts of the city." She said, "I will not go with you but I will send two of my men with a stretcher." Together we brought MaRa and Mary Magdalene to Irisa's house while it was still dark.

Then I collapsed, exhausted, but secure in the knowledge that we were safe in this house. I knew that MaRa would receive the help she needed to recover from her unknown illness. That night my healing faculties gradually returned to me, energies enabling me to recognize where to apply my powers. The black clouds that gathered above MaRa were not clouds of death. They were dark shadows, which she attempted to conquer with her own forces.

Mary Magdalene had also collected dark clouds around her, which continued to follow her. I sensed how she began to despair. Before I climbed exhausted into my own bed, which Irisa had prepared for me, I went to Mary Magdalene. I laid my hands on her heart and began to pray that the dark forces plaguing her did not overwhelm her. I battled against the darkness above her with all the power that I possessed, into the last corner of her being. I knew that I could not at that moment conquer the darkness completely, but at least she would be able to sleep securely that night. I remembered the day when Jesus begged me to conquer the demons in the woman. These powers returned to me with renewed energy. Then I withdrew and relaxed, but although I tossed and turned I could not sleep.

I resolved to go to Irisa, sat on her bed and said, "We must find a method of healing MaRa." Irisa smiled and said, "I have been with her every hour. Jesus conferred upon me many healing techniques. It looks as if I can at least reinstate her essential bodily powers. Keep calm, Miriam, you have achieved a lot. You have returned with something absolutely new. I also see that you have now really grown up. You were away for two years and I did not know where you were. A lot has happened in that time, and I am glad that you are here again. Here you are safe; no one knows that you are here. When you have rested and recovered from your experiences, I want to sit with you and exchange our news. Jesus is not in town at present. I will do everything I can to help your friend. I can remember her; I believe we met in Canaan. Don't be afraid, everything will be all right." A white light shone around her, and I knew that I was safe and could finally relax. At last I could find peace, in the knowledge that we were safe here.

We were content and secure in Irisa's house. When I awoke from a long and restful sleep I was finally aware of how long I had been away. The continuous silence of the women in the mountains had deeply affected my sense of time. When I went into the dining room, I saw that the meal was prepared for us, but first I wanted to see how MaRa was progressing. As I entered her room I could see that she was a bit better, and her strength was gradually returning, but she was still somewhat dazed. It was not always clear whether she was sleeping or in a semi–conscious state.

Nevertheless, an improvement was noticeable. I also went to see how Mary Magdalene was, but she was still asleep. So I went to Irisa, who embraced me and was obviously happy that I was rested, and we enjoyed our meal together. I was naturally curious about what had happened since the evening I had left Canaan.

She related that, following that evening, Jesus was suddenly and truly the Messiah. Everybody who saw him knew it. Then he left with his disciples for the Sea of Galilee. Sometime later he returned to Jerusalem. She told me that Jesus had become quite famous. People came to him from all directions and from neighboring countries. His days were filled with miracles. She only knew this from the stories of others. Since then, Jesus travelled through Israel from place to place with his disciples, stopping occasionally. At the Sea of Galilee he performed numerous miracles. It was said that Peter and Andrew went out fishing, and Peter returned three times to report that there were no fish in the sea. Then Jesus gave him a lesson as his teacher, and sent him out again. This time the nets were full of fish and everybody had enough to eat.

Not only had his disciples witnessed the occurrence, but so too had the local people from the village. It was also reported that Jesus was observed with bare feet, walking across the water with his hands lifted to heaven, as if he was talking to God. Irisa said, "Every day there were more stories about Jesus. Wherever he appeared the people went to him in droves." I learned that he constantly taught his disciples, and that another had joined their number while they were travelling. He had cured many sick people, and had even some who were at death's door, given up as incurable. He spent much time with his disciples, but now and again he returned to Jerusalem, staying with Lazarus at our house, so as not to endanger Irisa.

Whenever Jesus was in Jerusalem he gave Irisa instruction in his art of healing. Irisa said, "They were the brightest moments in my life. He is wisdom itself. Heaven touches him and he releases the people from their afflictions." I asked, "Why must he protect himself?" She answered, "You know, Miriam, the better known Jesus becomes, the greater is the uneasiness around him. Here in Jerusalem the ruling castes begin to consider him as their enemy. The simple people praise him, saying he has come as King of the Jews. Hence he has made enemies in the royal family and the ruling classes. But also some of his disciples cooperate with the Zealots: I cannot understand how they can support rebels whose only aim is to break the power of the Romans and chase them out of Israel. That is very dangerous. And your brother, Lazarus, is also actively supporting the Zealots. He is unwilling to give up the idea, that Jesus should inherit the throne of the people of Israel. But I only know this from reports and rumors.

"I try to see Jesus in the short periods when he is here, to learn more about his love and his supreme power. I keep away from the other matters. It is sad that the more he helps people, the more enemies he seems to have. The reports of his miracles always travel ahead of him, and where he appears it is almost impossible to approach him. His reputation is known far beyond the boundaries of Israel. Sometimes he disappears with his apostles, to teach them, and nobody knows where he is. You will see how the apostles have changed. You know the personalities he has chosen. But there are also petty jealousies, and some maintain that he has chosen renegades and that he has intentionally surrounded himself with enemies of the state.

"But Jesus is not concerned with such opinions, or with the interests of the state. He loves the renegades and rebels. He is really the Son of God; he loves every being the way he or she is. He is not a servant of the rulers or representatives of the state, but that is perhaps why they regard him with mistrust. Even the Romans keep an eye on him, although they have not taken any action up to now. My friends say that the Romans regard him as harmless, and insist that he does nothing dangerous against their interests. He does not endanger their power. One hears nothing seditious from him, and he has said no word about taking over the power of the state or about other political matters. All that he preaches is about love and reconciliation, and the power he invokes is the power of God." She paused.

I asked her, "Is my brother Lazarus in Jerusalem at the moment?" She replied, "As far as I know he is not at home at present. He is often away, but nobody knows where. Sometimes he is with Jesus but other times he disappears completely." Then I asked, "Where is Martha?" Irisa answered, "As far as I know she is at home. I think she would be very happy to see you after all this time, and to know that you are well. Nobody knew where you had gone and Jesus had made Mary promise not to say anything."

I asked, "And where is Mary now?" Irisa replied, "Mary often retires to her house. The more famous Jesus becomes, the more she withdraws herself from the world. Her younger son,

Jacob, is usually with Jesus and travels with him. He is as an apprentice to Jesus, and learns quickly from him. Mary sometimes comes to Jerusalem, but more seldom than she used to. I think she would cry for joy to see you again. Whenever I asked her about you she became sad and her eyes took on a misty appearance, as if she knew what fate has in store for us. I know that she misses you. She often tells me that you should have been the daughter she never had."

I asked Irisa when Jesus would come to Jerusalem again, but she could only tell me, "One never knows when he will reappear. But if he were coming I would be the first to know it." Irisa suggested that I should use the opportunity to rest and relax while Jesus was away. And she was naturally interested to hear of my experiences. I was also not surprised to hear that Jesus was becoming increasingly well known. His presence and his self–confidence attracted people looking for a new leadership. I was unhappy to hear about the disturbances in Jerusalem, since I knew that the king was powerful and nervous, and that the Roman governor could be influenced by him.

I went into MaRa's room, to find out how she was. She was now fully conscious, her eyes were open and she recognized me immediately. She took my hand and smiled feebly, saying, "I thank you from the bottom of my heart. I would not have been able to leave that place without your support and I would not have escaped from the mountains, and been able to live normally again.

"In the previous nights I have only dreamed of Jesus. He redeemed me and released me from the burden I have carried for thousands of years, but which I had voluntarily taken upon myself. He was with me in spirit for three nights, and never left me. I am sure that I will see him again soon. Here the light of his spirit is present and I recognize the sisters who have received me and accepted me in their number, even after I have been separated from them for so long. I accept that my arduous way is not yet at an end, a path that I chose for myself, but that Jesus has relieved me of my greatest encumbrance."

MaRa asked me about Mary Magdalene, and I said, "I believe she is still sleeping." I told her that Mary Magdalene, in whose eyes she and I had presumed to see wildness and rebellion, was in fact very loving and tender, and that she had attended to MaRa day and night on the journey to Jerusalem. She was loyal and devoted. MaRa said, "I am aware that she has a wonderful spirit, Miriam, and has suffered a lot. But I am sure that Jesus will visit her; in the nights when I had my visions I dreamed that she should prepare herself for meeting the Messiah. She has a great and loving soul. Nevertheless, I was never able to help her in the last years. The power we once had has slowly diminished. We have maintained this ancient order so long, but when it disappears it will be lost forever. But I am not sorry and I am not sad. I know that the Messiah, for whom we have prayed since time immemorial, has come. A new era of redemption starts with his coming on Earth. Therefore I do not mourn over what is past."

I took her hand and said, "I think you do the right thing, trusting in Jesus. Let us enjoy these days, since I feel that Jesus will be in Jerusalem again soon. Or perhaps we should go to him. In any event, you need peace and quiet for the next few days, and Irisa and I will be here, if you need somebody.

Apart from that I want to thank you: I know what you have given me with your last reserves of energy, and which nearly cost you your life. I have now grown up and feel myself to be a woman, although I am not sure what that will mean to me. But you have initiated me in something which nobody else could have given me." I kissed her hands and asked her if she needed anything. She said that what she really needed was peace and time to think about the changes coming in her life. "I have to get used to being able to communicate again: to listen and to speak. Now a new life commences for me. You can leave me for a time. But before you go, would you bring lamps to light the room and water in which I can wash? I will withdraw into prayer, to break with the past." I left the room and was very happy, for I knew that everything was in order. Jesus prepared the way for us, which we had not felt for a very long time.

In the corridor I met Mary Magdalene. For the first time I saw joy and contentment in her eyes. This wild and temperamental woman from the mountains now radiated love and an inner security. I could not restrain myself: I approached and embraced her. "Come with me. There is something for us to eat. You can strengthen yourself." As Mary Magdalene approached the well-stocked table she seemed shocked. She was not used to such lavish meals, and had never experienced them. Tears poured down her cheeks. She told me that it reminded her of her childhood, but she had never seen so much good food and drink. She was not sure whether she could eat everything on her plate.

I said, "Sit down and take your time. In this house everything is relaxed and peaceful, and you can enjoy yourself — what our souls have so long desired. What terrible things have you experienced, Mary Magdalene? As a child you could not flee from them. Can you remember when you were by the river, you asked me what I was bringing you? I know now — it is the message I received in my youngest years. Mary Magdalene, I should tell you that the Messiah, whose coming was announced in the ancient scriptures of our people, is now present amongst us. Before I came to you I spent many hours in his company. The most important message for you is that you have been selected to meet him." She gazed at me with a distant look in her eyes, which had an amber glow. Golden light radiated from her eyes. The wildness I had seen in her in the mountains was softened by an inner beauty.

I said, "Come with me, I want to show you something." And I led her into the room Irisa had set aside for us. It was probably the first time that somebody had washed her hair. The care that women receive in our culture was new to her, and she was astonished. I felt a love for this woman, a deep friendship, a trust and solidarity. It was a great pleasure for me to comb her hair, which was soft but had never previously seen a comb. It was a joy to rub oil into her hair and to give her the clothes that Irisa had laid out for her.

She cried as if her heart would break, but the tears were of happiness, that she could relinquish the sufferings of the past. She leaned her head on my shoulder as if the fear that she had experienced had changed to trust — a completely new experience for her. She asked, "Where have you brought me?" "We are in Jerusalem, Mary Magdalene." She replied, "I have only heard of it in stories. I sense a different energy from that which I have always known. When I first felt it, it bothered me, but the peace of this house absorbs all irritations. But where will we go from here? Where do I belong?"

I stroked her head and said, "Don't worry about those things. We are in a house that is frequented by the Messiah, where all friends are welcome. And not far from here is my family home, where you are also welcome to stay. Nobody will recognize you, since you no longer wear the red veil that identified you as a priestess. What you have learned inside you will remain. But be careful with your knowledge, since you grew up among the wild women. When you move around outside you should be careful to withdraw your energy somewhat, that the Jewish society does not recognize your potential, since they have an unpleasant habit of stoning women whom they label as witches. Or they drive women out of the comunity when they do not conform to the rules of the men. Women are not permitted to be independent or have their own ideas."

She swallowed hard and asked, "Where has God sent me?" Then she was silent for some moments before she took my hand and said, "But I trust you. I know that I am safe here, that I and my wild spirits are protected." She paused and said, "I must thank you. I know what you did for me last night. You really possess supernatural powers. That makes it possible for you to drive the dark demons into the last corners of my being, so that they no longer have power over me. I have indeed perceived that you have given me peace of mind and in joy in my heart again. Nevertheless, I sense that the demons still live within me. I don't know where they come from or wehre they will go, but at present they have no chance: this house is filled with love and peace."

Irisa entered the room at this point and I said, "Mary Magdalene, I would like to introduce you to your hostess and to my dearest and most intimate friend, Irisa. She is a Roman and comes from another culture, but in her heart she is one of us." Irisa moved spontaneously to Mary Magdalene and embraced her warmly. "You are welcome in my house. Please consider it as your home while you are here. I will look after you as long as you need. I have sufficient rooms that you can stay here."

That afternoon I decided to return to the house of my family, to find out what was happening there. I knocked at the door and it was opened by someone I had never seen before. He asked me, "Who are you?" and I replied, "I am Miriam, the daughter of the house." The young man apologized and said, "I will find Martha for you." I entered the house and when Martha saw me she burst out crying and said, "Miriam, you are here again, thank goodness. Jesus had always said that you were in good hands, and that I should not worry. But if he should tell me where you were, he would be betraying old friends. He said I should be patient. But believe me, it was very difficult for me." Then she embraced me and I was glad to have returned.

I asked, "Who are all these new people in the house?" She said, "Lazarus has employed new staff. They are our servants, Miriam. Jesus often visits us and stays with us, so Lazarus thought we needed more support for when Jesus and his visitors are here." I asked her, "Then where is Lazarus at present?" She turned away from me, unwilling to answer, so I held her arm and asked, "Martha, I am old enough to hear the truth. What has happened?" She said, "He would cut my tongue out if he knew I told you. But you should know. Jesus does not agree with him, but Lazarus does not even listen to his advice. He has joined the subversive group called Zealots, and has taken a leading role in their activities. He is constantly with them and is amongst the activists advocating a rebellion of the Jewish people against the Romans. But he refuses to tell me anything about it. "When he comes home and Jesus is here they behave like old friends. They love one another and Lazarus behaves as if Jesus were his brother. Occasionally he accompanies Jesus when he travels through the country. I think he is with Jesus at present, but he does not tell me about his activities."

She looked at me. "I am so glad that you are here again. When I am alone here, the soul of this house seems to sleep, only awakened in the presence of Jesus. It has been difficult to live here as if I was alone in the house. I was sometimes very lonely." I said, "Why don't you come to Irisa? I think you would find an old, familiar acquaintance there." So we both left our house and returned to Irisa's house.

Martha and Mary Magdalene were overjoyed to meet after such a long time, and embraced each other and shed tears of happiness. Then I saw something I will not ever forget: they laid their forefingers on the other's mouth and looked into the other's eyes. I knew that it was their pledge, never to speak about the past. They sealed the knowledge inside themselves so that only they and their hearts knew about it. I led Martha to MaRa, whom I had previously prepared to expect us. MaRa was much better, and when Martha saw her she laid her head in MaRa's lap and cried. I believe Martha had previously thought she would never see MaRa again, since she knew how dangerous it was during the many years that MaRa was in the mountains. I left the two of them together.

The following days were very peaceful. I sometimes left the house in my traditional Jewish clothes, which gave me the right — as a respected Jewish woman — to walk the streets undisturbed. I often wandered through Jerusalem and was very interested to hear what the citizens were saying and thinking. One day I was in front of the King's palace, and suddenly remembered Salome. I wondered what had become of her. Wherever I was, I did not hear a word spoken about Jesus. It was as if nobody was willing to speak about him. But I noticed that there were more Roman soldiers than there had been previously. One day I desired to accept Magda's invitation to visit her in Canaan. But I had did not have her address. I asked Irisa, but she did not know either. She said, "Unfortunately I only met that wonderful woman on that evening. But I am sure that when you go to the Temple somebody would know where she lives. As far as I know she is well known in Jerusalem. She is an esteemed healer, and a respected wise woman."

That evening I went to the Temple. I did not know who I should ask, so I sat on the steps and waited. A few minutes passed, when suddenly Magda emerged from the Temple and came towards me. Her complete being and her light radiated joy when she saw me. She said, "I knew that you would come to seek me this evening. I was just waiting for you." She took my arm and said, "Even though I sometimes remain in the Temple, the times have changed. Come with me. Unfortunately, here is no longer a place for the ancient wisdom. The head priests Annas and Caiaphas are completely in control here, but at least they tolerate me and allow me to work at home. Many people visit me to receive the gift of my healing. But here is not the right place to discuss such things. Sometimes I come here and light a fire in a wing of the Temple that they have left at the disposal of the priestesses. But I believe even this small privilege will not be permitted much longer."

Magda was extraordinary, as ever. She did not refer to my absence. She acted as if we had just parted yesterday. She brought me to a small stone house, which was very snug and comfortable. She lit the oil lamp and led me into a room that was filled with celestial energy. She lived alone in the house, and I sensed the healing power of God. She placed some dates and water on the table and gave me some bread, laughing. "I also know the habits and rituals of the Essenes, Miriam."

Then she sat next to me and looked at me. As she removed her headscarf her white hair fell about her shoulders. She said, "I know why you have come to me. God has told me. You are well prepared to accompany the Messiah. You have brought those with you that I have dreamed about. The Lord has called them for some time. But leave them at Irisa's house for the time being. Their powers are not yet prepared to appear on the streets of Jerusalem."

She looked into my eyes for some time and said, "Miriam, the holiest existence the world has ever seen is now among us. How long have we prayed that God would send this invaluable treasure to us on Earth? Jesus is present and God's love has returned to redeem humanity. Many nights I have dreamed that the path Jesus has chosen will not be easy. He will need people like you and me. He has selected the most difficult way to carry our fate on his shoulders and to liberate us. I see in your eyes that you know a lot. You can visit me when you like. You do me a very great favor when you come to me in the evenings. I don't think it will be long before Jesus reappears."

I asked her, "Would you like to come to Irisa's house with me?" She refused, saying, "No, it is not my house. You are well looked after there, but my house is here. But I will accompany you to the house, since it is now very dark. I have no fear in the streets; nobody attacks an old woman. But you are a young woman. I will walk with you to the house. And I will be very happy when you come tomorrow." I returned to the house with her, and resolved not to tell anybody where I had been. The two different worlds should not come into contact with one another. I do not know why I thought like that, but I was sure it was right.

Irisa had looked after the two women who were recovering from their terrible experiences. She had infinite patience with them, knowing that they had suffered difficult times. Her powers of healing also had to be attuned to the spiritual requirements of the house. Sometimes we talked to one another and sometimes we were content to be silent. Occasionally I would ask Irisa to narrate some stories about Jesus. She told me about his wonderful qualities and miracles, a few of which she had witnessed herself.

I risa said, "I am sure that the Almighty is present in Jesus' words. I have seen him perform miracles which only God can achieve." She had tears in her eyes as she described so many mysterious and wonderful miracles that

Jesus had performed in the last two years. It was evident that no human being can accomplish such things: only the Almighty himself is capable of such wonders. She continued, "We Romans have gods, but what I have seen Jesus perform outstrips the powers of the Roman Pantheon. He shows me each time I see him that there is an all–powerful source of light, and he embodies it." She went on, "I have seen despairing and sick people come to him. Whether the soul or the body was sick, Jesus found the cause and healed it. You cannot imagine how it happens. Sometimes I have observed how even the most severely afflicted invalids prayed for help, whereupon Jesus would kneel before the person and pray completely within himself — as I have never seen anyone pray before. And then suddenly the miracle occurred, and it was as if there had never been a sickness.

"Once, I was travelling in Capernaum when a leper was brought to Jesus. Nobody dared to touch him. But Jesus went directly to him and said, 'You should not come to me. I should come to you.' He continued speaking quietly to him, but I was too far away to hear what he said. Then Jesus knelt before the leper and prayed, and the leper was healed before our eyes: first the leper could just stand up, but after a time life flowed into all of his limbs and he was able to move normally. Then he knelt before Jesus and praised him. Weeping with joy and full of devotion he praised the Lord."

"But there are still cynics. When Jesus performs a miracle, those who are near to him fall on their knees, while in the back rows there are people who murmur disapproval and even antagonism, claiming that he is a magician and is misusing his powers. There are always different opinions on the subject.

In my heart I cannot comprehend that some people do not understand what a wonderful gift his love is, how much he has and what a force it is to save us all. In your absence, Jesus visited Lazarus very often. There were always many who sought him, and asked for his help.

"Once a young girl came to him, and when he asked why she had come, she replied, 'I don't know. I lost my parents and live on the street, begging. I have been blind in both eyes for a long time, andsome kind people brought me to you, saying that you could give me my sight back. You can help me and you can save me.'" Irisa wept as she told us, "Jesus began to cry, and gathered his tears in his hands, which he then applied gently to the girl's eyes as he prayed to Him with whom he always spoke. Jesus said, 'Your eyes have not been able to see, but within yourself you have seen God. Your soul is saved.' He found a good family for the girl. Everyone who comes to him finds a home. That is the blessing of his love.

"There is also a report that he awakened the dead. No sickness seems immune to his ever–healing love. No human suffering is too great to prevent him curing it. For the last two years Jesus has travelled around doing good deeds for all people. He has ordained all his disciples, who also travel around alone, praying and baptizing the people in his name. But the most wonderful miracle I have seen was before the gates of Jerusalem, while we were on a hill outside the city. Jesus was preaching. It was absolutely quiet and the starry heavens lit up the night. I cannot recollect his words, but suddenly flames emerged from his mouth and engulfed us all. Every one of us could see how the flames spread above us and illuminated all of us. Our souls rose to Heaven and were filled with a hope and love that we had never before experienced. That night I came home and the flames have never left me. Before I went, Jesus had told me to heal the sick. He said I possessed powers of healing, and that people who come to me would find release. But you will see it yourself. You will be surprised what has developed in the two years you have been away. Jesus' arrival is always foreseen well in advance of his actual appearance. The people are waiting for him before he is here." I took her hands and asked, "Do you know when he will return to Jerusalem?" Irisa replied, "I have heard nothing up to now. But as soon as I have some news I will let you know immediately; you will be the first to know."

That evening I resolved to leave the house and to visit Magda. In the gathering dusk I dared to walk alone through the streets of Jerusalem. Suddenly somebody advanced towards me. I had tried to avoid encountering someone anyone on the way, but this person came directly toward me. I stopped and tried to avoid him. Suddenly the person stood in front of me and grabbed me, so that I could not escape. He wore a dark cloak and looked at me with evil, dark eyes, but the face was covered so that I could not identify it. I was not even sure that it was a man, since he or she hissed the words, curses as if they were a snake's poison: "I know you. You are from the brood of that man who travels through the country. But believe me; we will take steps to block your way wherever you go and to destroy you. Don't believe that your strength is greater than ours." Then this being spat at my feet, turned away and disappeared in the darkness.

I did not know whether I should return directly home. It was a great shock to me. I decided to continue to Magda's house, since it was now not far away. I knocked on the door and she opened it. She seemed to be weakened, but she asked me to come in. She looked at me and asked what the matter was. I related what had passed on my way to her, and she let out a despairing sigh. "Miriam, in this town there are various forces active, and I believe this one came from the king's magicians. They collect increasing numbers of shadowy sorcerors around them. They creep around the town at night, intimidating the citizens and searching for the friends of Jesus. They are spies, and I would not be surprised if they were paid by the high priests in the temple. They are snakes that cannot do any good."

Then I asked Magda what had happened to her. She hesitated and then said, "I was in the temple today and wanted to kindle the holy fire, as I have done for years. Suddenly a gray, shadowy man stood behind me, mantled so that I could not see his face, and his sinister energy held me in its grip. With my remaining strength and a prayer to God I was able to flee from the temple. He hissed after me, 'Here is no longer a place for you. Don't dare to come here again.' I was able to return home, where I finally felt safe. I don't know what is happening in the temple. It seems to me that the high priests have allied themselves to untrustworthy magicians and dark unknown forces. The temple of the priestesses, which was formerly open to us, is now closed. I believe that evil rituals take place there, of which the public knows nothing. I sense that this costs me much energy, and I hope that Jesus returns soon. Something evil is happening in Jerusalem. Jesus' light ascends and helps the people but the opposing forces become increasingly powerful. They hide behind spies and dark presences, which creep around the town."

Then she said, "I believe it would be better for you to avoid visiting me for some time. When I have something important to tell you I will send you a message. I know where you live. But we must start to protect ourselves." I replied, "Before I leave I would like to know whether you want to tell me something more. I see so many pictures in you, describing the way of the Lord. I have visions also, which I can neither understand nor interpret."

Magda lighted the oil lamps and said, "As I told you, God's most valuable gift lives among us. We recognize and must follow him, in the person of Jesus, our Lord. Let us not discuss the way; rather let us help to fulfill the purpose for which he is here on Earth. But now I beg you to leave me alone." She went to the door of a neighbor and knocked on the door. A young man appeared and she asked him, "Would you be so kind and accompany my friend home? You surely know the safe ways in Jerusalem."

She turned and embraced me and said, "Let us be careful. Curious things happen here, things that are not good for us." The young man brought me back to Irisa's house, and bade me goodbye. I entered the house somewhat depressed. This evening the house was quiet and I withdrew to my room. Later I told the other women of my experiences in the streets of Jerusalem. Under Irisa's protection we resolved to avoid being seen in public, at least for the time being.

Some days later there was a knock at the door and Lazarus stood on the threshold. I was overjoyed to see him again and embraced him, not daring to ask where he had come from. He said, "Jesus is on his way to Jerusalem, and will be guest in my house. I estimate he will be here in two days. I will take over the preparations for his arrival. When Jesus arrives, I will let you know and send someone to accompany you and to ensure your safety. Miriam, I think it would be better if you remained in Irisa's house for the time being. Jerusalem is not safe anymore. I can move around freely, since I know the safe streets and ways. But for you they are not safe."

Our group of women waited two days until there was a knock at the door and Martha entered. She said, "Jesus will be there this evening, and you are all invited to come. In two hours I will send someone to pick you up and bring you to us." Then she left. MaRa had recovered enough strength and wanted to go with us. But I wanted to be sure to pass the news of Jesus' arrival on to Magda, since I was not sure if anyone in our circle had contact with her. I told the women to go on ahead, since I wished to bring somebody with me, and would follow. I was very careful this time going to her house, creeping through the streets of Jerusalem, and this time it was as if a guardian power was protecting me.

I knocked on Magda's door and when she opened it I said, "Come with me Magda. The Lord is in town again. I would like you to accompany me." She collected her warm shawl and we left immediately. It had become cold in Jerusalem and we sought the safest ways, until we arrived at the house. I knocked at the door and we entered. I was surprised that not many people were there; apparently Jesus and Lazarus had managed to find their way to Jerusalem without attracting much attention. As I entered, MaRa, Mary Magdalene and Irisa were already there. They had had something to eat, but otherwise we were alone.

272

Jesus and his apostles were in the house but had withdrawn. One by one a few of the apostles appeared, none of whom I had seen for two years. I greeted them all. First came Andrew, who greeted me warmly, and his brother Peter. They had changed in those two years, as if they had left their pasts behind them. They were new beings, quiet and introverted. Eventually all were present, and they sat around a table together. Some faces I scarcely recognized. We did not speak to each other much, and Jesus had still not yet appeared.

There was an indescribable atmosphere in the room. I felt it would surely be a special evening. All of us had captured the atmosphere and spoke hardly a word. I reflected how it would be when the apostles, after two years with Jesus, would react when they saw MaRa, whom Jesus knew from long ago in Canaan, and Mary Magdalene, whom he had never met. I had also not seen Jesus for two years. I was curious about what would happen this evening. Neither Jesus nor Lazarus had appeared, so we wandered around the house, anticipating. It was getting very late when Lazarus finally joined us and ordered pitchers of wine to be placed on the tables. I helped him, but still there was no sign of Jesus.

At last, Jesus entered around midnight. Apart from his apostles there were four or five others present, whom I had not originally noticed. One of them, a dark-haired man, seemed familiar to me, and I racked my brains as to where I had seen him previously. But I could not remember. The apostles seemed unmoved by Jesus' long absence this evening, as if they were accustomed to it. But we who had not seen him for so long were very excited, and we all waited expectantly to see what he would do. Then he sat down at our table. I noticed how much he had changed. He smiled, and I sensed how noble and majestic he had become. The beauty of his radiance lit up the room, as he looked at us lovingly.

He said, "Now it is time to meet again." Looking at MaRa he said, "Have I not promised that we would be reunited? I am happy that you have recovered and that you have left the solitude of the mountains in order to continue your mission." Then he looked at me and I sensed a deep and profound love flowing to me. "You are now a grown woman, Miriam, and not a child any more. I sense profound changes in your heart. Welcome home!"

I could not do anything else than walk to him, kneel before him and lay my head on his feet. At this moment time and space were no longer present. When I looked at him he said, "The ways that we should take are prepared for us. You don't need to tell me anything. I know it all. The strength that is born within you is welcome and a support for me." I began to cry, since I did not know exactly what he meant. Nevertheless, my soul recognized the profound meaning of his words.

I said, "I have brought two friends. Do you remember Magda?" Jesus looked at her and I made space for her to kneel before him. She also laid her head on his feet. As she raised her head Jesus regarded her and said, "Wonderful mother. I can do no more than thank you for all that you have done for me. Your path is matched identically to mine. I thank you in the name of the Lord, our Father that you have chosen this way, in our names and in the name of God's glory." He laid his hand on her head and said, "Blessed are you, carrier of light. You were always present for light and healing."

Magda began to speak: "Lord, I do not know words to answer you. But I would like you to know that there is much unrest and many disturbances in Jerusalem, and I can sense them around my house. The high priests in the temple and the king and his family are no friends of yours. They are very wary of what you do and their spies are everywhere in the town and look for all who recognize and support you. Nobody dares to speak about you in the town, in fear for their lives."

He heard her calmly and patiently. "I know, Magda. I have no fear for myself, but I am more worried about you all. Jerusalem is no good place to be at present. But I have a mission here." Then he looked around at us all: and told us, "I beg you all to leave this town with me tomorrow. We shall travel to the Sea of Galilee. We can find accommodation in Tiberias. We will be absent from Jerusalem for some time, but before we go I have something important to do, a commission I have received from the Lord whom I serve. Magda, I beg you to accompany us to Tiberias. I would like you to be with me for some time. Nevertheless, Jerusalem and those who are seeking the light need you. You should eventually return, when the situation in Jerusalem has calmed down. Each of you must decide whether you will follow the path that destiny has in store for you. I have chosen my way, and I will follow it unconditionally. You are free to choose whether you are willing to serve your destinies, for which you are assembled here." Magda bowed again to Jesus and returned to her original place.

Then something occurred that we could only observe in astonishment: Mary Magdalene stood up, as if remotely guided from another world, appearing to be driven by a

275

force other than her own. Her whole body trembled as she advanced towards Jesus. Then she stopped before him, and continued to quiver all over. She fought with her wild, disordered spirit and simultaneously with the love that her blazing eyes revealed. A shudder shook her whole body. She seemed to be unable to approach Jesus more closely, so he stood up and advanced towards her, stepping close to her. He held her shoulders and looked into her eyes. Then she collapsed and fell to the floor. The trapped spirits within her continued shaking her, as Jesus bent over her and prayed.

What we had witnessed moved us deeply. We women sat there and started to cry. Jesus' prayer seemed endless as Mary Magdalene shook and her body experienced severe cramps. Then Jesus finished praying and held her head and placed his hand on her heart. He spoke and the words resonated through the worlds: "Darkness and gray spirits, I command you to leave this being and return to your own world. Return this soul to me!" Then Mary Magdalene trembled anew, until she finally lay motionless on the ground. Jesus stroked her forehead and spoke holy words. She opened her eyes and knelt before him, holding his legs. He stood still, apparently unmoved. Her tears flowed over his feet. Then she dried his feet with her hair, as if ashamed of the outburst. She looked up at Jesus with tear-stained face and said, "Forgive me! Please forgive me that I have touched you with my tears."

Jesus knelt down to her and took her face in his hands, looking into her eyes. "Nobody before you or after you has so profoundly recognized my suffering. You are blessed amongst my followers and blessed among women." Then he turned and sat down again, leaving her kneeling there. A light began to germinate in her, although she was still unable to move. We all were transfixed, deeply moved by what had occurred between the two of them. Then she moved again, knelt before him and said, "Lord, I don't know how and why, but I love you above all. I did not know until this moment what love is. But my heart overflows with love when I see you. Please do not leave me alone. Let me always be near to you. I will serve you and be your servant. Wherever you go, please take me with you. I beg you, please don't send me away." Then she began crying again. She cried as if she would never stop, and repeatedly wiped away her tears with her hair. Her body quaked again as if the world was shaking, breaking through her anguish. But to me it was as if all of us women had experienced her tears.

Jesus looked up and turned to Peter. "Bring me the holy oil." Peter disappeared and returned with the oil. He placed it on the table next to Jesus. Then Jesus said, "Mary Magdalene, look at me." He passed the oil to her and said, "Anoint me, here in this house. This is the final dedication which I have awaited, from your hands." She did not know what to do, so Jesus took the oil, poured some on her hands and said, "Anoint my head, so that I can anoint you." Mary Magdalene stood up and she was surrounded by a golden radiance. With the oil in her hands she said, "I do not dare to touch you, Lord." Jesus smiled and replied, "Touch me. Only thus can we heal mankind." Then he bowed his head to her and she stroked the oil over it. Then she knelt before him and he anointed her. He looked at her lovingly and said, "Now return to your place."

Jesus requested that wine be served to all present. Then he began to speak, first to his apostles: "I have not come to Earth to judge. I have not come here to destroy. Rather I am here to reconcile, to support and to elevate those who live in the blessing of the light. Everyone in this room is already chosen. And others will join you, perhaps not in this epoch, but later. I have chosen my twelve apostles, in order that you bring the message of my name to the world."

Then he requested a jug of water and went to each of his apostles, saying, "I baptize you in the name of the Holy Spirit. Go out and speak in the name of the Lord. Love and bless all you meet." He took the head of each of his apostles in his hands and prayed for him, a prayer to God. This ceremony reminded me of the ritual with which John baptized. But the baptism which Jesus gave his apostles was slightly different — a baptism of light, and ordination of their souls. It seemed to me that I could see each of them in the possession of his light. All of them, whether I was familiar with them or not, appeared in their own light. They accepted the authority that Jesus had bestowed upon them, each and every one. Then Jesus sat down.

Then Jesus spoke again. "I am here with the sword of justice. I separate the wheat from the chaff. But I am not here to unleash a war between races or nations. Nevertheless, there will be many wars in my name, of which I cannot approve. God has given me the sword thatI carry, to free everyone who suffers the slavery of society and to destroy whosoever speaks untruth against the Lord. My message is love and the forgiveness of all sins. My fire is the enlightenment that extinguishes forgetting. I am also here to help the women of the world in attaining and maintaining their own power. The primeval rights of the Earth and of the mother have too long been forgotten and ignored. I have chosen twelve men as apostles, but I will also choose women to be my apostles, to carry my word out into the world and in my name when I am no longer here on Earth."

There was silence in the room. Each one of us knew that these words of Jesus had awakened something unexpected in us. I knew that Jesus was the source of all hope for each of us in the room. But with these words we were reminded that he would not be on the Earth forever. It released fears in us, fears we did not want to acknowledge. Then he continued, "This day is destined to be our last in Jerusalem for a long time. Only much later will I return to this town. I beg you all to accompany me to the temple tomorrow morning. I will visit those who claim to have the right and the message to speak for my Father."

He ordered more wine to be poured. Then he said, "Magda, come to me." Once again he took the holy oil and baptized her, saying, "Let the Holy Spirit be with you. You are one of the three who speaks the female language in my brotherhood. I have chosen twelve male apostles, and you are the first of three female apostles. In this life and in many successive lives, you should go out and proclaim my name until the glory of my name is known throughout the world. Everything I am and will be is present in your heart, in your vision and in your being. You are the first woman of my choice, and for that you have dedicated your life." As she began to kneel before him, Jesus took her head in his hands and said, "No Magda, I am not here for you to kneel before me. I am here to kneel before you. I shall bow down in obeisance before every being who serves the Lord with all his or her heart,

279

with all his or her might, with all his or her strength." Then he stood up and embraced her.

Next he went to Mary Magdalene. He took her hand and she stood up. He led her to the place where he had been sitting. Then he took the water and baptized her. He said, "I baptize you as my second female apostle in my name. You will go out into the world in my name and announce my message, so that it will never be forgotten. This is the promise of my soul. From now on you will travel with me and always be at my side. I baptize you in the name of the Father and of the Holy Spirit, that you are blessed and recognized to eternity. You serve me eternally and you love me eternally." Then he took her head in his hands and kissed her on the forehead. He looked at her and spoke to her very quietly: "But I am not here to give you the blessing of womanhood. I am here to be the Messiah, not a man at the side of a woman. I am master for all. And if you choose this path, the subsequent times will not be good for you. But one day the praise for my name will also be for you." Mary Magdalene looked at him humbly and said, "Lord, I am your servant. Whatever you instruct me to do, will be fulfilled in your name, and I will serve you in Heaven as on Earth. I do not know what my destiny is, but I lay my fate in your hands." She returned to her place and Jesus sat down for a moment.

He seemed for a moment lost in thought, then he said, "At the moment somebody is missing who should be here; it is a pity that Simon cannot be with us today. But it is my wish that we all visit him in his house. It will be a meeting of great pleasure to all of us, which I wish to share with him." He paused for a moment and then continued, "Tomorrow you will witness how the power of the Lord will revive and reinstate the Temple of Solomon in Jerusalem. At present it lies oppressed and buried, under the walls of those who misrepresent and misuse the knowledge and love of the Almighty with false words. I shall go there and destroy the temple of lies. I shall go there to reinstate Solomon's Temple, which in ancient times served the lore of God's baptism, to ordain all beings in the fire of His glory and His light."

Then he looked at me and said, "Miriam, come to me." He baptized me with holy water, and God's blessing flowed over my head and liberated me. Jesus said, "You are also blessed. The Holy Spirit comes to you, so that you are present in God's name to eternity. You are the third of them whom I have chosen: my third female apostle. I became acquainted with you as a small girl, and recognized the flame of the Almighty in your heart. You will also proclaim my name now and in later times. You will serve in my name until I return to the Earth in the far distant future. Your destiny is linked to mine." I opened my eyes and looked at him. My heart said, "I place my fate in your hands, my Lord Jesus, although I do not know what my destiny is. I will always serve in your name, wherever it leads me. Teach me. Teach my soul all that I should know to proclaim why you are here."

He stroked my forehead lovingly and said, "I have prepared an important mission for you. My heart is filled with pleasure concerning what is planned for you. Every sacrifice you make in your life will be rewarded with a gift from the Almighty. Your path is prepared." He stood up, lifted me to my feet and embraced me, saying, "You are welcome for all time and in all heavens."

Then he said to the three of us, "You are united forever. I beg you to take care that nothing worldly comes between you, only love. It is implanted in all three of you. The light of Christ will be present after our times, and far into the future. And now I beg you to accompany me once more; I will teach you, as I will teach others in this room."

Jesus requested that wine be proffered. Then he stood up, went to MaRa and held her hand: "Come and sit next to me." Then he requested a chair be brought next to him.

Jesus began to recount, "Your story is old, as old as the story of the gods. In earlier times, a great ancestry existed in many heavens and on this Earth. But gods change when on Earth, due to their forgetting who they are; they no longer know their identity or their mission. You help them with your love and your light. The Almighty Mother sits in front of you, she who succors the world of the gods. But she has to witness the downfall of those that she wishes to promote."

Then he looked at MaRa and said, "You have left your appointed place in order to enter into the darkness of the Earth, to seek and to find the lost gods. Your name will never be erased or forgotten. The black ring that you carry inside you is the ring of the Earth's darkness, the potency of the spirit that will not serve God. You have so long carried this ring within you, to prevent further harm coming to the Earth. It almost cost you your life. You should thank Miriam and Mary Magdalene for saving your life. Their love rescued you from your original mission, and brought you to me. With all the might at my disposition I cannot free you from the ring inside you, as long as it is your wish to carry it.

"However, I can free you from this ring, if you really wish it. It is your decision alone. If you give me back the ring that you are protecting until you are freed from this burden, then I have to return it to the Earth. You know that other beings wish to possess this ring. You must choose: do you wish to keep the ring or will you return it to the Earth?"

MaRa reflected a moment and said, "I really don't know how I should decide. The first time that it I had doubts about the ring was when I experienced how it started to poison the community of ordained women, which I guarded with all my strength. It has contaminated my body and soul, and polluted the whole Earth. But it also changes me. It is difficult for me to reach a decision." Jesus looked at a dark-haired man and said to him, "Come to me." As MaRa saw the man her eyes lit up. Then I remembered where they had met before: that time in Canaan when Jesus had prophesied that they would meet again.

Jesus spoke to MaRa. "Come to me. Do you recognize this man?" She replied: "Yes, I recognize him from previous times. I sense that my soul is at home in his heart. Nevertheless, I still do not know how I should decide. What will happen when I give up what my sisterhood has bestowed upon me and choose another path for my life?" Jesus was quiet for a moment and then said, "You have two possibilities. Either you carry the ring alone within you, or you release it now and go with this man and seek a new life with him. Find new perspectives for your redemption and your resurrection."

It was a singular moment for us all. We knew that there must be a reason MaRa and the man from Damascus were meeting for the second time. But Jesus offered them the choice, to take a decision together which would change their lives.

Then the man from Damascus said, "When I saw MaRa for the first time, I knew instinctively that we belonged together. Since that time I have only returned to Damascus once. I am a rich man, and can afford not to work. I have returned to Jesus and have travelled with him. I was permitted to experience and learn so much with him. I still do not know where I come from, where I am going, or who I am. But when I see you, then I know my way." MaRa was deeply moved by his words and replied, "I do not know why, Jesus, but I beg you to relieve me of this ring. Every word I hear resonates in my soul. I will enter this new life and leave the old life behind me. Thus I am prepared to answer the call, to proclaim your word to the world — wherever you send me."

Jesus was silent for a moment. And then said, "So your decision is made. I will take the ring of darkness from you and release it unto the Earth, to expose the enmity between the worlds and the struggle between light and darkness. It will someday seal my fate. But I thank you. With this decision you have heralded my path and my fate on Earth, and have carried out God's will, whatsoever the Lord, my Father, will decide from now on. I take the dark ring of redemption, to free the concealed destiny."

He laid his hand on her abdomen and I saw a shining ring of darkness leave her. He raised the ring to heaven, saying, "Lord, it is Your will and Your decision to return this ring of darkness to the Earth. I lay my fate, now sealed, in Your hands. Whatever you decide, I will follow this path on Earth."

Perhaps I alone saw all of what followed. Shining brightly, the ring disappeared and returned to the place of its origin on Earth. Jesus shivered, and I saw how drops of blood appeared on his forehead and ran down his face. I ran to the kitchen and brought a towel. I asked him, "Lord, allow me to clean your face of blood." He nodded agreement and I saw he had tears in his eyes. I wiped the blood from his face, and could not prevent my own tears from flowing: the pain that he experienced was also my pain. I loved Jesus so much that I could not bear to see him suffer. I knew then that it was not his sorrow alone. When I had cleaned his face, I took the towel back to the kitchen. I prepared to wash the towel and saw something astonishing: an impression of the face of Jesus was on the cloth. I burst into tears and cried as if my heart would break. I laid the towel on my heart. I have kept the towel my whole life long, always carry it with me and will not give it out of my hands.

I went back to the room, deeply moved by the gift Jesus had given me. I kept the secret to myself. I returned my attention to what was happening in the room. Jesus called for the holy oil and some water. Then we witnessed something wonderful: Jesus married MaRa to the man from Damascus, whose name was at that time Sharon. He said, "Go on your way. When the time has come, travel through the country; you should also baptize and proclaim the name of the Lord. Blessed are your ways you will travel together on this Earth. I invite you to accompany us to the Sea of Galilee, until the time comes to leave us. Together!" Jesus paused, apparently deeply moved, and then said, "From now on we shall experience the most wonderful years on Earth. The fruits of the Lord will be available to us, and all of you who are present, and some others not yet here, should partake of them. I want to share the blessing of this time with you.

"I beg you all to accompany me tomorrow to the temple in Jerusalem. Let us not travel there together, but split up and all take different paths to the temple. We shall agree upon a time to meet there. I pray you all to go there but try to avoid being recognized. I am taking a great risk. When I have completed my mission at the temple I will disappear from the town. We will then meet at an appointed place outside the gates to Jerusalem. We will leave the town, and for a long time we shall not return."

He asked Lazarus to divide us into groups, tell us how each group should approach the temple and how we could leave the town unobserved. We assumed that Jesus had something planned, which he had not wanted to divulge until the time came. Nevertheless, this evening remains in our memories one of the happiest in our lives. We were so spiritually united with him and with one another, that we were unable to express it in words.

Jesus, Lazarus and the other group organizers planned their actions for the next day. We would meet in Simon's house on the way to Galilee. At last all plans for the next day were completed, and we retired to our rooms for the night. It had been a long time since I had slept in my parents' house. The other women slept in Irisa's house, where we would meet next morning. Lazarus would accompany me.

When I awoke the next morning, Jesus and some of his apostles had already left. Then Lazarus said, "Come. It's time to leave." He, Martha and I walked through the town to the square in front of the temple. We made our way unnoticed through the stands of the merchants and sat down at the prearranged place, as agreed between Jesus and Lazarus. I observed the hustle and bustle. It was a curious feeling, seeing the salesmen peddling their wares in such a hallowed place. Soothsayers, clairvoyants and faith healers were also present, promising and preaching, offering to save souls directly outside the temple. As I observed the temple I could not see any thing that could give redemption or salvation. Inside and outside, the temple was crowded with salesmen, customers and crowds who had gathered for one or another reason.

Suddenly Jesus appeared among them and positioned himself on the steps, so that he was visible to the crowd. Then he turned to the temple and said, "Citizens of Jerusalem, is this the place and the art by which you praise and honor the Lord? Have you forgotten that in former times the original building housed the holiest temple of the Jewish people? You tore down the holy Temple of Solomon in order to erect pillars of worldly power and to repress the power of the Lord's word. You have polluted and desecrated this house of our Father. Holy words have not been heard here for a long time. The name of the god here is Greed. The demanding hands that gather money in this temple are also equally greedy. They promise you God's redemption for money. But God cannot be bought or bribed! Your sanctimonious words of praise cannot awaken the temple buried under these walls."

Then I saw that some high priests had appeared. White-faced, they heard what Jesus was saying and angrily asked, "What do you want here? You dare to insult our house?" Jesus replied, "You! Your house? Is it not the house of the Lord, the only God? You are not God's servants; you serve yourselves. And this monstrous building, in which you hide yourselves, is filled with your wealth. With your sanctimonious speeches you oppress the people, and deny the power of God and that which He has given me. But our power and authority lie outside your sphere of influence. I have the power in my hands to re-erect the ancient temple. But I will not do so."

Then Jesus raised his hand, from which an enormous flash of lightning emanated. The priests jumped backwards in fright. The steps in front of the temple broke apart. Flashes of lightning sprang from the Earth. Jesus went along the rows of stands and overturned them one after the other. He was angry and shouted to the merchants and salesmen, "Leave this place immediately! You have no right to be here. This is the place for God's word. You have forgotten the might of the Father, as you have forgotten his name." A new lightning flash struck between the steps and it seemed to me that the whole building quaked.

Jesus addressed the priests: "You see I do not need a day to re-erect Solomon's temple, or to split your heads or to destroy this false temple of yours as a witness of your hypocrisy. But I am not here to bring hostility. God has led me to this place to bear witness to his might, and has authorized me to offer you the chance of conversion to His way. The Lord has given this inheritance into your custody." Then he turned and said, "Blessed are those who can see the light. Blessed are those who feel the power of the Almighty and sense the radiance and glory of the golden Temple of Solomon. Gold is the color of the omniscience, the omnipotence and the love of the

Lord. That is not the gold of statues, icons and taxes, stolen from the Earth. Gold was the character of this room and of this place, hallowed by the fire of the omniscient wisdom, revealing God Himself."

As I watched, the Earth opened up and the Temple of Solomon was for a moment visible. His Power and His glory were for this short time evident. The countenance of God marked this vision. Then the Temple of Solomon sank back into the Earth. Only the golden statues, which had decorated the ancient Temple of Solomon, remained. Jesus spoke again: "How many prophets and how many messengers of God do you need, until you finally accept the evidence of your errors, and return to your origin in God? You should remember the origin of birth, how God created you and how the divine people was born out of the Earth. This race was divine, originating from the light of the Holy Father, chosen in His name. I will only return to you when you have completely repented for your sins. If you would understand this for a moment, you would be forgiven. But I have only seen hostility in your eyes, not the recognition of truth, of Him who has sent me here. Hence you will not see me again on this place, unless God wishes it."

With these words Jesus left the square in front of the temple. Many people had fled out of fear, particularly when the flashes of lightning occurred. I looked at the priests who had emerged from the temple. They were petrified and their faces white with fury. Instead of appreciating that Jesus had resurrected the Almighty Power of God on this square, the eyes of the priests were filled with hate and they hurriedly returned to the temple and closed the door behind them. We

289

then left the square unnoticed, as agreed on the previous evening. I was quiet for a time and then touched Lazarus on the arm and asked him, "Where does all of this lead? Jesus has started a war. He has encouraged the opposition and hostility of those who rule the town, the country and the people."

Lazarus just smiled. "I have been hoping for this confrontation. He is the king that I wish to see on the throne of our people. I am ready to fight for that, and if necessary to endanger my life." I could not reply. I was speechless. For the moment it was more important for us to leave the town and proceed unnoticed to the appointed place outside the gates of Jerusalem, so we moved on. We met the others, and Jesus instructed us all to travel in small groups, taking different paths. He instructed us to meet next at Simon's house. Jesus had created an uproar in the town before the Romans had a chance to intervene. It was obvious that the lies and hypocrisy of the priests would lead to riots and rebellion. Before Jerusalem could be cordoned off and searched, we were already outside the town and on our way to Canaan. A door behind us had closed.

I was very happy when Simon's house appeared in the distance in front of us, the house that I had left two years ago. And I was also happy to see Simon again. Thanks to Lazarus' leadership and the donkey that we had at our disposal, the journey to Canaan was relaxed and uneventful.

We were affectionately received. Simon was already waiting for us and greeted each of us individually. He appeared to be very happy that we were there again. It was the first time that I had the chance to see him with adult eyes, to observe his being, which seemed primarily to be evidenced as a generous host. But it was clear that there was more to him. He was no ordinary person. Encounters with him were not from this world. I always remember the day on which we sought Jesus in the desert, and the time with him in Canaan before I travelled to the holy women in the mountains.

Helena Salome was very happy and excited to see us again. She told us that she was married, and did not live in the house any more. Her husband had nothing to do with the movement to which we belonged. Nevertheless, she was very happy. She said, "But I have a surprise for you."

She led me into the hall in which we had celebrated two years ago, and there sat Mary. She approached me joyfully und we embraced each other long and silently. Great joy streamed from heart to heart. She whispered, "My daughter. You have a place in my heart, and I have missed you so much." When we finally released each other, I asked her if she had been in the house the whole time. She said, "No. Jesus sent me a message. I remained a long time in my own house, since I need stillness and tranquillity now and again. I am no longer young and Jesus' life becomes increasingly exciting. That is very strenuous and provocative. At home I can find the peace I need. But when I received the message that a surprise waited for me, I could not refuse to come here. And when I see you I know that you are my surprise! I am really astonished how grown up you are in just two years. You are no more a girl, but a young woman."

Mary asked, "Who else will be coming here?" I replied, "Oh, you will be surprised. You know some of them. I look forward to our days here. I remember the wonderful nights in Canaan, in this house, as if it was yesterday." Woman servants arrived and gave me a room. One after another or in groups the rest of the party arrived and were shown to their rooms. MaRa and Sharon also had a room together. Simon greeted every new arrival as if he had departed only yesterday, his art of welcoming his guests. He seemed to know all of the apostles well, and conversed with them freely. It was evident that friendships had been formed in the past two years.

After the long journey, all were glad to withdraw to their rooms. Before we retired Simon said, "This evening you are all invited to a festival at my house." I could not sleep, so I went out into the garden. I wanted to find peace under the trees, remembering the nights we experienced, when Heaven and Earth blended in one another. Then I sensed someone behind me.

It was Simon, who said, "You love my garden as much as I do. When I need peace and quiet, I often come here. You have chosen a good tree, a good place to relax. May I keep you company?" I said, "Yes, of course." I tried to find the words I wanted to say. Then I plucked up my courage and said, "I would like to thank you for the wonderful days that I experienced in your house two years ago; you were part of some of the most memorable days in my life. Unfortunately, I did not have enough time then to get to know you and to thank you."

He smiled and said, "This house was designed for that purpose, and I had prepared it accordingly. You were away for two years, but Jesus was often here during that time. Sometimes he was alone and sometimes his apostles were here with him.

But my house is large enough to accommodate them all." I asked, "Did you travel around with Jesus sometimes?" He answered, "Only seldom. Every now and again I receive a message from him and I go to visit him. But I return home soon after since there is business to attend to, for me and for my family. I must admit that I sometimes get the urge to visit him, even when I work here. He has invited me to accompany you all to the Sea of Gennasaret." I was silent for a moment and then said, "You know that I met you a long time ago." He nodded and said, "I know." I considered for a moment, and asked, "You know you are a remarkable person? But I cannot describe you. I remember hearing about you in Qumran. And now you live here, wealthy but unostentatious. Why don't you join Jesus and announce his presence to the world?"

He answered, "But I do. Only I don't need great words to show myself. When I am here on Earth I don't make a fuss in public. The worlds and the tasks that I influence take place within me. Sometimes I enjoy pleasant hours with my brother Jesus. But at present I see that he is the one who should show himself to the people. I feel no compulsion to do that. Wherever I can support him, I do so. Wherever I can be a host to him or to you all, I do so."

Despite my deep respect for him we conversed for some time, and I was surprised what a benign, affable and agreeable person he was. Something wonderful radiated from his eyes. It was different from the emanation from Jesus' eyes, but just as divine. I began to feel tired and said, "I think I would like to retire to my room for a while. As I have learned, the nights in Canaan are long, so I would like to collect my reserves of strength together." He looked at me and said, "You should not

293

be afraid. In my house you will not be pursued. You are safe here and always will be." It was the first time that I had been so closely associated with someone as omnipotent as he, who was able to read my thoughts and give answers to questions that I had not posed. On the other hand it was also clear to me what subversion Jesus had aroused in Jerusalem. We were fugitives who had left the town in secret. I retired to my room for a time. On descending I saw that a splendid meal had been prepared, as so often happened in this house.

I asked Jesus whether he had invited others for the evening, and he replied, "No. I think the next days should be peaceful. I have caused a great disturbance in Jerusalem. We will now remain in this house, and see what Heaven has in store for us. We have to make extensive preparations. I must instruct you and the other apostles concerning certain matters, and prepare you for our mission. For that purpose I require the shelter of this house and Simon's support."

The evening proceeded without any notable occurrences. During the meal I had the opportunity of speaking to several apostles and becoming more acquainted with them. I particularly liked old Jacob, whom I first met two years ago. He was a friendly, affectionate person, and told me that he had previously been a high priest in the old Jewish tradition, in Jericho. But he left his post in the temple to follow Jesus. He recounted that he discovers the truth with Jesus every day and with every step. Then Matthew joined us, and I asked him whence he came. He replied, "I cannot remember how my previous life was any more. But I have no family and nothing to leave behind. That made it simpler to join Jesus and to accompany him every day."

Judas Iscariot also joined us. I remembered the evening when Lazarus quivered with disgust at his presence, so I took the opportunity of conversing with him. He was a quiet, good–natured and profound young man. I was now adult and impertinent enough to ask him, "Judas, my brother told me that you were in a school for magicians in Jerusalem." He replied, "Yes, Miriam, that is true." I asked him, "Would you tell me what you had learned in the school?" He replied, "There is an ancient magic of our people, which is retained in secret teachings. My parents sent me to the school and I was initiated in the use of the magical techniques. But in the time when I knew your brother, some changes were taking place: some of the graduates decided to serve the powers of darkness. I was happy to follow the call of Jesus, since I was not sure if I was not myself affected by the call of the powers of darkness. I also heard from an acquaintance that members of the school were serving the king. And I must admit I do not know what they do with these magical powers. But I am informed that they keep the king alive, since he is said to be ill. They influence the mind of the king and also that of his new wife. I have relinquished all my magical techniques and tools, and laid them at Jesus' feet. Now I travel with him."

I said, "Judas, it seems that you are not completely convinced in what you do." He replied, "Yes, I am! Believe me, Miriam. In my education I was initiated in matters that have long affected my soul. I have seen worlds I do not like to discuss. That is the root of the sadness that you see in me. I have rejected these initiations, since they contain other powers than those of Jesus, which harness their own energies. Every day I try to learn through the blessing of the Lord. I seek the path of devotion with Jesus. When I observe Jesus performing miracles, I have never seen him harness the forces in the ways that I learned. It moves me every time, how he contacts God, deep in prayer, and how God's power is transferred through Jesus. He does not want the power for himself; it comes directly from God's throne.

"No, I am completely convinced that his way is right. But believe me, how I was initiated is still in conflict with what Jesus teaches and it sometimes creates an inner conflict for me. It will be some time before I am completely free of my past schooling."

Then he changed the subject, asking, "Do you know that there are murmurings amongst my friends? Apparently some of them are not happy that Jesus has also chosen three women apostles. It doesn't fit into their prconceptions. The idea is also somewhat unusual for me, but I find it good nevertheless. It will not be an easy path for you. We men can appear in public any time. We are free to do what we want. I don't know how you women manage with society's taboos and restrictions for women. But you have my support. You are women, and I respect you as our equals, even though you carry different knowledge and different magic than we do as men." He ceased speaking and stood up. I was thankful for the conversation, since I had also detected a growing feeling of uneasiness in the room.

It was a long evening. Simon seemed to like celebrating deep into the night. He often sat with Jesus and they talked to one another, but I took the opportunity of talking to him when I could, too. I also saw how Mary Magdalene often sought to be near to Jesus. Sometimes he permitted her to be near, since everybody in the room could see that she was a woman yearning for this man. Jesus treated her at all times with great respect, sometimes permitting her to stay and sometimes turning away to do other things. He did not encourage her feelings, but it was obvious that she was deeply in love with him. I could sense how she fought to control her feelings. I felt that she had chosen an extremely difficult task. To be in love with the Lord is simultaneously a blessing and a punishment.

I had also loved Jesus above all, right from the beginning. But I was grateful that I did not love him as a man, that he had not conquered my woman's heart. Despite Jesus' respect for her, he did not appear to reciprocate Mary Magdalene's love. I admired him for his masterly charm and personal magnetism. He treated as all the same: with great respect, so that each one of us had the feeling we were somebody special for him. He treated Simon like a brother, and when they were together the intimacy between them was something exceptional, and only between the two of them. We women also received the same respect and consideration that he gave to the men. For him we were independent beings and were always treated with sincere love and esteem.

Jesus sat often with MaRa and Sharon and joked with them. He bestowed his blessing to them, because their partnership was a great source of pleasure to him. The evening was a wonderful experience for all of us. Every one of us had the opportunity of meeting every other person present. It was very informal and relaxed. I must admit that, by the end of the evening, I had developed a great respect for each and every person that Jesus had gathered around him. All were honest human beings with noble characters. They were from varied backgrounds and professions. Some of them had even been scorned by society, as in the case of Matthew, the customs officer.

I went to my room with the feeling of being home. Before reaching it, I met Simon. He approached me and kissed me on my forehead saying, "Welcome in my house." After these words I went to bed, and slept peacefully.

The following days were calm. Jesus was particularly relaxed and happy. He was constantly concerned with our well–being, and was increasingly like a father to us. Sometimes he left the house with his apostles, returning a short time later. We never knew what he did, but we presumed that he chose some from of the circle of apostles and was training them in some way. The days passed and we had more or less forgotten Jerusalem, and I was grateful for that.

On the fifth day my brother Lazarus said to me, "As far as I know we leave soon for the Sea of Galilee. You will then become acquainted with another family property, which you have not yet seen. We own a large house there." I asked, "Will we all be able to live there?" Lazarus replied, "Not all. Jesus is usually in Peter's house, and he has other friends there who would be pleased to accommodate him. However, I do not know exactly when we leave." I asked Lazarus, "Do you believe we will ever be able to return to Jerusalem? I think Jesus has made many enemies there."

Lazarus replied, "We are not yet connected with Jesus in the public eye. Don't forget, he protected us by splitting us into small groups or single persons, so that we would not arouse suspicion. But the times are very turbulent in any case. There are many critical voices in the population, hoping that there will be a new king of the Jews. They rely on his hereditary right as a direct descendant of David and hope that he will be the new leader." I replied, "The others regard such an idea with suspicion, and will do what they can to avoid it." There we ended our conversation.

On this evening, Jesus asked us to meet together. He came and sat in our midst, while Simon stood at the back of the room. Jesus bade Simon to come to him and to sit next to him. Then he began to speak: "At present this nation and this people live in uncertainty and oppression. My Father has sent prophets for a long time, to spread his word, but to no effect. Here in this room, together with me, are beings from the holiest of heavens. You do not know who you really are. But what I see, and for which I thank you, is that everyone in the room has chosen to go with me — without knowing what is involved, without knowing what the future will hold, and what my intentions are, without conditions and questions. I have come to Earth at my Father's wish. Peace has been extinguished for so long, and the fires of love and peace have not burned on this Earth for a very long time. Each one of you in this room carries a key to this place; every one of you carries a key to God's kingdom, which you brought to Earth with you.

"I would be nothing if I were alone, and my message worthless on Earth; it only lives through you. What value is a realm to a king, when all subjects are ignorant slaves? A true king can only be satisfied when his subjects are knowledgeable, lead happy and fulfilled lives and realize their aims in life.

Each one of you should understand that you all aspire to the divine knowledge. I know your qualities and your aims. I have a deep respect for all of you. Many aspects of God's rule are present here. But the world and this land will not recognize you as you deserve, although you serve humbly.

"Now I want to begin my central mission. I have come neither to awaken the dead, nor to redeem the living nor drive out demons. I have come to take over the grievous suffering and the karma of humanity, from which the human beings are unwilling or unable to save themselves. This is the will of my Father. I do not know what my future is. Those who are blind to these matters will never recognize you. Simon and I carry the key to all heavens in our hearts. I cannot open a Heaven without him and he cannot open a Heaven without me. For this Earth we cannot at present open a heaven, we can only deliver it from suffering, edify those whose light and love are strong enough and free those who have forgotten but wish to return to their spiritual home. Truly, truly I say unto you, Heaven on Earth is prophesied, but many years and many lives will pass until my seed, which I have planted on the Earth, starts to grow and my message is understood.

"Much will be written about our experiences. The powerful and influential will pervert our history to their own ends, to rule the world in my name but to their own advantage. I will not be deterred for one moment from doing what I have to do. You will go with me and I will confer God's inheritance on you, each according to his or her needs. But you will need to immerse yourselves in many other lives, to inherit much later what you sow here. Understanding will require patience. I have been immersed in deepest darkness. I am the seed that penetrates through the darkness. My being is born in darkness, to bear fruit at a later time. The time is not yet ripe, and the traces will be lost until the resurrection sometime in the future."

"You are all divine beings, rulers and angels from the highest Heaven in my Father's kingdom. From today onward, you can manifest and proclaim the glory of God. But, believe me, not one of you will have a simple destiny. You can decide to withdraw today, in which case I would ask you to leave this room. I cannot be more honest than that. I can only state the truth. The destiny of the Earth is not yet ready for us. Each one who fights for God's realm on Earth has access to Heaven and Earth simultaneously. But redemption will not come from human hand."

At that moment one of Simon's female servants entered the room, to refill our cups with wine. She was a beautiful woman with long hair, and Jesus said to her, "Come to me. You serve in this house with so much devotion and tenderness. You do not yet know who you are. I will tell you. You are my angel, who prepares my way. Simon, would you release her from your employment? I would like her to accompany me too."

Then he looked at her and said, "You come from the highest level of the angels who praise God in the heavens. My angel, who protects me in heaven, please protect me on Earth as well. Spread your powerful wings and follow me with every step. I will need you to accompany me and to safeguard my person." She lowered her head and her long hair covered his feet. She folded her hands in prayer and said, "I have so much wished to accompany you."

Then she looked at Simon and said, "Master, you were always so good to me. I don't want to desert you." Simon answered, "When Jesus wishes you to go with him, I cannot stop you and I would not do it if it is your wish. From today you are independent. I have brought you from slavery and now you are completely free. You were an attentive and benign servant and have served my truly every day. Now you belong to the circle of the Lord."

Jesus said to her, "Stand up!" Then he stood behind her and raised his hands, as if he had opened her powerful wings, which extended over the whole house and radiated fire. They were like a powerful protection of flames. Then Jesus stood in front of her and said, "From now on you shall carry these protective wings behind me. I shall need them! You will be my protection against attacks from other worlds. From today on, your name is Seraphim, my angel, who accompanies me on all paths."

He turned to his mother, Mary, and asked her, "Give her some clothes, that she is no longer dressed as a servant. Give her some of yours that she can travel with us." His angel knelt in front of him. It was clear that she was infinitely grateful and her eyes were filled with thankfulness. Jesus said, "You will go with the other women, and you will be well looked after. There you are welcome and will be safe and secure." Then Jesus stood up, and as he passed Mark he said, "Your affectionate glance at the Seraphim has not escaped me, Mark. But you will have to be patient for a while."

That evening was holy for us. An atmosphere of peace and benevolence reigned. We knew that something special had occurred. We were a community of friends, convivial companions who celebrated until deep into the night.

It was late when a servant appeared, a well–built man who had just brought more wine from the cellar. Jesus saw him and said, laughingly, "Simon, I don't know, but I think I shall have to ask for all of your servants." He looked at the man and said, "I also need you. With the power of your body and spirit you can protect me in all worlds. I will need a good bodyguard. With Simon's permission I would request you to serve me instead." Simon laughed and said, "If you take all my servants, I don't know how I am going to host you when you come next time."

Jesus went to the man and held his hand over the man's heart: "You are my bodyguard. I beg you to take over my bodily protection, since you are strong and observant. We shall not always be among friends. I would be happy to have you by my side." The man bowed to Jesus. Then Simon said, "Unfortunately, Jesus, he does not speak our language. I found him somewhere on my travels and kept him with me because I liked the warmth in his eyes. He was loading wine barrels in the Aquitaine. But he has not yet managed to learn our language." We saw in his eyes that he had not understood. Then Simon spoke to him in his own language, and he understood and nodded approvingly, as if he was saying, "I would love to serve you, Lord."

From that moment on, the man was always near to Jesus. He had no name, since Simon claimed that he did not understand his own language, and only communicated in broken Greek. Hence Simon had never discovered his name. He named him jokingly, "Guardian of the Wine," which he always used. He, the guardian of Jesus, had accepted his task. From that moment on he watched with eagle's eyes each and every person who approached Jesus. He was always on Jesus' left hand side. Wherever Jesus was, his guardian was present and guarded him. I began to ask myself what Jesus was preparing, and why he was gathering people to protect him in this world. But I did not want to think about such matters, but preferred to concentrate on Jesus' statement, that we would for some time be able to experience Heaven on Earth.

The next morning, Jesus informed us that we would resume our travels in two days. Then he asked Simon, "Would you come with us to the Sea of Galilee?" Simon said, "Yes, willingly, if that is your wish." Then Lazarus said, "Simon, I have stayed in your house and enjoyed your hospitality so often. I would be very honored to invite you to stay in our house this time." It was agreed, and I was very happy that he had accepted.

Later that evening someone knocked on the door. We opened the door and found a messenger, completely exhausted, who said, "I must speak to Jesus." As Jesus entered the messenger fell on his knees and said, "I must bring you the news, Lord. John the Baptist has been imprisoned at the command of King Herod. He had ordered his arrest and imprisonment." Jesus asked, "Where is John now?" The man replied, "He is in a prison near to the Sea of Galilee, where the King has a palace." Jesus asked, "Why was he arrested? What happened?" The man replied, "I am one of John's followers, and I have been with him for some time. But John had increasingly anarchistic tendencies, and his speeches against the King and his followers were increasingly loud and aggressive, and he listed the sins of the rulers. He criticized openly the King's new wife and called her a whore and heir to the devil. John was unable to restrain himself. Nobody was surprised when the soldiers appeared and carried him off. Even John had foreseen his fate. He looked the soldiers straight in the eye and said, 'Now you will fulfill your destinies and I mine.'" Jesus turned and left the room. Through the doors I could see that he fell on his knees and prayed.

Then those of us in the room all began to speak at once in confusion. We had heard that John had made provocative speeches at the River Jordan, which had very much displeased the King. John had chosen a dangerous mission, and played with fire. The news spread through the whole country and nobody was surprised that the King had him arrested.

Then the apostles began to chatter about John's arrest, and when Jesus re-entered the room he became angry. "Close your mouths. You have no idea of the situation. Had he wanted to avoid the situation, John would have acted otherwise. But he chose this destiny. This great prophet knew exactly what he was doing. He did it to precede me and to break the might of the King. He sacrificed himself for that purpose. I never want to hear another word or thought on the subject in this circle. Pray for him, because his fate is one of darkness and danger from now on. The King will show no mercy towards him." With these words Jesus closed the subject, just adding, "We leave tomorrow."

Then he turned to the messenger. "Could you convey a message from me to John?" The man replied, "Yes, I know some of the guards in the prison. If you wish, I can pass a message on to him." Jesus said, "Then tell him that I will be coming to the Sea of Galilee, not far from him, and will contact him. I don't know what I might be able to do for him, but I am near to him with all my thoughts and with all the strength of my being. Please beg him to cease attacking the King. I know John. His fire burns in all worlds. Hurry to him now, and deliver him the message." I have to admit, as we went to bed that night, we all had serious misgivings about John's situation. The King and the powerful elite had for the first time dared to imprison one of Jesus' followers. We did not know whether we would all suffer the same fate.

On the following day we started out on our journey to the Sea of Galilee. We had enough provisions and animals to carry us and our luggage, so we could proceed with only short pauses. We stopped a few times to sleep. But Jesus appeared to be uneasy. As we sat together Simon came to Jesus and said, "Jesus, my friend. I have contacts in the King's palace. I could arrange for you to visit John in prison." Jesus answered, "I think it better not to visit him in prison." Simon suggested visiting John himself, in place of Jesus, to which Jesus agreed. On arrival at the Sea of Galilee, Lazarus approached Jesus and asked him where he would like to stay. Jesus replied, "If it is possible, I would like to stay in your house. Please find accommodation for the others with our friends."

For the first time I was in the house of my family at the Sea of Galilee. It was a beautiful house, which appeared to have been the family's summer residence. It did not have as many rooms as our house in Jerusalem, but there was enough room for five people — Jesus, Simon Lazarus, Martha and I. Lazarus and Peter attended to the accommodation of the others.

Simon disappeared in the evening, and when he returned he told us that he had been able to speak to John. He offered to intercede on John's behalf, and to use his connections to have him released from prison. But John had refused. Simon also asked John if he would like to see Jesus, but this he also refused. However, he did have a message for Jesus, which Simon related: "Your assignment is not yet completed. Your path has not reached its goal. Do not endanger yourself by contacting me. My fate is sealed and my destiny is increasingly fulfilled as the end approaches." Simon told Jesus, "John wishes you to know that the voice of God is so strong within him, that it will break the chains of the sick King."

Jesus withdrew and did not wish to speak to anyone. But Simon seemed to be unaffected by the events. He sat with me and we talked to one another. Jesus remained absent for some days. I wished to explore the town and so I crept out of the house now and again and wandered through the streets to the sea. I was somewhat sad that I had never before had the opportunity of becoming acquainted with this pleasant place.

One day I was wandering through the streets when a veiled woman passed me, and as she passed whispered, "Don't stand still, but bend down as if you have dropped something. I know you. You belong to those who accompany the Messiah. Is it possible for me to see him?" I asked, "Who are you?" She answered, "I am Salome, the daughter of the Queen. Can you remember? We met once in Jerusalem." I asked her when she could come to us, and she replied, "It is easiest for me to leave the palace at night." I told her the way to our house and said, "Come to us shortly before midnight. I will inform Jesus. I will come to the gate and say whether he will see you.

I hope I can help you." Then we acted as if I had picked up something from the ground, and she went on her way.

I hurried back to the house and sought Jesus. He was sitting with Simon and they were deep in discussion. I said, "Please forgive me for disturbing you. Lord, I met Salome on the street. Do you remember? The daughter of Herod Antipas. She would like to meet you, and I have arranged that she should be at our gate shortly before midnight, since she is only able to leave the palace at night. If you wish I will wait for her and bring her into the house." Jesus said, "So let it be. If she seeks me she should find me."

Shortly before midnight I waited at the gate, but there was no sign of her. I was wondering if anything had happened to her, when I saw her approaching. She said, "I apologize for being late, but I was unable to leave the palace earlier. I had to wait until all were asleep. Can I see the Messiah?" I replied, "Come with me. He is expecting you." Only when we had entered the house did she remove her cloak and veil. She was simply dressed, to prevent being recognized. As she removed the veil I saw this beautiful woman again, with black, curly hair.

Jesus was waiting for her, and she fell on her knees before him, saying, "Thank you, Lord, for the opportunity to speak to you." Jesus asked, "What is the matter, Salome?" She answered, "I don't know how to help myself. I know that John the Baptist is true to you, and his imprisonment is the work of my mother. For months she has been inciting Herod, my step-father, against John. But John is not willing to take back his insulting words about the destruction of the whole Roman province. He advocates the destruction of the realm, and the destruction of the King's powers, and nothing can stop him. My mother, Herodias, has managed to persuade a Roman visitor to permit the imprisonment. She understood how to steer the conversation to the subject of John, and to ask provocatively how Herod could tolerate someone advocating the downfall of the state, and hence questioning the occupation of the Romans. Here she had found her husband's sensitive spot, so that he felt he had to protect his honor with the Roman occupiers, and immediately issue orders to imprison John.

"But John did not even stop there. He shouted so loud in the prison that he could be heard in the palace. Repeatedly he advocated the destruction of the Roman province and spoke of his own death without resurrection and his sins and atonement. He will not cease this provocation, and my mother becomes increasingly angry. I have repeatedly begged her to release him, since I know he will not harm anybody. But her heart is full of hate. She clings to the sovereignty and authority of her husband. I am sure she will insist on his death."

Jesus said, "I know much of this, but what is it that troubles you so?" "Jesus, she tries to use me, because she knows that her husband regards me with lascivious eyes. She knows that she no longer has power over the King, and now she tries to use me for her purposes and to turn my words around to her advantage, to avenge herself on John. My mother is cold and calculating. I really don't know what to do."

Jesus thought for a time and then said, "There are destinies that are unchangeable. Everyone contributes to his or her own fate, even though this is not immediately visible to the outside observer. But inside there is an unchangeable part that has to be redeemed. I beg you to return to the palace. Accept this part of your fate, since you will not be able to prevent it, whether you pacify your mother or not. A sinister constellation of stars and a dark flame have hung over the palace for a long time. Believe me, the sacrifice that John has made will free you, even when you do not yet understand it." Salome replied in tears, "Oh Lord, what a tragic fate you predict for me." Jesus said, "No, Salome, it is not a tragic fate. It is the power of those who intrude into such fates, in order to sustain the spark of light. That is you, Salome. In this sinister palace you are the only flame of love and light, even though you cannot propagate it. You are this light."

Salome asked if she might return to see Jesus, to which he replied, "No, Salome. It is dangerous for you to come to me. It would endanger me and all my companions. And it would be dangerous for you too. I beg you to understand, you belong to my companions. You are one of us. But don't let anyone know it. Please return to the palace now. There will be other times, but first some predestined events must take place, and irrevocable fate be fulfilled. God will support you, and I will also be near to you, to help you endure your sadness. Believe me."

Salome left the house and I accompanied her outside and to the gate. I really liked this woman with her dark eyes, her profound wisdom and that inner spark that identified her with us. I said, "Salome, I shall pass the point where we met every day. When you seek me, I will be your friend. But it is now time for you to return. When you need something, I will be at the same place at the same time — whether you come or not."

Then she left, and I returned into the house. Jesus had retired but Simon was still awake. At first, I thought he was meditating, but as I entered the rom he looked up at me affectionately. I sat down next to him. I felt very tired, so I lay down with my head on his legs. He sensed my tiredness and stroked my head, saying, "Nobody knows it but it is a fact that I guard the destinies of all these beings. Believe me, Miriam, if I could change Salome's tragic destiny I would. But every soul chooses its own way, and will follow it until the end. The powers of the karma are very strong in this country at this time. Most of the doors that I guard are closed. Only a few are open, to permit the beings to be freed from their karmas. But the time will come when this situation will change. Then I will have other possibilities. Then the doors of God's blessing will be re-opened. Until then I have to wait, and guard your destinies with all my might. But I cannot change them." I asked him when this of which he spoke would come, and he said, "An era will come long after the present — A time when much that is impossible today becomes possible. A time when we do not need to return, to break the dark chains of our karmas and to carry them with us. A time when the karmas are liberated from the beings, because a new epoch is arrived."

I asked, "Simon, since you are guardian of destinies of beings, do you know my destiny?" He replied, "Yes and no." "Can you tell me something of my destiny?" He replied, "Believe me, if you had a fate at present, when Jesus is on Earth, it would have changed again. Your destiny is coupled to his path. The only thing I can tell you is that you have chosen it for yourself freely, and the choice was made in heaven, before God's throne." "And you?" I asked, "Have you also chosen freely?" He replied, "I choose nothing. I am there where I have to be. I appear where I can, and I am where Jesus is. Sometimes we appear on Earth separately, but when we appear together we bring great possibilities of change to Earth. With our combined power we can create great changes. The time will come when I appear before him and assume the leadership, as another being. But now is his time. And I protect him on his path."

"Simon, I cannot sleep tonight", I said, "I'm so wide awake. There is so much light from you and Jesus, but dark clouds are following us. I feel their presence." Simon asked, "Are you afraid of the dark?" I thought for a moment and said, "Not really. Not personally. But I am afraid for those that are not able to endure the darkness." Simon replied, "The world is dark. You must fear for very many beings on Earth. Your fear will be endless, which helps nobody. You must simply accompany us with your strength and vigor. That is the best you can do for us, then you help demolish boundaries between reality and unreality." I told him of my fear, saying, "Simon, I don't believe I can." "Yes you can, you will tear down many boundaries for Jesus. That is why you came to him." I pressed him further, asking, "But what should I do?" Simon smiled and said, "You don't destroy boundaries through doing, but by being. Through your presence."

This was the most wonderful conversation with Simon I had ever had. He possessed a profound wisdom. I imagined it to be like the goodness of my Father in heaven. I never heard a bad word about anyone. He was quiet. He was present without pushing himself into the foreground. I noticed that Jesus was more relaxed in his presence, as if he felt protected.

The next day Jesus said, "I would like us all to go down to the sea. It is time for us to move forward. Lazarus, could you call Peter, Andrew and the others? I would like to go fishing."

As Jesus walked through the streets, I noticed for the first time how it was when Jesus appeared in public. As soon as somebody recognized him, the people emerged from their houses and approached him, calling, "The Messiah" or "The King." Others came to him with requests or questions. The path from the house to the sea was complicated by the mass of people who blocked the way. One man said, "My mother is very ill and lies in my house. She cannot leave the house any more. Could you help her, Lord?" Jesus looked at him and said, "She has been helped. Go home to her." Later I heard that he went home to find his mother in good health, and she remained healthy for many years.

Jesus was no longer limited by space and time when performing his miracles. We who had witnessed these miracles could write books about them — about every day and about every miracle. Such things did not interest Jesus. It was easy for him just to let his life flow, without planning it. Many beings had experienced his wonders of healing, resurrection and forgiveness. For us the miracles were a daily occurrence, since the people continued to stream to him. But those of us who accompanied him to the Sea of Galilee got to know another side of Jesus. We received a lesson from him. He was a strict with us, but remained always a divine teacher.

When we arrived at the sea Jesus asked the apostles to send the people away. He had an incredible authority when he wanted to be alone; when he wished, the people acknowledged his wish and left. He created powerful vibrations around himself, to form a circle of protection.

When we were finally alone he turned to Peter and said, "Peter, would you like to go fishing again?" Peter replied, "Lord, are you jesting with me again? To let me fish unsuccessfully until you send the fish to me?" Jesus said, "No, Peter. You have become a fisherman of human souls, but you will become even greater. Your soul shall grow further. In your mastery you will mature more, so that the vision that is buried in your heart can materialize in the world." Much as I had asked Simon, Peter asked, "How can I do that, Lord?" Jesus replied, "Learn from me. Learn to believe in the impossible and to act beyond boundaries. Just follow me. Come with me on the water." In the evening twilight, Jesus approached the water and said, "Peter, walk on the water with me." Peter answered, anxiously, "It is impossible for me to do that, Lord."

Jesus turned to Peter and said, "Without belief you cannot follow me. Either you believe what I say now or you can return to your house immediately. Then you will no longer be with me." Peter was visibly shocked and said, "Lord, I will believe in you. Give me the strength to believe so unconditionally that I can do it." Jesus then walked on the water and said, "Then follow me. Come!" We could hardly believe our eyes: Peter followed Jesus and they walked together over the water, to the middle of the sea, where they stood with one another.

They returned after three hours. When they were about thirty meters from the shore, Jesus said, "At present your belief only lasts two to three hours. Now it has disappeared again."

We could not restrain our laughter as Peter sank into the water. Jesus continued calmly to the shore while Peter had to swim the remaining distance. Jesus then requested that a fire be lit. He had previously instructed Andrew and others to catch enough fish for us all, and then prepare a meal for us all.

This evening Jesus taught us the fundamental laws of belief. During this time I began to seek a nearness to Simon. As we sat by the fire I sat next to him. With him I experienced a sense of security that I found with no one else. After we had eaten, Jesus commenced teaching us the laws of belief.

Jesus gazed out to sea and began to preach. "Does any one of you believe he knows who I am? Do you believe or do you know? Look out to sea. Do you perceive nature in all its aspects, as it exists at every moment? This sea teaches us belief; I can only walk on the sea because it believes in me and I believe in it. But I am looking for the same true belief in your hearts, which stretches you beyond your customary boundaries. If you knew what it means to truly believe then you would know how I function. Belief alone can move mountains, cross boundaries that previously limited us, and lead you into everlasting light. What do you think I do when I touch someone, heal and liberate him or her? Or awaken him or her from the dead? I believe! But I do not believe in the limits prescribed by our earthly life. I trust our Father and His will so implicitly, that I am able to break through the earthly boundaries and take the souls with me — to heal or to reanimate from death.

"You must start to trust me, but first trust yourselves! You were all born with the power of God within you; it is latent in every one of you. This is a power that you will never lose and that you retain in all lives forever. Then you do not need to believe in me, but in yourselves for all time and with all of your being. Saturate your belief with your love. Bless your hope with trust. Believe unendingly and forever, until you no longer know where belief starts and finishes. Trust my Father, for He believes in you every second. The Father in heaven, with His infinite love, thinks only of you — otherwise I would not be here on Earth, otherwise I would not be on this mission."

"You have seen how Peter transcended his boundaries for a short time by trusting and following me. But in the future you must believe in yourself, Peter. Every one of you can only believe in your heart, until the end of time. Nature knows the mastery of the true belief, and thus the elements serve God's estate — how could it be otherwise? This sea shall teach you devotion, to walk in belief, without sinking. But you do not really believe. You still regard me as walking Messiah, whom you follow with each step that I take. But where is your belief in yourselves? Where have you left it behind?"

Then Jesus stood up and left us alone. The echo of his words still resonated in our hearts. I looked at Irisa and she was crying. I looked at the others and they were all shocked, particularly his disciples. But Mary Magdalene and I were not affected so much. Our eyes met and we began to know something that could not be described in words. She smiled and I smiled in return.

As the others withdrew to their various quarters, I asked Lazarus to remain with me on the seashore. I wanted to look out to sea and to learn under the stars, to learn what they could teach me about belief. Mary Magdalene remained with me too. As we looked out to sea a bond was forged between us, one that would remain between us until the end of our days, unspoken but bound in our mutual love. After a time I broke the silence and asked Mary Magdalene how she felt. She replied, "Miriam, for me so much has changed, and you know I love him above all. I am prepared to follow him with every step, to accept every sacrifice, just to be with him. I cannot think otherwise: only to follow his path, wherever it leads."

I was really touched by her words. Although I had known and followed Jesus for many years, I had not had such extreme feelings for Jesus. I had never before experienced such an unconditional love as that of Mary Magdalene. Then I said, "It is time for us to return home. We will bring you to your house." She showed us where she lived; as all of the others, she was accommodated with friends of Jesus. Then we returned home. Jesus had already retired and Simon was also absent. So I went to sleep with the wish to find the unconditional devotion, which Jesus embodied, in myself.

The next day I went, as promised, to the agreed place to wait for Salome. But she did not come. As she did not appear, I decided to go into the town. I had heard that a market was in the town, and since I wanted to purchase a few things for us. I made my way there. It turned out to be a terrible experience. As I made my purchases, the women who were standing around began to murmur, and I could hear some of what they were saying. Unashamedly, they exchanged comments, referring to me: "Look at her. That is one of the whores who accompany the so-called Messiah. He gathers prostitutes around him. Women without honor, who don't have a man of their own and live together with the men, as in a temporary marriage." I looked at these women, and had no reply. But I did not look away: I looked the women straight in the face, into their loveless eyes. My heart said, "What base and common women you are. Your hearts contain only evil thoughts. But I do not want to change your thoughts; you have to live with these vicious and shameful ideas. If you would only know how pure and loving Jesus is, then you would know how polluted your souls have become." Then I left the market, and refused to visit it again.

I returned home and told Simon, Jesus and Lazarus of my experience. Lazarus said, "Miriam, I have prophesied that this would happen. In our houses you are protected, and we live here in a way the outside world neither understands nor likes. But as you continue to follow Jesus you will encounter such attitudes frequently. The vicious glances and the evil thoughts will follow you."

I went to Jesus and said, "Lord, it is all the same to me if that is the price I pay. They can call me a whore if they wish. That did not hurt me as much as what they had said about you in the marketplace." He replied, "Miriam, these people do not know what they do. But I wish you to forgive them. That is the only way that we can change this world. Do not evaluate any of them who judge you, just love them as God loves them and as I love them." I began to cry. "Jesus that is the most beautiful lesson that I have ever received from you. I beg you, never let me deviate from this thought." He looked up and said, "Also forgive those who have chosen a gruesome destiny, such as those who killed John." Then he left the room and I heard him leave the house.

We learned later that John was killed on that day and that his head was cut off and, in a disgusting act, served at a festive meal of Herod Antipas. Shocked and disturbed by the news, I continued to go every day to the appointed place to meet Salome. We received the news that John's body was released to be buried near Nazareth, where his parents lived. Fear and disgust swept through the town. It also affected us. We were warned about what measures the head of state was capable of taking when somebody offended him. We also received news of preparations for war by Herod and his family.

Every day I visited the place where I was to meet Salome. But for a long time she did not come. As I returned home one day I overheard a conversation between Jesus and Lazarus. Lazarus said, "Jesus, it would be better if you would marry. There is already too much disquiet in the country, due to your appearances and to your presence. You know that Miriam and Mary Magdalene are both of royal blood. Should you take one of them to be your wife the people would recognize you as king in the old tradition. Then many of the difficulties due to your unconventional actions would disappear."

I was shocked by the Lazarus' words, and heard Jesus' answer: "I will not do that, Lazarus. And I would certainly not do so to become king of this country. My kingdom is not on this Earth. I know your secret wishes. I know the desires of some of my followers, who oppose the state. But I am not here to be an opponent of the state and to take over the throne. Believe me, these women are so divine to me that I would not misuse them in that vulgar way. I know I challenge boundaries and am very unconventional, but how can I overcome the evil spirits when I don't exceed their boundaries?"

I went to my room and hoped that nobody noticed me, and began to reflect on what had happened that day: the occurrence in the marketplace, how the women regard us and the suggestion from Lazarus. Suddenly I realized how much freedom we enjoyed with Jesus. How often I have seen men and women enslaved by marriage and by society's demands on them, and simultaneously their inability to live without it. In the Jewish society men were permitted freedom without marriage, whereas unmarried women were scorned and cast out from society. These women were thrown out of their families and often ended in abject poverty.

I felt myself to be protected — by my brother, by Jesus and by Simon. In their houses women were free to live in security, without having to sacrifice our freedom or our honor. I had seen how Jesus had married MaRa and Sharon. I was conscious that this was something really different. It was if Heaven had married them and not the world. I spent the day in my room, since there was a peculiar atmosphere in the house. The day after I went again to the place where Salome would meet me, and she was there. She was very disturbed and was pacing back and forth, impatiently waiting for me. I asked her what was the matter and she replied, "It is horrible, Miriam, it is so horrible. I can never return to the palace and have left it forever. I have brought a few things with me. I cannot return to that fetid pool of barbarism. You cannot imagine what my mother did to me." She covered her face again when she saw other people approaching, and I said to her, "Come with me to our house. We will take a less-frequented way. We will find a solution for you." We arrived at the house. Only Martha was there. Jesus, Simon and Lazarus had gone out.

We hid Salome in our house, and she told us her story. "A few nights ago, my mother persuaded me to dance for her guests that evening, the holy dance of the seven veils, which I had learned as a priestess with the Nazarenes. And do you know what she did? She told Herod that I was in my room and unwilling to dance unless the head of John be presented to me and served on a salver during the feast. Naturally I knew nothing of my mother's dreadful plan as I entered the room to dance. In the middle of my dance the head was brought in and I fell unconscious to the floor. The scream I let out came from deep in my soul: I could not believe that my mother and stepfather were capable of something so gruesome and disgusting. I will not return to their palace. Even more repulsive is that, to maintain their own innocence they claim that this evil act was my wish! I don't know what to do, but I will never return home."

I said, "First I will get some clothes from us for you to wear. Then you should tame your wild curly hair, which is your most recognizable characteristic: I would suggest tying it in a bun or binding it with a hair band. Also remove your most exotic jewelry, Salome. You should appear as a modest woman, and then I will ensure that nobody recognizes you. Let us now wait until Jesus returnsso that he might tell us what we should do. Perhaps we can find a place for you where you would remain undetected." When Jesus, Simon and Lazarus returned they also heard the gruesome story. Salome related how, in the previous nights, John had filled the prison and surroundings with his shouts and his words of God. The walls of the palace had even shaken with his anger. "You do not know who you have imprisoned." John had shouted, "A holy man! I am on this Earth to baptize in the name of God. I am here to persuade you to repent, and to find forgiveness for your sins. That is the only way to find redemption. But in your thoughts I only sense the evil of your preparations for my death. Believe me, my death will be your death a thousand times over."

When Jesus heard this he said, "They don't know that they have killed the holiest amongst the holy ones, and so have sealed their fates with the traces of their own blood. My friend John, who has paved the way for me, is dead. He paid the price of my advancement with his life. Now we will accord with his will, as that is the will of the Lord above." Then he bade Martha and me to collect Irisa. When our Roman friend arrived that evening, Irisa would offer Salome a position in her household so that she would remain completely undetected. Irisa would claim that she had purchased Salome in a market and that she came from a foreign land. Jesus asked Irisa also to take Magda with her, back to Jerusalem. I asked, "And what am I to do?" Jesus replied, "You stay here, with Mary Magdalene. I wish you two to remain here with me for some time. There are things for us to do."

The next morning the others left, as did MaRa and Sharon. As I bid MaRa farewell, I knew that I would not see her again in this life. She planned to go to Damascus and to see how she could spread Jesus' message throughout the world. Jesus also bid them farewell and gave Sharon a walking staff, saying, "All of your paths in life are contained in this good piece of wood. Wherever you go with this staff, knock on the ground with it before you start: it will tell you how and whether you should proceed. The prophetic truth that you have within you will reveal your lives to you both. But your mission is in

Damascus." He blessed them both and said, "I don't know whether I will see you both again. Neither your paths nor mine are yet clear. But now you must go. Go first to your house in Damascus. After all that MaRa has experienced, she will require much attention. You, Sharon, should give her the healing she needs."

Jesus went to his room and returned with a pot of holy oil for MaRa. He said, "You may anoint individuals with this oil, and free and heal them. But it will also heal you. Whenever you stroke some oil over your heart, you will find relief from your suffering. You have carried a great load, and pre pared much for me. But now you must no longer share my dark destiny. I do not want that. You have earned a life in peace."

We bade them farewell, and I could not restrain my tears. Mary Magdalene also wept as she said goodbye to MaRa. She begged MaRa to forgive her for being so wild and disrespectful when they were in the mountains. But MaRa said, "Your ferocity broke the chains that have tied us holy women down over the centuries. I am now aware of that, and I am grateful for it. You have sometimes pushed me to my limits, but on the other hand you have in your way freed me. Miriam, you have also helped me to recognize my limitations, and I thank you both from the bottom of my heart." After an affectionate and moving farewell, they departed. I was sad to see them go, but consoled in the knowledge that MaRa was in good hands and would enjoy a more pleasant life.

I could not say the same for myself and Mary Magdalene. Even though we were together with Jesus, we knew in our hearts that it would not be an easy time. The uprisings were becoming more violent and more frequent, and we understood that the public was divided into two groups: the first insisted increasingly that Jesus was the long–awaited Messiah, and that he would finally become the worldly king of the Jewish people; others viewed Jesus with envy and suspicion. With the execution of John, the King had put fear into the hearts of the inhabitants and created an atmosphere of hate and violence. Jesus decided that we must leave Tiberias and move on. As we were preparing to leave next morning, Jesus decided spontaneously that he and his male disciples — without us women — would set out for Capernaum. He requested that Lazarus take Mary Magdalene, Seraphim and me to Jerusalem with him. Simon also bade us farewell, since he wished to return to his own house. I was sorry that we should split the group, and in particular that Simon would leave us. After bidding Simon farewell we made our way to Jerusalem.

After some days we arrived. Martha made the house comfortable for us and set aside a bed for each guest. I had returned to my home after a long absence. From the day we arrived, Lazarus was away every afternoon. He never told me where he was going and what he did. So I visited Irisa now and again.

I also began a friendship with Salome. She was a playful, beautiful and clever woman, and the more she was removed the influence of her family, the better I got to know her as an affectionate, supportive and loyal friend. I also enjoyed spending time alone with Irisa. Mary also appeared and stayed for some time; at the Sea of Galilee, she had resolved to come with us. I also visited Magda now and again, although she had withdrawn from public life. One day I reminded her that she wanted to teach me her healing knowledge, which she had promised me some time ago. She answered my request by saying, "What can I teach you? In the presence of Jesus and in your time with the holy women you have learned everything that you must know for each occasion." I asked her what she meant, but she did not answer. She had indeed withdrawn into herself, as if her powers had accumulated inside her and she did not wish to discuss them.

In Jerusalem it was rumored that there was considerable unrest, and that a rebellion against the Roman occupation was being prepared. One day I returned from visiting Irisa and met Martha, completely distraught and in tears. It was some time before I could calm her down, and then she told me, "Miriam, there was an uprising. At Irisa's house you would not have heard about it. There was a massacre in a suburb of Jerusalem." She could hardly express herself. "Do you know where Lazarus is? He has disappeared. He did not return home."

As he had not returned, we left the next morning to look for him. Jerusalem was marked by the disturbances, and we were confronted with a shocking sight: many Roman soldiers were visible and obviously watching over the town. There had been many dead and injured citizens, and it was difficult to pass soldiers' checkpoints. But we explained that we were citizens of Jerusalem. We asked everywhere about my brother Lazarus. But no one could help us, until we arrived at the place where the corpses of the dead citizens were gathered. My heart stood still as I recognized the body of my brother. I did not know whether I should scream or rampage. But I pulled myself together for the moment and called Jesus from within me. Then I went to the Roman soldier and said, "This is my brother. Please let me have his corpse." Martha could hardly believe it, and I had to prevent her from collapsing. I shook her and said, "Pull yourself together. We must bring my brother away from this place. Do you know where the family grave is?" She nodded and I said, "Then we will bring him there."

Outside of Jerusalem there were caves where families laid out and watched over their dead. I did not know what I should do, so I told a completely distracted Martha, "You remain here, even though it seems intolerable. I will go to Irisa and ask her to help us. We cannot remove the body alone." I made my way to Irisa's house as fast as I could, and told her what had happened. She immediately requested some of her servants to accompany us with a stretcher, to help us bring Lazarus' body home. I don't know why, but I had the feeling I must contact Joseph of Arimathea, though I had not seen him for so long, to see if perhaps he could help me. I went to the temple and asked for him, but he was on away on business. So I returned as fast as possible to the place where Irisa's servants were preparing to bring Lazarus' body home. Martha had calmed down and told me, "The family grave, where your mother and father lie, is outside the town." We brought Lazarus there.

We wrapped him in linen strips, as was the old tradition. I don't know why, but I did not cry. On the other hand, Martha was inconsolable, and I had difficulty calming her. Although she helped me, I had to do most of the work. I prayed to Jesus, "Please come! Please come! Please come! Please do not leave me alone now." I sent him the message with every heartbeat in my breast, in thought and prayer. But Jesus did not come.

Martha and I observed Jewish custom, and remained three days and three nights by Lazarus' body. As Martha prepared to sing the traditional Jewish death dirge I covered her mouth with my hand and said, "Please do not sing that. I don't care if we are being watched and judged by others, and even if they find us cruel and unfeeling. But I cannot hear that bawling here. I want to think of Jesus and of that which I have learned from him."

On the third day we had given up hope of meeting Jesus. So I decided that we should leave the grave and return home.

Halfway home I could hardly believe my eyes: Jesus was walking towards us. I approached him, remaining very calm and said, "Jesus, Lazarus is dead." Jesus asked, "Where is his grave?" I returned and led him to it. He said, "Move that stone away." I could not move it alone, so Jesus helped us move the stone to one side. Then called into the grave, "Lazarus, get up! What are you doing there?" I could hardly believe my eyes, as Lazarus opened his eyes and, after three days in his grave, walked toward us. All his wounds had disappeared and I did not know whether I was looking at a ghost or at a new human being. He was surrounded by light.

Then he went to Jesus and embraced him. "Where have I been, my brother, my friend? Three days and three nights I was with you. What am I doing in this cave? You have brought me to Heaven and consecrated me. You have shown me the gate to Heaven that I guard. What happened?" I said, "Lazarus, you were killed in the uprising in Jerusalem. You are crazy. How could you let yourself be persuaded to do something like that?"

His resurrection had changed him. He said, "I remember now. I was so far away, as if I was on a long journey with Jesus." Jesus looked at him and said, "That is true. But when you arrived at the gate to Heaven I brought you back. The consecration that you received from me will make a new human being out of you." Lazarus said, "The war of the Zealots was wrong. It was not your wish, was it?" Jesus Replied, "No, it was not my wish. Let us now leave this place. It is not right for us to be here at the moment." Jesus accompanied us back to our house. Seraphim could not believe her eyes when she saw Lazarus. She fell on her knees before him and said, "My God, he has become a saint. You were resurrected from the dead. You have crossed the threshold and have returned to life." She fell on her knees before Jesus and wept. "Get up!" he said. "There is nothing to cry about. Here is something to celebrate."

Jesus stayed with us. We had witnessed this miracle with him, and Lazarus was his friend and brother. But I did not yet know how it happened to me. Not only had my brother returned to me, but also a new life. Jesus said, "I cannot remain long in Jerusalem. I have only come for you, Lazarus. Now I should return to Capernaum. But I believe that your face is not any more so welcome in Jerusalem. You and Miriam should leave this place and go to Simon. Leave this house. Seraphim and Martha should remain here." Then he said to Mary Magdalene, "Come with me. We are going on a journey." Mary Magdalene packed and left with Jesus. We prepared ourselves for the journey to Simon's house, and left Jerusalem behind us. Although Martha remained in the house, I was pleased to leave Jerusalem after all that we had experienced there. I had witnessed death and life there.

Before my eyes everything died and was resurrected, through the hand and blessing of Jesus. That was burned eternally in my soul.

Lazarus and I were accommodated in Simon's house. We all had room enough to relax and to recover ourselves. Lazarus had changed: a new meekness and humility had come over him and I sensed that he had become very attached to Jesus. A few days later, Lazarus expressed a desire to leave the house and to go to Jesus. I asked him, "And what should I do? Where should I go?" He replied: "You had best remain here. I cannot take you with me, since it is too dangerous for you. My face is too well known." I remained behind with mixed feelings, particularly since Simon was obliged to travel on business. So I remained alone with the servants in the house, and used the time to reflect on the recent occurrences and experiences, and to process and order my thoughts.

It was clear to me that Jesus had involved himself in a revolution. He was not concerned with the strict rules of the Jewish people. It was already rumored, particularly in Jerusalem, that Jesus did not observe the Sabbath, and that he even healed people on that day. He was a revolutionary who broke all social and political rules. He was not interested in the established standards of behavior created by society. He moved about freely without concerning himself with etiquette or the boundaries of convention — on the contrary, he even violated them openly.

I often thought of Mary Magdalene, who accompanied him, and where they were at this moment. But inside myself I knew that the revolution he had started would be liberation for all of us. Although these thoughts were strange for me, I was sure that Jesus broke the rules in order for human beings to truly and conscientiously live following their inner spiritual needs; that much I had experienced with him. Through Jesus I was able to live fulfilling the needs of my heart, my freedom, my thoughts, my feelings and my existence itself. But where would this way lead us? We all experienced reticence and even resistance to the radical way that Jesus had chosen. And it was obvious that every day there would be more opposition. Through the activities of my brother I was automatically involved, and was subject to the accusation of being an enemy of the people. Hence I was content to be in this house, where nobody outside knew or recognized me. We all joined Jesus in enjoying our spiritual freedom, but in the world outside it was different. All initiations and practices that I had experienced with the Essenes and the divine women of Ephesus were completely foreign to the life of the common people and hated by their leaders.

I was safe and secure in Simon's house. There were enough servants to make my life comfortable and to serve my needs. Then Simon returned from his journeys in foreign lands, where he had been conducting family business. It seemed peculiar being alone in the house with a strange man. Although I was accustomed to wandering from one place to another without developing roots, as I had since childhood, this was still an unusual experience for me. Our time together was spent strolling through his extensive garden, or taking meals together. We had much time to talk and learn about important issues — spiritual and worldly. Thus I was able to know new aspects of Jesus and new perspectives of his work. It was clear that Simon and Jesus came from another world, where different cultures existed.

Simon said, "Many of us, including yourself, live with the memory of these old cultures, from the time when the divine laws were universally observed. These cultures have disappeared and are only known from afar. Nevertheless we decided to return to Earth time and time again — despite the increasing strangeness with each visit. Jesus and I are not bound to this existence; we live a life bound to the culture of light and love. We only aspire to lead people back to these old values when our time comes."

Although I had not heard such things before, they found a resonance in me, and I knew that Simon was right. I began to understand that Jesus was not a revolutionary, bringing something new. He attacked the standards and authority of society when they did not serve God. I asked Simon his opinion of the Jewish people, since we were a divine people, among whom I had grown up. Simon said, "Every race of people on Earth is divine, and many scriptures bear witness to peoples who carry within themselves the sacred origin of God's word. When Jesus and I were travelling together in Asia we came into contact with many of these cultures." Then I asked him, "Why are you in Jerusalem, of all places? Why have you chosen these people at this time and place?" He reflected a moment and then replied, "Because here is the beginning and the end, which concern the whole world. Here is the cradle. Here peace was born and here peace died."

At this time I did not really know how to evaluate these words. But I recognized that Jesus and Simon were two beings who looked beyond the present. They did not live in our time, but embodied God's timeless vision. Through them we had the possibility of growing out of the present limited human existence. During the following days many ideas and impressions passed through my head, and I dreamed of past and future times. I also dreamed of war and of darkness. I dreamed of beings with whom I was somehow connected, which always fought to retain their inner light and radiance. I also dreamed of a time that would come later: a time of change, of departure and of transformation. I dreamed of fires, God's grace and glory of His light.

During my stay in Simon's house, a self-confidence and tranquillity grew within me, such as I had never previously experienced. I began to realize that until this time I had been a homeless nomad. But here I found a sense of having arrived, which was completely new to me. It was then that I gradually realized that the love between Simon and me had grown strong, and in the protected atmosphere of the house remained for the time being our secret. We were together in Simon's home for some months, and apart from occasional news of Jesus the time belonged exclusively to us. I began to look after the house and do the shopping. Nobody in Canaan seemed to notice, as they assumed I was the new servant. We were not interested in enlightening the inhabitants as to our true relationship. It was the calmest and most wonderful period in my life: I found a home in Simon's house, which provided a security previously unknown to me.

Then one day Simon said to me, "Come Miriam, we must leave now. Jesus has sent us a message that we should come to him. He is in the region of Capernaum, where we will find him without problems." I took his hand and said, "I don't know if I want to go with you. How will we show the people what we have experienced here?" He replied, "Don't worry. Just come with me." So we set out in the direction of Capernaum. It was a pleasure to travel with Simon, since he always sought accommodations where I had a room to myself — to protect my reputation! Whenever we wished to eat he found an appropriate restaurant. Hence the journey was comfortable, supported by two of his servants, who tra velled with us and always attended to our wishes. When we arrived in Capernaum, Simon found good accommodation for us. Then he went to search for Jesus.

When he returned he told me, "There is an enormous crowd around Jesus. For weeks he has been gathering them here. He prays every evening and the people come from all directions to hear him. He has invited us to come to him. Here he has found a place where he will not be treated with hostility, as he is in Jerusalem. Your brother Lazarus is here and Jesus has sent somebody to Jerusalem to inform the people who wish to come. Jesus is staying with a customs officer, Zachariah, whom I have also gotten to know. He is a nice man. But I have heard the opinion expressed that by living with a customs officer Jesus associates with the dregs of society. But that does not seem to bother him." Simon said to me, "Now you should relax. You need the rest. This evening we will go to Jesus together and meet him in Zachariah's home. He will wait for us there."

As promised, Simon collected me and took me to the house. Zachariah was a large, strong man who was very happy to see us. He invited us to join him in his evening meal, during which he told the story of how he met Jesus on the street: Jesus had approached him and asked him if he could be a guest in his house. Jesus had told all his followers to find their own accommodation, and then had stayed some weeks with Zachariah. I was surprised at the relationship between Jesus and Zachariah, and wondered if the latter knew who was living with him. They behaved as good friends, having a good time together and enjoying one another's company. So I experienced Jesus, Simon and Zachariah from a different point of view, as I had never previously experienced them. They joked and behaved as children freed from all worries. I must admit, I felt very happy in their company, and was able gradually to distance myself from the troubles of the past.

Then Jesus suddenly asked, "You know, Simon, she carries your child within her?" Simon answered, "I didn't know it with certainty, but I already sensed it." Jesus reflected and asked, "What will you do about it?" Simon replied, "Naturally, I will do what is necessary. She can stay with me." After a brief pause Jesus said, "It would be best for you to marry. Then I would know that she is well looked after with you. This will be important in the difficult times ahead of us. And I would know that her future is secure. I wish this for all women who are close to my heart. I have fewer worries about the men, who can travel freely here and in foreign countries. I have already given MaRa into a good partnership. When Miriam lives in your house as wife and partner I will be very happy. Since I see that you love one another, it will not be difficult for you both. On the other hand, Magda is an old woman, and will accompany me when I die. I have no worries on her account. For Mary Magdalene, who has accompanied and served me loyally in the previous weeks, the situation is somewhat more difficult. I love her above all and secretly am sometimes as her partner. But I cannot become her husband. God will find a way for her. Every day I feel increasingly the importance of my purpose here on Earth and am aware of what the future has in store for me.

"The child you are carrying, Miriam, is a soul which wishes to unite the worlds. Nevertheless I cannot spare you certain things that will happen, since you have chosen to follow me. You should know that the time is drawing near when I will die and rise again from death. I wish you and Simon to be with me during that time. You will not have the chance to draw back and look after your child and family in peace. The child in your womb shall accompany me, although it has not yet an earthly form. The time is drawing near when the visions and prayers that I carry in my heart, and for which we are here on Earth, begin to become reality. I must take the appropriate steps to fulfill this purpose."

"A great multitude has come to me from all directions. But I will withdraw for the next seven nights, to bring God's word to the Earth, and I would like you to accompany me. You are my dearest friends. Zachariah is also a member of our group, since we all belong to an old family. We have been together in previous lives and always find one another to be together again, and will do so in the future. In this time we have chosen a particularly difficult responsibility. But I know I can trust you to support me, just as I have supported you in the past."

As I heard what Jesus said, I was at first shocked. I had many nights dreamed of his departure and rebirth. I was also sure that he would choose a worldly death, and that we were prepared for something that would go beyond normal bodily death. Suddenly my dreams and visions were unified within me. I had known for some days that I carried a child in my womb and sensed the powerful light under my heart. I looked at Simon and I was convinced that I would be well protected and was safe with him. I was happy that I would see Mary Magdalene again, and I was not surprised when Jesus admitted that she was his lover. Otherwise nobody had suspected anything, not even his disciples or close friends: it was their secret story. Her heart had found a difficult partner for her, but I was delighted that she had Jesus' love, since that is what she had always longed for.

That evening we met at the foot of a hill. We did not need directions, since a great mass of people were going there. The crowd was enormous. Jesus had not yet appeared, but I detected Irisa in the crowd, and Simon and I made our way to the group. We met our friends from Jerusalem again. We all rejoiced at the reunion. Mary arrived with Joseph of Arimathea, who brought a friend I had already met, named Nicodemus. I was also very happy to see all the disciples again and greeted them all. They had grown big and strong, and were like pillars at his side. Peter greeted me particularly heartily. It was clearly evident that Jesus had schooled them regarding their responsibilities and they all had grown in stature. Everyone could see why he had chosen them. Simon greeted them with great respect, and it was noticeable that the respect was reciprocated.

Jesus had asked his disciples to bring bread and other provisions to feed the mass of people, but the crowd grew and grew! Then one of the disciples came to Jesus and said,

"We have not enough bread for all." But Jesus only laughed and said, "Distribute the bread" — which they did. The wonder was that the supply of bread continued, as if a perpetual source existed — as if the loaves were constantly replaced as they were distributed. All present could experience this wonder. Everybody was fed without the food supply coming to an end. Jesus was very relaxed when he appeared and greeted his friends from Jerusalem cordially. I sat next to Irisa, since I was very happy to see her again. Salome and Seraphim were also there, and I felt as if I was in a large family.

Irisa only looked at me with her warm eyes, without saying anything. Intuitively she recognized my pregnancy and made no comment, but only smiled and asked, "Are you happy?" I nodded and said, "Everything is in order. And how have you been?" She replied, "We have had good times since you left us. It is clear to all of us that we are preparing our–selves for something important. When the news came that Jesus had called us to him again, we were very happy and left home immediately. I believe something very special is going to happen. Look how many people are here, and how many are touched by him only through his presence. Nobody else could do that. I am beginning to appreciate the value of the gift we received, to get to know Jesus so well. Now that the masses stream into his presence, it is gradually becoming clear to me."

As it began to get dark, Jesus had the oil lamps lit so that the night sky was brightened. We were somewhat disturbed by the presence of Roman soldiers, who had evidently received the command to observe the proceedings. They were watchful and disciplined, but remained some distance away from us.

Nevertheless, their weapons and their readiness to intervene were clearly evident, should it be necessary.

Jesus was incredibly calm and radiated a wonderful goodness and love. He spoke to people and went to his disciples. Now that they were grown into true disciples, with their love and understanding they were also able to answer the questions and to advise and help people who came to them.

As it grew later Jesus mounted to the top of the hill, so that everyone could see him. He asked us to come and sit with him. At this moment the Roman soldiers advanced towards us and tried to block our paths to Jesus. They asked, "What's going on here?" A captain approached Jesus and asked, "What are you doing?" Jesus looked at him and said, "Your master has ordered you what you have to do. My master has commanded me to do what he wants. Let us both do what our masters command." The captain replied, "My master has sent me here to watch the proceedings and to intervene if there are disturbances of any sort." Jesus said sympathetically, "I promise you that there will be no disturbances here."

"But don't you recognize why you are here? You are indeed a Roman, but nevertheless one of our number. Don't you also seek my message and don't you follow my call?" The Roman soldiers below had not heard the last words, so the Captain went to them and instructed them to withdraw to the edge of the crowd. He returned and told Jesus, "I have ordered the legionnaires to observe the crowd, and only to intervene when I give the command, in the event of disturbances. But my heart wishes me to remain here, so that I can hear your words. Would you permit me to remain here, Master?"

Jesus looked at him and answered, "That is why you are here. I am grateful to you that your soldiers will watch over us, to enable me to preach the word of God in peace." I witnessed the conversation, and I was fascinated to observe how Jesus managed to reverse the situation to fulfill his wishes. The Romans were no longer our lurking enemies, but had become the guardians of our security. He had converted our enemies to being our friendly protectors.

Jesus climbed to the peak of the hill and we accompanied him, remaining under one of the olive trees on the hill close to him. We were privileged to be so near to him, and to hear every word. There was much jostling, as everyone tried to find a good place to hear Jesus; his disciples made sure that that everyone found a place where they could hear him. Every age group was present, young and old, including families with children. All present waited patiently to hear what Jesus had to say. Nevertheless, it was some time before the crowd was quiet.

Finally Jesus spoke. "Citizens of Israel, I thank you, that your hearts have followed my call to come here today. Some of you have come a long way, and the voice of your hearts,will be rewarded. Heaven has sent the most sacred messages, which I pass on to you now. Every one of you is searching for the way of life. I have come here to explain, to illuminate and to prepare the way for you. Every one of you is welcome here, whether friend or enemy. You should all recognize your neighbors here as friends. There is no place for enmity or jealousy here. We are here to ring in a new culture in the spirit of love, which unifies all people and all races the world over. I am aware of the news that has spread through the country — that you hope that the king of the new Jews stands before you, who will permit you to rise up and correct injustice and poverty. But I have to tell you: I am not here to rule, as a king in this world. I am here to preach the justice of heaven.

"I am here to bring you salvation. God will convey to you the precise words of your deliverance, which you will receive through me here tonight. Every one of you is blessed. Every one of you who has heard the voice of compassion will never again be forgotten, and in the future will find life in eternity, will never die but always be re–born. I address you all, people of Israel, people from foreign lands. Look at those who surround and support me. They have long accompanied me and have heard the word of God. But every one of you sitting here has discovered the voice of God. The circle of followers at present surrounding me have heard the voice of the Lord for some time, and will come to you. Then they will depart in all directions to carry my message to those who are waiting all over the world.

"I see many among you who carry the access to God's world within them. This evening they will meet each other, and will be one hundred and eight in number. They will support and accompany me and all who care for the Earth, who care for humanity and who will spread the word of God. Tonight you will listen to me, but in the future they will guide you and show you the way. They have also learned the divine truth. I would ask every one of my hundred and eight supporters to stand up, so that people can recognize you as the emissaries of God's word. You are the guardians of the gates between Heaven and Earth, so hear my words and recognize one another in your hearts. Your hearts open and you create a ring of love and compassion around me, because I am the embodiment of the Light of Christ, the embodiment of all love in all worlds. I am here to light the Earth with my love, to save and to heal the world. I am here to lead you, so I ask you to stand up and be recognized."

Throughout the crowd, from the front to the very back, men and women suddenly stood up as if hypnotized, and the crowd regarded them. Slowly but surely, one after the other, they got to their feet and stood proudly there. The atmosphere was magical.

"Guardians of the Lord, my Hundred-and-Eight, every one of you has heard my call, nobody is missing. I bid you to come forward to me. People of Israel, do not be envious. Then when one of the Hundred-and-Eight will ascend, so too will you. And when they are active the Earth will be saved. Now they shall come to me!" Jesus asked the crowd to make way for the Hundred-and-Eight, so everyone who had stood up and answered Jesus' call now found a way through the crowd to him. Then Jesus looked at Simon and asked him, "Have you recognized them all?" Simon replied, "Yes I recognize them all." Jesus said, "Then from now on you are their guardian. The Hundred-and-Eight who guard the highest gates between Heaven and Earth, I have called them here to form a supporting ring around me that maintains the Light of Christ. I give them into your hands, to lead and guide until their work is completed."

Then Jesus resumed speaking. "Citizens of Israel, the Holy Spirit is present here. Father, Son and Holy Spirit shall unite in these nights, and will appear to each and every one of you. Father, Son and Holy Spirit shall establish the Holy Trinity on Earth again. The Holy Spirit is among us, embodied in the name of my friend. His voice and his name may not be known to you, but you should know that he who embodies the Holy Spirit is here tonight. His fire will combine with my fire, so that the Holy Spirit and the Light of Christ join together in heavenly harmony. The divine unity has not been evident on Earth for a long time; war and enmity have the divided and repressed the people of this Earth. Tonight the Holy Trinity shall unite the people and open the gates to new hope on Earth." Then Jesus turned to Simon and said, "Simon, I know that you do not wish stand up and be recognized by the people. But I bid you: fetch the flames of the divine fire from heaven, and let them descend on to the Hundred–and–Eight, so that all can see them." Then the wonder occurred: one hundred and eight flames sank down on each of the chosen ones, so that each of them was bathed in holy light.

Jesus said, "People of Israel, people of the world, you have seen the flames of unity over each head of my supporters. That is the first sign of the holy nights. You should follow these flames and recognize them; they light the way between Heaven and Earth to God's realm. You have witnessed the miracle of this holy night. For all who have found their way to me tonight I say, the inheritance of the appointed holy ones is available to you all. Accept the holy inheritance. I say unto you, observe the wonder but do not cling to it. Tonight you have been nourished, and you have been permitted to see the Holy Spirit among the initiated. Return to your homes and to your beds. Tomorrow we will meet again and you will witness the next miracle from God's throne. Take the message of conciliation and love from this night into your everyday lives. Find reconciliation with the war in yourselves: that is the beginning and end of your destinies. To the Hundred–and–Eight, I ask you to remain a while with me."

Jesus waited until the crowd had dissolved and only his chosen ones remained, along with a few of his intimate friends and associates — including ourselves. It was really wonderful how Jesus had called and a hundred and eight souls had found a piece of God's realm within them. It was clearly visible in their eyes. Jesus said, "Not everything that you bring here is good. You are guardians of Heaven and have also created hell. Hence I bid you all, stay with me here tonight and seek no other place to sleep. Then the hell that lives in your souls can find salvation. This is God's first message of your liberation." I saw the scared look in many eyes. One woman, whom I had previously seen in Canaan, stood up, went to Jesus and knelt before him, saying, "Lord, I have experienced Heaven and hell. But when your message is true, that we belong to your circle, please show us how we can find salvation. When we are chosen to bring peace to the sufferers of hell, please show us the way."

Jesus replied, "For that you have to go through fire. These ways are not unknown to you. But today is somewhat premature. The message of salvation from God's heavenly throne shall extend over six nights before it finally reveals itself on Earth." Jesus laid his hand on the woman's head and said, "You have my blessing. You belong to the circle around me who will spread the word. I will free the flames which every one of you has experienced in seven days, so that you will always carry them above you to announce the news of the coming salvation.

"Now you should all find a place to sleep on the hill; this place will signal your salvation. Lazarus and Thomas will also stay here, since they also belong to the circle."

Then Jesus joined us and sat down and remained with us for a while. Suddenly he said, "The days will be light, but the nights will be dark. Be not afraid, my companions, for I am in your presence. Bear the darkness of night with me and fill the days with light." Then Jesus withdrew, alone, and slept. Only Mary Magdalene stayed and watched over him, while Zachariah acted as his bodyguard.

During these nights, the servant from Simon's household also took care that nobody approached Jesus while his disciples took up protective positions around him some distance away. Seraphim had also decided to remain nearby in these nights, and to spread her protective wings between Heaven and Earth. Nevertheless, we decided to return to our accommodations, and as I gazed into the star-filled heavens I sensed the light of the child under my heart. Simon put his arm around me and accompanied me to the house where we were staying. He said, "You should not worry. I am looking after you and protecting you. The darkness of night cannot harm you." Then he withdrew, and I sensed that he had resolved to return to the Messiah and to immerse himself in the darkness with him. Simon sought an appropriate place to which he could withdraw for the night.

On the following morning Simon collected me. He was very attentive and said, "Come with me, we have an invitation to Zachariah's house. Jesus is waiting for us." On the way we met Magda, whom I had missed during the last weeks. I was surprised and asked her, "Where have you been so long?" She replied, "Miriam, actually I wanted to remain in Jerusalem, but the Lord had called me. My soul sensed that he will bring the reconciliation I seek. That is why I left Jerusalem, although I originally did not want to come." I asked her, "Where are you staying?" She replied, "I have only just arrived, so I have not arranged anything yet." She was already an elderly woman, so I looked at Simon and asked, "She could stay with me, couldn't she?" He nodded and I said, "We are going to Jesus. Would you like to come with us?" Her eyes lit up and she said, "I would like nothing better. I have missed the Lord; I have not seen him for so long."

We walked to Zachariah's house together. Jesus was already there. The house was a small but very inviting and we remained for several hours. Jesus conversed for some time with Magda and I took the opportunity to speak to the other women, including Mary Magdalene. Jesus had bound us all together in a bond of friendship, so we knew that we could love and trust each other. Mary Magdalene was happy and sad simultaneously, and I did not say anything, since I sensed that her love for Jesus was a wonderful prize but on the other hand a great burden to her. She would never get what every woman wants for herself. Nevertheless, she was unconditionally devoted to him. You could see that in her eyes.

I excused myself and retired to my room, since I knew that it would be a long evening. Magda accompanied me to my room, and I requested a second bed be installed in my room for her. Then I said, "You can stay here, dear friend." She was not as convivial as in earlier times, and I sensed that age was becoming a burden to her. But light still radiated from her divine qualities. We decided to rest for a time. When we had recovered, Simon collected us and accompanied us to the meeting point, where thousands of citizens were assembled. We climbed to the top of the hill to find the place where we were on the previous day. I sat next to Simon, and everybody else was there. Only Jesus had not yet appeared.

Jesus arrived in the evening and blessed all present. I observed everything from afar. Then he spoke to his disciples and let food be distributed. There was enough for everyone. We hoped that the miracle of the previous day would be repeated. I was not hungry, and I sensed that my body was slowly getting used to the fact that another being lived within me and also needed space. Jesus spoke to the Roman captain who came over to u, and provided us with protection as he had on the previous evening.

As darkness fell and the stars slowly became visible, Jesus let the lamps be lighted. He sat so that everyone could hear him. Jesus said, "Through your and my devotion and love, you will this evening witness the establishment of the law of reconciliation. I am on this Earth to bring deliverance. You who are listening record my words in your hearts. Here is the law of God's glory, imprinted on the hearts of each and every one of you who is blessed. Here I will proclaim the law of innocence, which will purify your souls." He requested that his male disciples mingle with the crowd and baptize everyone who wished it. Then Jesus came to us and said, "Mary Magdalene, Magda and Miriam, you should also baptize the people. Prepare them with the baptism in water." We spent several hours baptizing all who came to us, each one with the Holy Spirit. We washed their souls clean.

When this was finished Jesus stood up and said, "The cleanliness of you souls is the ecstasy of your hearts. Blessed are those whose hearts are as innocent as the children. Blessed are they who no longer raise the sword. Blessed are they who hear God's word. Blessed are they who carry the purity of heart into their lives. Become as the children! Do not demand the fruits of the Earth; only those who are pure can enter into my Father's kingdom. For each of you who wishes it, there is a place prepared in heaven. In the future you should embed this law within you, and cast out thoughts of revenge for injuries suffered. Rise up and love your enemies. When an adversary declares war, meet him with love and peace. When your neighbor is your enemy, forgive him.

"When one strikes you on your left cheek, turn the right cheek for him to strike. Do not resist an attack; who has war in his heart brings destruction to the worlds. Whosoever is killed by human hands should forgive the perpetrator. Who suffers injury should forgive. Only in this way can the perpetual circle of revenge be broken. Conquer the hostility in your heart. Start no new wars in your thoughts and feelings. Practice the law of forgiveness. Only thus can you break the bonds of your earthly inheritance. Let love rule every day of your lives. Vanquish those who do not love with your charity. Love your enemy as you love your dearest friend. Love those who you have never loved before. That is the law of heaven.

"Those who have heard me should pass on my message to the world by forgiving. Follow the path of prayer. Pray and thus find the path to our Father in your home. Moses came to give you the Ten Commandments. But I came to give you again the Lord's Commandment of forgiveness. The great wars can only be won by those that offer no resistance. Nevertheless, you should all be soldiers: soldiers of light and justice. You should not die in poverty, you should not die in melancholy and you should not die in suffering. With head held high at the moment of death you should recognize and fix your eyes on the face of God. The Lord has given each and every one of you on Earth the right of self-determination. Break your own will by praying in your hearts over and over again: 'Lord, Your will be done on Earth as it is in heaven.'"

Jesus then knelt and began praying before the multitude: "Lord and Father in heaven. Hallowed be Thy name. Born out of love and enveloped in that love, You reign throughout eternity. You are the beginning and the end. You are our birth and our death. Lord in heaven, forgive us our sins and forgive those who have sinned against us. Lead us to redemption, not by seeking revenge, but by donating forgiveness. Let us know that we are children of Thy kingdom. Forgive us every moment when we forget You. For Yours is the kingdom, the love, the power and the glory. You carry the name of eternity, which You have imprinted in our hearts and in our souls. Raise us up so that we can see Your face. Lead us into the light, from the finite into the infinite. Let love be the law of our lives, so that peace and joy reign. Father in heaven, let we the children of the Earth be the messengers of Your glory and Your name. For You are the birth of our souls, and so we can see Your eternal light, Your peace and your glory, forever and ever. Amen."

When Jesus had finished speaking these words, it was clear that he had prayed for the redemption of us all on the Earth. Nobody, neither his disciples, nor we, nor anyone else had recorded these words in writing, but we did not need to.

From this moment every word was written in our hearts. From that time onwards we prayed in his words, as if we had always known them.

Then Jesus stood up, raised his hands to Heaven and said, "Your will be done, Lord. As in Heaven so on Earth. Give us this day our daily bread. Let us bless the food of the Earth. We proclaim our arrival on Earth as a gift of Your benevolence, that all beings find their way and their purpose, blessed and happy." Then he turned to the people. "People if Israel. You have now regained the purity of your souls, to each of you who has heard my words today. Your souls have been cleansed of all guilt. Go out and teach the law of forgiveness."

Next he turned to his disciples and said, "You should also proclaim the law of the eternal light." Then Jesus withdrew, and his disciples requested that all gathered there return home. We also left the hill. I took Magda back to my room. Shortly before she went to sleep she said, "The child you carry under your heart radiates light into the whole room. You carry a wonderful gift for the Earth. This room is filled with God's grace. This child surrounds us with its light, and enables me to find peace again." With these words she slept, as did I.

Simon picked me up next day and we went for a walk together. We did not speak very much, but I felt the unity of our souls, between him, me and the child. I was also increasingly conscious of the presence emitted from the child. I asked, "Do we meet Jesus again?" Simon replied, "I will climb the hill to see if he is there. You can follow me later, if you wish." As I arrived at the top of the hill I found Martha and we sat together with Mary Magdalene and Irisa. A few minute later, Jesus and Simon arrived together.

Jesus approached me and said, "Before the evening begins you and Simon should come with me. And you too Mary Magdalene." We all withdrew together under the shade of a large fig tree. Then Jesus raised his hands to Heaven and water flowed out of them and onto my abdomen in which the child lay. He said, "This child carries the purity of the world in it, and I baptize it in my name."

Then he looked at Simon and me and said, "When these days are over you should return to Canaan. And when it is your intention, you should celebrate you marriage there." Then he turned to Mary Magdalene and kissed her on the fore-head, saying, "Do not be sad, my Mary Magdalene. Happiness from other worlds awaits you. The house of Simon and Miri-am will always be your home, just as it is my home. When these days are over I will remain here with my disciples for a time, since I still have things to do. Mary Magdalene, you should go with Simon and Miriam, to their house in Canaan. Wait for me there."

I looked at Jesus and asked, "Who is this child of mine?" Jesus replied, "I cannot yet tell you his name. But I will disclose it at the appropriate time. But I already know something which I can see in this child: it is a child of revelation, as I have prophesied." With the sense of light and lightness in my womb, we returned to where the others were sitting. I tried to hide my thoughts, since I wanted to keep them to myself. Mary Magdalene sat next to me and was most touching and considerate, and held my hand. As we sat there, more and more people arrived and gathered at the foot of the hill. Jesus descended to the crowd, mixed with the multitude and spoke to individuals. He distributed bread, water and wine to the people, and attended to them. His love was ever–present, and flowed to them all. His love enveloped all of us.

Then Jesus left for a short time and returned with the Roman captain. Twilight had not yet fallen. The disciples were gathered around a fire, away from us, and Jesus and the captain went over to them. They spoke together for a while, and Jesus appeared to be giving them instructions. I observed the starry heavens as darkness approached. I was amazed to see stars moving together and melting together in one light, within which were pictures I had never previously seen. The heavens covered the whole region in a dome of light, with a very bright star in the zenith. This star was greater than all the others. I had never seen a star of such brilliance. During this time the disciples were providing the populace with food and drink.

Jesus had left the hill. As I ceased admiring the miracle in the heavens, I became more aware of the Roman captain. He was watching his soldiers attentively, who were posted outside the crowd. Nothing escaped his observation. He had the gift of leadership through his presence alone. I had not previously seen this quality in Roman soldiers. The captain radiated a light that structured his company and sent the message of his authority to every individual soldier. On the other hand the soldiers were dull gray beings with red in their auras. When I was with the Essenes I learned that this had no connection to the red from the rainbow light–presence of human beings in their primeval behavior. The captain was different, and had understood why Jesus had selected him. Jesus was fulfilling his appointments on Earth, which were often arranged in Heaven long ago. The captain seemed to belong to them.

Jesus was not visible and Mary Magdalene sat apart from us. In his absence something singular happened to those who were waiting for him, and it became increasingly noticeable the longer they waited for the Messiah: the light quality of those who sat on the hill changed. I knew within me that Jesus was working with those who were gathered around him.

I could also see the light surrounding them, and was even more impressed than by the miracle of the heavens. The people around Jesus radiated more strongly than the stars, each as his or her own universe, with colors such as I had never seen on Earth before. The light of the disciples was clearly visible in the crowd at the foot of the hill, and radiated into those surrounding them. The light surrounding the Roman captain reflected the stars.

Jesus probably saw this display every day from us, since that we are creations that move the worlds of stars. The light on the top of the hill blended increasingly with that of the stars until they appeared to become one. The human form was no longer discernable and just a continuum of light remianed. After a while the light slowly faded and the individually were distinguishable again. I sensed the communication between Jesus and Simon, who was sitting next to me. Jesus then appeared at the top of the hill and approached us smiling, in quiet agreement with our feelings. He was happy that we had perceived the invisible — for a short moment in time, the unity of all beings in this chaotic world of ours.

Jesus chose a place to sit between us and the crowd, alone, as if he wanted no one near him. He was completely still, with his hands around his knees and fully conscious of the crowd. It was completely quiet, and we all waited. Everyone in the crowd had the impression that Jesus was in contact only with him or her, although there were thousands present. Then he stood up and went down the hill and through the crowd, which parted to make way for him. Nobody dared to touch him. Jesus stopped in front of a soldier and led him through the crowd to the top of the hill. The captain became increasingly observant, and watched Jesus and the soldier attentively. The astonished soldier sought the eyes of the captain, who nodded assent. The captain was at first somewhat irritated, since it was unusual to request a Roman to stand amongst Jews. Jesus then sat down and, although he spoke quietly his voice was audible even at the back of the crowd.

He said, "Who of you can believe that God's kingdom is near, when he or she cannot accept that neighbors, who live in the same country, cannot be regarded as brothers and sisters? The arrogance in such hearts fills them with hate. The Jews consider themselves to be God's chosen people and the Romans believe that they can rule the world by force of arms. Although you are neighbors you hate each other. But I say unto you: every being on this Earth was born of God's creation. No being is born from nothing. But the Earth suffers the fate of forgetfulness and the karma of rebirth. Believe me, you people of Israel, believe me, you Romans: if you are Jew or Roman in this life, the roles could be reversed in your next life. Open your eyes and look into your hearts. Today you are Jews, in the next life you could be Roman warriors, just as deadly and vengeful. How can you believe that you are really

God's love, when you condemn him who kills you? Or when your neighbor is your enemy? I say unto you, in order to propagate love in the world you must love him who offends as you love yourself.

"In particular you should love your enemies; they are your key to the kingdom of heaven. It is easy to love someone who has an easy destiny or enjoys your friendship. But to love those who banish you into exile, enslave you or kill you is to pass through the eye of the needle to God's love. Whatever you sow, you will reap. Sow good and you will harvest good; sow evil and you will harvest evil. This is the foolishness of the world that has lost the aspect of God's creation. The farmer who prepares his field and only cares for the seed that he sows does not recognize the creation in all its aspects — the sun, the rain and the wind, which are God's gifts to the farmer's seeds, his ears of corn and his bread.

"Extend your horizons; recognize the sun and the divine principle which lights your path. When you walk stooped over, with your eyes on the ground, you will never recognize the divine wonders of daily life. You should be like the birds: they neither sow nor harvest, but the Father in Heaven looks after them every day. Look to the heavens, where the Father gives life and shares it with you. Do not look down so much, at the dusty sand. Observe whence life's nourishment comes. Then the Father lets the sun shine, lets the wind blow and lets the clouds send rain. When you look up you will see that the Lord looks after you every day. Look only at the Earth and at the earthly life, then that is the dust and the heaviness that you carry to your death. Look up to the Father himself, and you are raised to heaven.

"You will recognize the fundamental quality of God's love in the eyes of every being you meet. Recognize that every being on Earth is only doing his job — whether Jew, Roman or any other nationality on this Earth. A soldier, who has the assignment to be a soldier, must be a soldier. But why should you despise him for that? A farmer must be a farmer and a king must be a king. But when you scorn him for his profession you attract bad energy and it corrupts your souls. I say unto you: go through life without prejudice. Go out and love, and renounce your own wishes. Forbid all prejudice in your heart. Then prejudice goes with you at death, and will reappear in your next life. The judgement of your forbears is still contained in your inheritance and burdens the Earth. Every being, every creation of the Lord and every human can any moment decide that he is free to love so that God may recognize him. Accept your enemy as your friend. Accept your destinies. But in particular, love those on the Earth who can do nothing on Earth but persecute, kill and disinherit. But believe me, you will take this love with you after death and into the next life, so that the Earth inherits this love too." Then Jesus stood up and indicated that the soldier should go to his captain.

Jesus then turned to his disciples, who were nearby, and waiting for their next instructions. He let them bring water to him and then said, "Take the jugs of water and come with me." They went through the crowd, and repeatedly sprayed the water into the rows of people, repeating the sentence, "God in heaven, release them from the inheritance of Atlantis with your love." Then he said to the crowd: "You can all go home. You are all liberated from something from which you could never have freed yourselves alone."

As Jesus walked up the hill to us, I sensed how exhausted he was and as the crowd dispersed I saw even more clearly how lonely he was. His body seemed to carry a heavy load. When he arrived he said, "How could they have forgotten how heaven's laws and the seal of creation were in accord with one another?" As he spoke, a thousand rolls of thunder and flashes of lightning displayed God's anger. Surprisingly no one was hit by lightning, but the crowd dispersed rapidly, fearful of being struck down.

Then Jesus spoke again. "The anger of the worlds, between all heavens and all Earths, the anger between the gods, angels and the enlightened masters and mistresses cannot be soothed. There is no way for me to avoid being the sacrifice, in order that this primeval anger — which has divided the worlds and divided Heaven and Earth — can be mollified, finally, to redeem you all."

Then he looked at us and said, "Many of you are greater than you believe, but you have also left God's kingdom in some way, even when you follow and serve me with each step I take. Great rulers and gods sit here, who were amongst the most powerful in God's heaven. But your freedom has created great anger between the worlds. The fact that you are willing to follow my footsteps is positive, as the first sign in Heaven that you are willing to soothe the anger that you have caused.

"All of you who follow me were not found and chosen because your beings have attracted my attention, but because your souls cried out for the seed of love that they found in me. I have not come to erase the adverse traces of the simple people, since they are only fellow travellers, following some leader.

"I am here for you, as your sacrifice, so that you can finally recognize and serve the highest aims in humility, which are God's laws. But believe me; the anger that you see in Heaven is neither from me nor from my Father. It is the anger from primeval times, caused by enmities and wars between the rulers of the worlds and those who carry the light.

"The Earth is only a small stage in a greater theatre. I can liberate those below from the seal and the karma of Atlantis, but I cannot do it for you. You must break this seal yourselves, by returning to the path of your own spiritual authority and recognizing God deep inside yourselves. Only then can you overcome that which you have withheld from God."

Mary Magdalene, Irisa and I stood up simultaneously and Jesus beckoned us to him. Jesus' words had moved and shocked us deeply. Mary Magdalene knelt before him and asked, "Lord, how can we take this path? Tell us how we can liberate the world." He looked at her and replied, "Go and serve. Be willing to die, be willing to live, but serve the Earth with every fiber in your body and serve the knowledge of your heart."

Then Irisa asked, "Lord, give me the strength, that I can make my contribution to the redemption between Heaven and Earth." Jesus replied, "Love and heal. Serve by bowing in obeisance to every being and healing him or her."

Then I asked him, "Jesus, what can I do to redeem that which you require, and to follow you?" He replied, "You must return to an ancient land as a sign that the countries that were previously ruled by great kings in the name of God can rise up and return to their ancient glory. Go into that ancient land that still carries your tracks as pioneer, in advance of others who will follow later. Many lands have died, and the traces of their light are buried under the earth. They are trapped in darkness. Believe me; that only happened because you left your place. You preferred to withdraw into your own personal heaven. But nobody will find redemption when he is unwilling to return to his own kingdom and serve God in his own domain." Jesus looked at me more profoundly and meaningfully than ever before. His words shook my world.

That night we all wanted to sleep on the hill. Mary Magdalene, Irisa and I had clear visions of our respective ways, resulting from Jesus' prophesies. I was submerged in waves of dreams concerning the past and future of humanity. I dreamed of primeval times and of lines of light under the ground, which combined in a divine matrix, upon which the human beings used to wander. I also dreamed of the change from how the world once was — a sphere of light, impregnated by love. On the network of these light–lines, I saw God's dominion, borne in the hearts of great rulers who reigned over the Earth. I also saw that many had left their appointed places on Earth; some went to Heaven and others remained, while darkness covered the lines of light — which were eventually extinguished. As the times of darkness approached, those who were aware of the connection between Heaven and Earth had disappeared, to protect themselves. Those who had trusted their support and guidance were left behind, helpless.

At daybreak Jesus awakened us. I looked for Simon and saw him meditating, undisturbed by all that was happening around him. The Roman captain was also still there. I had the feeling that my dreams of the previous night had brought hope for the future. Jesus had lit a fire and begged us all to sit by it. He stoked the fire and looked intently into the flames.

Gradually he approached the fire even more closely, and said, "We have not much more time, since I have decided to be the sacrifice of this age. I do this out of my own free will. I sacrifice myself for the destiny of the Earth. I know you all from primeval times. We were previously happy with the dominion of God. Since then the peoples of the world have grown apart. There were times when the divine inheritance was single and indivisible. Since then this inheritance has been divided into a multiplicity with many names. But believe me, beginning and end have only one name. Each of you can only recognize himself through love. If you and I did not possess this love we would be unable to follow this path on Earth.

"As it is, the Earth will not make it easy for us: the darkness that has come between God and humanity hinders us. You know that each one of you takes a predestined route. You must start to dig the earth with your own hands, to reach the buried light. Your knees will be sore with all that praying and your hands will be torn and bleeding from all that you will dig out of the earth. Your hearts will be so tormented by the persecution and humiliation that you must tolerate in the name of God. But I beg you not to give up. I will not give up either.

"Step by step we must do away with the separation between God and the Earth, between Heaven and humanity. That I will do with my love, with my own hands and my own body, in order that the invisible gates are opened for everyone. To restore hope of returning home to those who have gone astray, and to make prayers available to those who have forgotten how to reach God through the language of the heart. That is your mission, which you should fulfill with every breath that you take, at every moment on this Earth. When you leave here — and none of you will remain in this place — you will be refugees in my name. And my name will be sought in all worlds. Nevertheless, I beg you to go out and spread the news of the love that I have imprinted in your hearts. Even when I shall no longer be near, I will always be with you and protect you.

"Truly, I say unto you Mary Magdalene, my old friend Joseph, Miriam and the rest of you, when I am no longer here you shall leave this land and be the ambassadors of a new light. Do you see the sun rising? Just as the sun rises you shall proclaim the new era of God's kingdom. But just as the sun travels through the shadows of darkness before it sheds its light and warmth above the horizon, so shall you make your ways through the darkness into the light. Here in my presence and in Simon's presence you can recognize momentarily the light from ancient times. But what use is the light if it is trapped in Heaven and loses its brilliance? The light has only arrived when it is anchored in the Earth, when those that rule, those that love and those that serve have access to it.

"Take this message with you. I am not here to rule. I am not here to conquer. I am not here to redeem you or the Earth. You must all return to the places where light is sealed under the earth, where it can be released through the sweat of your brows, to be resurrected on Earth. Each one of you has long ago agreed with God on your destinies."

That morning he went to each one of us and named a place, countryside and a country, of which some of us had never heard. He gave the names to every one of us — his disciples, and all of us who were present. Even the Roman captain had a place named. We now knew that we would soon leave and distribute ourselves over the Earth. Jesus already knew some of these places, and explained that some were so far away, that the distance was many times the extent of Israel. He also named a place for everyone, where a "seal of light" could be perceived and resurrected through the spiritual qualities of each one of us.

Jesus was then silent for some minutes, after which he said, "From this day onward, the path will be long and difficult. What you do to break the seals in this life, in the name of God, will enable you to be resurrected in the eternal light. What you achieve will prepare the way for others that they too can find their place in God's kingdom. Believe me; a time will come in many hundreds of years, when my words will break the seal of the trapped light. You call me Christ now, but in those later times my being will exist in the hearts of every human being. Then Christ means nothing else than unity of the love of the Father and the Son. But all beings are the sons and daughters of the Father in heaven.

"You cannot know how much God wishes you to return to His kingdom. Then the Father knows every child of His who has left His presence and got lost. The Father weeps for every one of you, every one of his children, who have left him — enough tears to create an infinite ocean. This ocean creates the love in which we will all find ourselves again in God's image. Believe me; no being can find redemption on the surface of this Earth of clay, sand and fire, without recognizing himself in the cosmos of creation. Only he who recognizes himself on Earth can recognize himself in heaven." Then he stood up and left us. We returned to our houses and slept, a sleep that wrapped us in silence.

During the day Magda looked after me. She prepared herbs for me, and when she returned she said, "These will help you against nausea." Her healing capabilities worked wonders for me, and I was very grateful to her. My body needed the tranquillity. In the evening Simon picked us up. He was in a very good mood, and we made our way through the crowds until we reached the place on the hill where we had sat previously. Jesus was already there and was obviously pleased to see us. More and more people were arriving so that we were increasingly engaged in finding places for them and speaking to them when they had questions or problems. I also resolved to help, since the numbers were so large. It was sometimes quite touching; some of the crowd were really moved, and attempted to hold our hands or even kiss them. For the first time I was aware that also the followers of Jesus, like us, were revered, and even worshipped. As every evening, Jesus let bread be distributed to everybody, and I began to understand the significance of his feeding the people. This evening it seemed as if it would never end.

Then Jesus stood up and we quickly sought a place near to him — which was our privilege. I sat next to Simon and leaned against him. Tiredness spread through my body. Then Jesus began to speak. "You know that my love is always with you. This love will never leave any of you who hear me tonight. Even when others deny me and spread false messages on Earth in my name, my love will remain with you until the end of time. My love is as great as that of the Father, whose son I am. It is His will that I am here on Earth. Believe me; it was your prayers that called for God's intervention, the plea of those who live in slavery on Earth, and not in freedom, as He wishes. God has shown you His mercy, which is the reason that I am here, to return your place on Earth to you. Tonight God will return your places to each and every one of you. You may ask me, what the significance of having your own place is." "So hear what I say: every one of you has a place in heaven, your own place, where you can see and recognize God. But you also have a place on Earth, in freedom and God's good will. When I look into your eyes I only see those who have lost, forgotten or given up their places. Tonight each of you shall receive the gift of his or her place, according to God's will. Your own place since time immemorial." Then Jesus stretched his hands to Heaven and began to pray, so that all could hear him. "Father in heaven, I pray to you, I send you my words of adoration, to beg you: for each one who no longer knows and no longer recognizes his place on Earth, has lost his place in Your kingdom and wanders obliviously on the Earth, open Your gates of heaven, Lord, let the flame of Your love guide him, that he can return to his place in Your kingdom, which he left long, long ago. Let each one find himself again, in his very own peace and where he can always see You. Let Thy will be done unto eternity, Father, and may You hear Your people, who are praying to You from the place of their origin."

Then Jesus raised his hands, with his palms towards the assembled crowd. Light streamed from his hands, with a beam to each person. At the foot of the hill all those who had come to Jesus stood up. It was a very moving moment, and somebody started to sing. One by one the others joined in, so that it was as if the whole hill below us was singin, "Hosanna to God in heaven, praised be the king of all worlds, Hosanna, praised be the Messiah, who has returned our spiritual inheritance to us." All people sang joyfully together, and it seemed as if Heaven and Earth were in harmony. The people wept and embraced one another. We on the hill were deeply moved. Many of us could not restrain our tears after what we had witnessed. The crowd would not stop singing, until the captain came to Jesus and said, "Jesus, I beg you to consider that I cannot answer for things which go beyond my orders from my superiors. I am also deeply moved and I sense where my place is, but I would beg you to close the meeting here, to avoid turmoil and perhaps even political agitation. I implore you, I do not want any trouble." Jesus looked at him with compassion. Then he turned to the crowd and said, "For today I beg you to return home. Heaven and God's throne have bestowed a great favor unto you, more than you can imagine. Tomorrow you can return. Blessed be every one of you, in the name of the Lord."

Jesus looked understandingly at the captain and said, "Stay with us." Then he turned to us; we who were always near to him remained — his disciples, men and women, also Zachariah. He requested that wine be brought, which he then raised to Heaven and blessed. He let his male disciples distribute the wine and knelt down and looked at us, saying, "Today, at this very moment, your place in Heaven is prepared for you. As in ancient times you can again take your places in sight of God's throne. God has today fulfilled my promise to you." We did not know how it had happened, but every one of us sensed, in his or her own way, how we'd entered into heaven. Jesus came to each one of us, laid his hands on our heads and said, "Your place in Heaven is prepared for you to eternity." He wept as he said it.

As he touched my head a tear fell on my hair. This tear would remain with me always. His love cleansed my being again. That night I was immersed in everlasting love. It felt like a single explosion within me. Everything twitched and tingled and I was filled with devotion. Then I slept. When I awoke, many were asleep around me. Jesus had already left, but none of us wanted to leave this place. Simon had evidently stayed awake as watchman, and when he saw that I was awake said, "Come, I will bring you back to a more comfortable place to sleep." He awakened Magda, and explained that we were returning. I held his hand as he helped us find our way back to the village in the darkness.

I asked him, "Simon, what happened just now?" He laughed and answered, "What happened is what has occurred since the beginning of time and what will always occur, but you all have just forgotten it." I then returned to my room and he kissed me goodbye and said, "Sleep well." Magda and I retired to bed. The room was filled with an infinite peace, which reminded me of my times with the Essenes. In that moment I sensed that I had in those times experienced much sadness and had suffered a lot. I immersed myself in this new primeval peace, and laid my hand on my abdomen, where I felt the child in me and held it in my arms. I slept, bathed in this original light.

I was scarcely able to wake up next day, only vaguely noticing Magda coming and going. Then in the evening she awakened me gently, saying, "Come, Miriam, it is now time to return to the hill. I will bring you there, since Simon is already there and did not want to awaken you. He has an appointment with Jesus."

We returned to the place on the hill, which had virtually become our own, and I talked to Irisa. She asked me, "Are you going to return to Jerusalem?" I said, "Not at first. I believe we all go to Canaan first. Don't you want to accompany us there?" I did not tell her why, but after our conversation I talked to Simon and asked him, "Shouldn't we ask them all whether they would like to come to us in Canaan?" Simon nodded and said, "The nicest times I ever remember at home were with all of you. I would like to ask all of them to be my guests again. We want to celebrate a wonderful feast, such as has never previously taken place, the finest and most memorable of all feasts." I looked at him with joy and gratitude. He was a wonderful being, who created so much happiness. He was modest but radiant. I felt so much love for him, so full of respect and admiration.

Jesus withdrew for a time and returned with Peter. Both stood in front of the crowd, and when all were silent Jesus sat down and asked Peter to sit next to him. He sat for a long time while bread was distributed and the disciples were helping those who needed assistance. The crowd was waiting for Jesus to commence, but he just sat there and radiated his love to all present. His eyes and his heart emitted a supernatural light.

After a very long pause he finally began, "Today I want to tell you about the Father in heaven, my Father and your Father.

Every one of you is a child of this Father. We were all born from this source. My Father wishes you to know that He is happy today for He has found his children again. Heaven conveys happiness and good fortune to you all, an eternal happiness from time immemorial. You should know that the Father requests nothing from you demands nothing from you and expects nothing from you. No tribute for your right of birth. He only requests that you fill what He has given you with your love and your peace. The Father wants you to know you are not created to bring bad luck or tragic destiny. You are created to be happy, to live with free will and in spiritual liberty. You were created to receive the fruits of Heaven and of the Earth. But those who have turned away from God have brought you another message. The Father in Heaven wishes you to know that whosoever oppresses or enslaves you cannot be conquered by revolution and war. Far too much destruction has already taken place in all worlds. He wishes to see you as ambassadors of peace.

You were baptized with water on previous nights. Tonight you will baptized by fire. This fire will end the conflict in your souls, sooth the rebellion against God and erase the guilt of forgetting. I shall not bring you this baptism. Simon will bring this baptism to you." Simon stepped forward and stood next to Jesus, who continued, "We are two pillars; my friend Simon is the herald of the world of salvation. Wherever you may find him he will be recognizable, in order that you can follow him in future times. He will proclaim our Father's regime of peace. He and I are here to sooth souls and free them from suffering. Recognize him today when he baptizes you with fire, so that he may identify you in later times. I proclaim him now, so that he can foretell and prepare for my return to Earth in the future, even after I have left this Earth and this life for a very long time. He and I are witnesses of the recurrence on this Earth. Engrave the image of our spirits in your souls and in your hearts. Wherever you appear you will be found by him or me."

Then he said, "Go out and baptize them with fire, Simon." He went into the crowd and baptized each and every one with fire above their heads, the flames exuding from his hands. Nobody could help him; only he could perform this miracle.

While Simon was baptizing the multitudes, Jesus stood up and said, "Peter, stand up, and come to me. I say unto you all, here is the rock on which my church will be built. He stands before you." He laid his hand on Peter's heart and said, "From now on you will lead my church. But believe me, citizens of Israel, the church that we bring will not comprise palaces or splendid temples. We will proclaim the word of God under the open sky, between Heaven and Earth. Go ahead of your congregation. We do not advocate the destruction of temples; they will destroy themselves through their false belief. Temples, churches and buildings will appear and crumble to dust; as they have come so shall they mix again with the dust of the Earth. Peter and my apostles, who I have myself selected, wherever you go you will leave only dust on the Earth. But your words will leave their impression on the world, until God's truth is assured. The fire that baptizes you is the redemption of your guilt. Receive the blessing that Simon and I bring to you, the liberation from your earlier culpability, with which you were born on this Earth. With these words I extinguish the primeval seal of original sin on this Earth, to which you have been bound in the past."

Then Jesus came forward, and fire also exuded from his hands. He helped Simon baptize the people who came to him. It lasted many hours. It was as if a magic surrounded us, and we were never tired of observing what was happening. Fiery patterns spread across the sky, the energy of which flowed to us as beams of light. This ritual continued until deep in the night until all had been baptized. Jesus and Simon then returned to their places and Jesus said, "Now you can all go home. Even greater gifts will be presented to you, but this night will now find its peace." The people left and were elevated and sublime. They were more beauteous and relieved of their burdens. They left as free beings, no longer enslaved and suffering under the burden the Earth's fate.

As Simon brought me back to my room I looked at him and asked: "Who are you? You are like him but are somehow so different." I was unable to say more, since my tiredness overcame me. He brought me to bed and then left. That night I dreamed of the child I was carrying in my womb. It was as if it possessed an infinite light that radiated through all worlds and everlasting love. The child had not yet a form nor had it a name, just everlasting love and light, and a gentle smile that touched my heart. That night I sensed that the child made me complete, a feeling that I had never before encountered. Many things had happened in my life and I had experienced many profound spiritual events. Nevertheless I had always felt incomplete. The child in my womb gave me the feeling that I had become complete, and not a half that always sought the other half.

The next morning I awoke and Magda was sitting on my bed. I looked at her in surprise and asked, "What is the matter?"

She replied, "I was just worried about you, Miriam. You were talking the whole night through, and never stopped." I asked, "What was I saying?" She replied, "I don't know. It was a language I did not know, and sometimes you were very agitated. Then you were sometimes very calm and occasionally seemed to be prophetic in your tone. So I thought it better to watch over you." I apologized, "Oh, Magda, you have certainly not had much sleep on my account. I am so sorry. I have no recollections of the night." Magda said, "No, I am not tired. Something was in this room that removed my tiredness and my old age. I was fresh and felt young again. I thank you for that. After many years it is as if I have become younger. I believe that with your incomprehensible words you have immersed me in a fountain of youth. I will go and fetch us something to eat." We ate together and I looked forward to the evening when Jesus would preach again. From this time onward his message would always be connected with the mountain, and would remain so to eternity. I could hardly wait for the evening. Somewhere in me was another great joy, and I was excited, as if I was a small child again.

In the late afternoon Simon picked me up. He joked with me on the way to the place where Jesus spoke every evening and where all were assembled. The streets through which we walked were completely empty; everybody had already taken their places some time before Jesus appeared. The atmosphere was peaceful and filled with joy, as if we had been miraculously transported to a holy place. Simon gave me his hand and guided me to the hilltop, where we sat down. The crowd had increased again since the previous evening — a tendency that had continued from the Jesus' first appearance; now there was hardly room to move at the foot of the hill. We were wrapped in a cloak of heavenly exhilaration. Each one of us felt secure and completely at ease.

When Jesus arrived he said, "This evening no bread will be distributed." When as many were seated as the limited space would allow, Jesus went into the crowd and asked his disciples to accompany him. When they were in the middle of the crowd Jesus begged the crowd to draw back enough to make space for him and his disciples. Then he requested the disciples to form a circle around him.

He then raised his voice so that everyone could hear: "Citizens who are present tonight, I will initiate something that will shape the future. You see the twelve, the holy twelve, who accompany me: uncrowned kings, true kings of light, whom I have over the last years collected around me. They come from various levels of society, and widely varying professions. They stand here uncrowned, yet they wear eternal crowns from heaven. Look at them. Be aware that they will continue my mission when I am no longer here. Their light shall embody the truth, which they will carry into the world. I will generate twelve stars, which will find their places over the Earth and proclaim God's word with my vision and in my name. All those gathered around me here are holy, genuinely initiated men, the embodiment of peace from all worlds. Follow them when I am no longer here. When you no longer can hear my words, listen to theirs. In every one of them you will find a firm rock of God. Twelve stars surround me, twelve bright lights from the universe, who submit daily to my teaching and my being, in the service of love. Sense the light of mercy that they transmit into the world. See how the Earth accepts it."

He turned to the crowd, asking, "Where are the Hundred-and-eight?" They stood up and Jesus said, "Make a circle outside the crowd." When they had done this Jesus said, "You, who have found me, feel the circle of God's might around you, which has come to Earth. Immerse yourself in the knowledge that God's seal gives you. Understand that you will no longer need words or explanations. Then Heaven is present. What you experienced today is embodiment of the seal of God on Earth. It has taken on the form for all time, in those who surround you and those who form the innermost nucleus."

Then he raised his hands to Heaven and said, "Lord, let the divine seal speak to them, which shall proclaim the joyful message." Above us the heavens opened up and brilliant light descended on the crowd. Every single person was immersed in an envelope of light, and the people wept with emotion. They started singing Halleluiah, and everybody joined in, as if the angels were amongst them. Jesus left the group and came up the hill to us. He sat in our midst and said, "Look! That is God's work."

The disciples were at first somewhat perplexed, but they remained where they were as the people streamed to them and bowed down before them. The Hundred-and-eight stood outside, around the circle. They were like God's watchmen, the embodiment of something divine visible on Earth.

Then Jesus stood up and said, "The seal of the Lord is within you. Now you can each go home. We have experienced the holiest of nights. Heaven and Earth have melted together and have found the truth in your hearts. Go and tell everybody who wants to hear that the message of God has arrived again on

Earth. The seal of darkness has yielded to the seal of light. I bless you all in the name of the Lord."

Then he was very decisive. "Now you should go. Everything you want is fulfilled. What are you waiting for? Stop hanging onto words that promise good things. Finally understand that each of you is the fulfilment of promise!" As the crowd did not seem to want to leave, Jesus approached them and drove them away. "Go away, go away! Don't hang on my lips anymore; they are sealed. Your lips must speak and your actions must speak for you. Your achievements must be so godlike that nobody can forget them."

Then he said to his disciples, "In particular, your actions must be so godlike that they can be remembered for all time." Then Jesus withdrew into himself and left the place. As I gazed at his receding figure it was as if I could see a light from Heaven falling upon him, which immersed and protected him. A celestial radiance illuminated the hill, as fire and light together. I thought I heard Jesus praying, but I sensed that he wished to be alone. Then Mary Magdalene came to me and asked, "Miriam, do you have a place where I could sleep?" I felt for her and said, "It is not easy to be with him." Mary Magdalene replied, "You know, I really don't know how to deal with him. Sometimes he wants to be very close to me, as if he really needs me, and at other times he withdraws completely and is untouchable — as if he didn't want anything to do with me. I need some peace and quiet now, since it is not easy to be with him. Sometimes he is human and sometimes he is God. But he is never completely tangible for me. He showers me with love and sometimes, and in the next moment he rejects me. I really need some space for myself."

I took her with me, saying: "Come, Mary Magdalene. We can certainly find a place for you in our room. It is not very large, but we will manage somehow." I begged Simon to accompany us, but he said, "Could you not ask one of the disciples this time? I have to remain with Jesus. I will remain here and guard him. I am his custodian." I went spontaneously to old Jacob and asked, "Could you accompany us? We don't want to return alone in the night. I do not know how many people are around at night." He agreed immediately; he was a wonderful and affectionate being. From the beginning one could see the Light of Christ in him, in its complete form. He was always prepared to help, always polite and always charming. I had never seen him refuse to help — as this evening. Thus we returned to our room.

When we were finally in our room Mary Magdalene started to cry. I sat next to her, stroked her head and started to sing — songs from my childhood, in our old language, ones my mother used to sing to me. Mary Magdalene cried bitterly, as if her heart would break. I said to her, "Here you will find peace." Magda sat opposite and looked at us sympathetically, saying, "It will never be easy for a woman to love a godlike man. Sometimes they are tangible and full of love, and then suddenly they withdraw and are untouchable." I asked her, "Have you ever had a man?" She smiled and said, "For temple servants it was not permitted to have a man. Sometimes I had asked myself whether it was a lucky or an unlucky circumstance for me. I have never in my life had somebody at my side to support me; I have only had my visions of the Messiah and my belief in God. Thus I was able to experience my own completeness and perfection in this life." She began to laugh and said, "But believe me; when I return to Earth in another life, I will live differently. This life has been dedicated to the Messiah, and no other man. I have met no other man who could fulfill my expectations." We laughed together, and found enough peace to sleep. I wondered as I drifted off whether Jesus would spend another night with us on the hill, since he had just dissolved the community that we were.

Early next morning Simon knocked on the door and asked me to come with him. We went to the house of Zachariah. Jesus was already there, alone. He looked at me and said, "Miriam, come to me." He embraced me and said, "You unify so much love in you. Your love and your child have helped me tonight. I thank you for that." I said, "I did not do anything, Jesus." He replied, "You don't have to do anything. You just have to be. Nevertheless, I have to thank you from the bottom of my heart; your love and that of the other women supports and carries me. Without this love I would not be what I am. If I do not have time to tell them myself, I would like you to tell the other women this. Without these women's love I had not been able to achieve what I have. Your love is so strong and supportive that I can plant my seed, my words and my mission in it. Every day, unconditionally, you give me this love from your hearts. You lay your love in my path, to give me security and joy on this Earth."

I would only understand these words of Jesus much later. What I realized at that moment was that he revealed the divine, female nature to me — and he had thanked me for it. I knelt before himand said, "Lord, I was unable to do otherwise, and I don't believe any woman who has followed you could have. I can speak for all women who are near to you. We do not know anything else than to follow you with heart and soul. That is our good fortune. That is our fulfillment." He just looked at me and answered, "You are all true priestesses." Then he ended the conversation. The men had begun a free-ranging discussion on all subjects and I asked them if they wanted to be left alone. They answered, "No, stay here."

I detected a change in Jesus. In his eyes was a mixture of joy and sadness. He began to reflect on something that stimulated the two moods. I sensed a tremor inside him. He said, "It is time to return to the hill." We accompanied him to the accustomed place of assembly. His disciples were already awaiting him. He instructed them to distribute bread to all who came, but then to send them home.

The evening was only for us. One of the disciples asked, "And what do we do when one of your Hundred-and-eight comes?" Jesus replied, "Then I will choose whether he or she should remain or not." Some understood and returned home immediately, and some wanted to stay. Generally the disciples were able to advise the citizens, but when some insisted, Jesus had to decide. He chose some of the Hundred-and-eight who could remain, but sent the rest home.

Then a woman came to him and said, "But Lord, I am sure that I may remain here." Jesus regarded her for a moment and said, "As you did not understand the message last night, you will not understand it today." She replied, "But I have come especially today." Jesus looked at her with loving eyes and said, "You can stay, but not because you want to but because I decide that you can. Do you understand the difference?" She was somewhat intimidated but was allowed to stay.

This evening Jesus remained secluded for a long time, until he appeared and descended down the hill to the captain. He was waiting with his soldiers to see what would develop this evening. Jesus spoke to him and returned with him. Jesus said, "Spend the evening with us. I am so grateful that you have made it possible for us to enjoy your protection during these nights here. I would like you to remain with us." We were all in a good mood and conversed with one another.

Meanwhile Simon spoke to the captain. Suddenly Simon smiled, looked at Jesus, laid his hands on the captain's shoulders and said, "It is nice to meet old friends." The captain was astonished but Simon only laughed. I had often experienced this situation between Jesus and Simon, as they looked into others worlds together, finding connections and relationships that were not available to our senses. It was always surprising how they could amuse each other with such things.

We were distributed over the whole hill, and Jesus made no sign of doing anything different this evening. He often withdrew and then returned. It was the first time I observed how he embraced Mary Magdalene as an affectionate partner.

Later in the evening Jesus said, "Come and sit next to me, John." John had become a wonderful being. I saw in him a being who reflected many worlds. Jesus embraced him affectionately and began to speak. "John carries the power of revelation in him. The gate to the prophesies of this Earth is within him. He will proclaim them in all worlds at later times in the future. He is clean and untouched by the world outside, and is like a younger brother to me. I love you, John. Do you know that?" John looked at him and replied, "And I love you too, Lord." Jesus looked at Mary Magdalene and his mother and said, "John. Promise me that you will look after my mother and Mary Magdalene. Give me your word that you will take them into your care when the times change."

It was the first time that his disciples had heard him talk like that; he had not yet mentioned to them that he expected such a change to happen. Some started to cry and said, "You will always be with us, Lord. How can you frighten us with such talk?" Jesus replied, "Nobody wants to frighten you. That is only your own fright. John, would you like to relate the revelation that you carry in your heart?" John looked at Jesus in surprise and said, "I do not carry a revelation in my heart." Jesus replied, "You do indeed. Even I do not have this revelation in me. You were born with it." John was somewhat confused and helpless. Then Jesus said, "You only need to look at Miriam. She carries a revelation in her womb, which wishes to speak to you."

Suddenly John fell into a trance and began to speak. I cannot remember the words precisely, but the pictures remain clear in my memory: a woman walking over fire, in childbirth pains, calling the spirits from all heavens, bringing fire, destruction and reconciliation, resurrection and affiliation. John spoke powerful words, as out of another age, of Heaven and Earth warring with one another to find conciliation, and of a child born to bring the antitheses together. Then he began to speak about Jesus Christ, whose being illuminated all worlds, all universes and all beings for all time with his love. He spoke about the Light of Christ that would rise and radiate throughall worlds and unite all in love and blessing.

Then he described how, in a later age, the golden sun originated and how someone whom Jesus has proclaimed will ride ahead of us on a white horse. He told that a time will come when all avatars in Heaven will arrive from all heavenly directions and unite in a cross. He described that when this happens the greatest destruction of all time will shake the world. At that moment those who have always believed in God and who have never given up hope of resurrection will be resurrected. He described a picture of four powerful avatars, walking towards one another, to reconcile the cross of the Earth and unite it in fire. He described one powerful avatar that will carry the fire from Heaven to Earth.

We experienced these images as in a dream. It was as if we were all in a trance. I could only hold my hand on my abdomen as John spoke, and ask myself what being lived within me. When John emerged from his trance he looked at us all and said, "Praised be to Jesus Christ, praised be the Lord, the salvation of all worlds who redeems our sins for all time." I looked around and saw that many were deeply moved by the experience, and some were crying. I saw eternal and unbounded knowledge in the faces of many. As we spoke about the experience later, we had all seen similar images within us, although we had no idea what John was describing.

Jesus looked as if he was in another world, and then said, "I will give each of you my blessing. Come to me and let yourselves be blessed with the Light of Christ, the light which I embody." He sat down and each of us came to him. He held our heads in his hands. When I received his blessing I sensed the light throughout my body; my whole being was flooded with his love, and I felt united with him. He was the goblet from which we drank. We were resurrected in his hands. Infinite love was in us and around us. The love was tangible and captured us all.

That evening we were drunk with love, without sentiment and without boundaries. We had drunk from the goblet of love, and were intoxicated from the wine. I cannot recollect how this evening ended or how I found my way to my bed. I only knew that I was completely happy, removed from this world and immersed in the godlike power of Jesus' love. When I awoke, Magda was already awake and said, "This love will be the way in the future. We must follow this love and embody it every moment. I know that we will carry it within us for all time, we will fill this love with life, let it die and be resurrected, until it is finally on Earth for all time." Then she came to me, knelt before my bed and said, "I know that we will always meet again, Miriam, whether in this or another life. I see that you will be many times on Earth, until we have succeeded in our mission. After last night I know that we will be able to bring this love to the people, and all will finally believe that this love brings fulfillment to the Earth."

Next day we started out for Canaan. Jesus promised to come to us as soon as possible. His disciples and a few more remained with him. Magda wanted to return to Jerusalem and Lazarus offered to accompany her. Mary Magdalene, Irisa and Salome travelled with us to Canaan. We were still somewhat intoxicated from the previous evening, full of love and enjoying the journey. Travelling with Simon was as ever a pleasure; he cared for our well-being and for our accommodation. We arrived at his house and were very comfortably looked after. The following day, Simon began instructing his servants in preparation for a great feast. He had the wine barrels tapped and supplies delivered. He estimated that Jesus would return in about a week, and during that time we were all happy and well looked after. Even Mary Magdalene seemed to have lost her sadness. We were all very relaxed and contented.

Since Simon did not observe the strict Jewish traditions as they existed in Jerusalem, we enjoyed a freedom of spirit in Canaan. Simon arranged that we would be married according to the official Jewish tradition, as he wished. He said, "It is better that way, that the officials in the town recognize our marriage, so you are legally viewed as my wife and have the right to inherit my estate, as will have our child." We did not discuss these things with the others. For the rest of the week Simon was occupied in preparations for the celebrations. At night we were separated. Nevertheless we experienced complete harmony during this time, full of trust, love and respect for one another. I felt that he knew at every moment what I needed, and took care that I received it.

Once we were alone in the garden and I asked him, "Why are you decorating the house so beautifully?" He replied: "For two reasons: first, so that we may have a great feast for our wedding, to celebrate once more with Jesus; and second, though is sad but nevertheless wonderful, this could be the last great feast when we are all together." He kissed me and said, "I don't want you to be sad; it's just like flowers, which also have their most glorious times, after which they fade and die. We should enjoy these moments and not think about the time when the flowers are fading and dying. That is the way you should see this feast of life."

Simon arranged for flowers to be placed all over the house. I don't know where he got them all, but I assumed he knew many merchants and traders. The house was perfumed fragrantly with flowers of all sorts. It was very pleasing. One day he brought me a wonderful scarf and dress, set with gold ornaments such as I had never seen before. He said, "I would like you to wear these when Jesus comes." I hardly dared to touch the clothes, since they were really very lovely and exotic. They were also beautifully embroidered. Simon said, "They come from Damascus. There are craftsmen there who make such things." I put the items aside, and admired them every evening.

A week later, Jesus arrived with his disciples. Zachariah was also there, and had brought a new man with him. The stranger was impressively strong and well built. Jesus requested that his disciples find accommodation outside the house, for which Simon generously gave them money. The feast was to take place next day and the decorated house was like a palace.

Jesus' mother, Mary came to me and said, "I have always felt you to be my daughter. Would you allow me to bath you, wash and comb your hair and clothe you, as our mothers used to do in ancient times?" I could not help myself; I started to cry, and at that moment remembered that I had no mother, but had the good luck to have such a wonderful substitute mother as Mary. I was charmed at the thought and agreed. She started to sing old sacred songs, then she combed and oiled my hair and dressed me and presented me with a gift. She said, "As I have no daughter of my own, I would like to give you something very special. It is a brooch from the ancient line of our family. I would like you to wear it." I could not help myself. I went on my knees to her and said, "I thank you from the bottom of my heart. You are like the original mother from all worlds, the mother of all mothers. You shine white through all the worlds and give me the gift of being the most loving mother of all times."

As I left the room I saw wine barrels everywhere. The whole house was brightly and festively illuminated with torches everywhere. I noticed that Simon had hired additional servants, since he wished to avoid any of us having to bother about organization and service on this occasion. Singly and in groups all guests arrived. Jesus was very fatherly and affectionate to me.

That evening Jesus started with a ceremony, whereby he let flower petals and holy oil fall into a bowl of water. He poured some of the holy water over the heads of Simon and myself, so that it trickled down our faces. This evening he performed a ritual that I did not know from our world. A great light appeared and bound Simon and me together in his name, as man and wife. For me this ritual consummated our marriage more within me than outside in the world, and the light shone in the room, gold and white. Everything was simple, but still sacred and sublime.

Jesus began to speak, full of love, as I had not heard him before. "We serve only one mother, the great creation. We are all the embodiment of this mother, whose impulse is fed every moment by my Father, the throne of God and his Glory. God's plan is rarely fulfilled on Earth. But today is the day when God's plan is fulfilled between Heaven and Earth. I want you all to enter into this creative act. Recognize and serve your mother, identify your brothers. These are the signs by which one will recognize you in the future. Creation and its plan want to be connected with the Earth again. The child you carry under your heart, Miriam, is a great contribution to the achievement of this plan. I would like the child to receive so much love and care that it can grow up without worry or adversity. I am sure that you and Simon will take care of that. The fate I must fulfill on this Earth shall remove all worry and suffering from this child, that it can make its way without obstacles.

"But hear what I now have to say. Simon, whom I have named my brother, and who will remain so for all time, will at some time in the future reappear on Earth and destroy all false prophets. His arrival shall be proclaimed with fire and passion. My way on Earth shall free the way for him to fulfill his mission, in order that we can one day reappear together on Earth. Then we shall be able to be seen in our own light, and not have to conceal ourselves behind locked doors or in secret passages."

Then he looked at his disciples and said, "Write this in your books, even though some may try to erase the story of Simon. All who attempt to falsify my story and my message or to use it for their own purposes should tremble and beware of your power and your wrath, Simon. Tonight the world enjoys the Power and the glory of God, brimming over with love and fulfillment."

Then Jesus said, "Simon, it is up to you as host, to formally open the feast." Simon did as Jesus requested, and let wine be proffered to the guests. The wine, which had been blessed by Jesus, was such as I have never drunk before. The wine literally glowed with the consciousness of Christ, as if Jesus were preaching again. Every sip was the blood of life. We were lively and full of joy. Jesus was very affectionate to Mary Magdalene, and this evening he publicly showed that he loved her for the first time. Some of the disciples were looking at them, but this evening Jesus was not concerned with such things. She was this evening his beloved. We celebrated, as if a thousand weddings were taking place in heaven.

At midnight Jesus suddenly stood in our midst. He went to his mother and knelt before her. "Mother, I beg you to release me as your son. From now on I am nobody's son, nobody's husband and nobody's friend. Tonight I shall penetrate into the being inside my being, and consummate myself as the descended Son of God. Please release me from your motherhood." He kissed her hands and said, "You were the most wonderful mother on Earth that I can imagine." Then he went to his disciples and said, "Release me as your teacher and master. From now on you are yourselves masters of your lives."

He went to Mary Magdalene and said, "Release me from your love." And to Simon: "Release me as your friend. This evening I will embody eternity for you, the endlessness from which I come and to which I return when my time arrives. Nothing on this Earth remains; everything perishes and leaves no trace. The seed that is sown on arth carries its fruit and returns to earth. In this night I will extinguish the transience in my heart."

Then Jesus left the room. In retrospect, it was the most wonderful of all celebrations we had experienced, but some were naturally very shocked. Mary Magdalene wept bitterly, as if her heart would break and I went over and tried to comfort her. "Mary Magdalene, don't you understand that he is taking you with him in this eternal love? You must realize that the earthly bond of a man–and–wife relationship is too narrow for him. He will take you with him in this eternal love, with which you will melt into union with him. I can see it. I can sense it in your heart and in your eyes." The disciples were shocked and elated at the same time.

Only Simon smiled, as if he understood, and took my arm. He was the wisest of us all. Past, present and future melted together in him. He was every moment happy, whether in his earthly life as the husband at my side and father of my child, or as a spiritual being beyond earthly bounds. Nothing tied him to this life; nevertheless he served this life and fulfilled it every moment with his generosity and his presents.

The other women were also shocked. Only Mary was composed, although she cried silent tears. I went to her and held her hands, and she said, "Miriam, I don't cry for myself. God could not have given me a greater gift than my son. I cry over him, because my visions show me his intentions, and I know that nothing can prevent him from doing what he has decided to do. We cannot even imagine the great pain and anguish he is going to experience. He will collect the suffering of all humanity in his heart and do penance for it. He will sacrifice himself. I have seen his way; he has shown it to me in many dreams in the previous nights. But he has also told me that I can never understand this from the human point of view. I can only understand it from the eternal perspective, through the endless love with which he blessed me. But the human being in me tortures itself with the fear of what is coming to him. Simultaneously the eternal Mary, which he has consummated in me, lives in Heaven and sees all. Here on Earth it is difficult to separate the two. I know that I will suffer great anguish, which will nearly break my heart." I held her hands and said, "Mary, whatever he intends, we will accompany him. Let the pain that he suffers pardon us, so that his suffering is reduced. I too have visions, perhaps not as definite as yours. But please don't relate them at the moment. I hope he waits until my child is born, but I promised long ago to serve and help him with every fiber of my being. Should he suffer hard times I hope that God will be merciful, so that I can be with him wherever I can serve him."

This evening was filled with tears, which nevertheless heralded an incredible happiness. One can scarcely describe our condition, how great joy and great sadness melted into one another and into us. The light that we experienced was not of this Earth. It was godlike. It could only come from God Himself, as could the ecstasy imparted by the wine.

I slept for the first time in my married bed, and was very happy. The memories and images of the previous evening could not cloud my contentment. As I went to sleep in Simon's arms I began to understand that great joy and great sadness can melt into one another in a divine combination. I did not know if this was an earthly law for all time. But at this time it was so.

I was awake early next morning and decided to go to the terrace to observe the rising sun. Everyone else was sleeping, but as I stepped out of the house Jesus was already there, gazing at the sun. I stood next to him, he put his arm around me and asked, "How are you, Miriam?" I replied, "Lord, how I feel is not so important. But how do you feel?" He replied, "You must know that where I come from — and where we all come from — we are always happy. We are all united and can accept everything with love: what was, what is and what shall be." I had a question in my heart and I wanted to pose it to him: "Jesus, why don't you marry Mary Magdalene? You love her, don't you?" He answered, "Miriam, if I were a man I would marry her. But I am here on Earth on a mission. I would not do her a favor by marrying her; she would only suffer more. Is it not enough that I am pursued with the ill thoughts and deeds of the people? I protect Mary Magdalene by not marrying her." I asked, "Will you all leave the house today? Will you go away again?"

"Yes, Miriam, I have a couple of month's time. I want to collect many people and contact many more, since I realize I should use this opportunity. My fate is sealed and I do not intend to attempt to avoid it. But I will use every remaining day for my mission, to contact as many persons as I can in their hearts and in their light." Then we heard movements in the house, as others had awakened, and Jesus left me and went to his room. When he emerged he informed his disciples that they would be leaving again today. After the previous day's feast, the prospect of all departing was on one hand sad but on the other hand exciting. Jesus left with his disciples and with the man he had brought with him, but with whom I'd had no opportunity to talk. Irisa and the others returned to Jerusalem, while Lazarus had chosen to go with Jesus. Simon and I remained alone in the house. This was very pleasing for us, since we finally had time for one another.

The next months were very quiet and I was much occupied in giving our child room to grow. Everything was calm and restful, almost idyllic. Simon cared for me continuously, except when he had occasionally to leave for a couple of days on business. When he returned from such journeys I would always ask him, "Have you seen or heard anything from Jesus? Do you know where he is?" Sometimes we heard that he was travelling around the country, that he was preaching and healing and that many people gathered around him. This lasted a few months and I was very happy that I was able to gather strength for what lay ahead. The child under my heart was mighty and full of light. It gave peace between Heaven and Earth and fulfillment within me. I enjoyed giving this feeling space to grow.

When I was in the fifth month of pregnancy my dreams began to be more disturbed. At the beginning I could not interpret them; they were vague and ambiguous, and I was very restless at night. Near the end of the fifth month, I awoke one night bathed in perspiration. I woke Simon and said, "Simon, let us go to Jerusalem. Jesus has called me. Let us leave. I must go to him." Simon looked at me seriously and said, "Now you should rest a little. Tomorrow we will leave early. I believe that your vision is a true one. Do you feel fit to leave?" I said, "I feel fine. My body is in good condition. But we should not wait much longer. I sense that something is brewing and I will be near him when it happens."

We left the house next day and Simon arranged for some of his servants to accompany us, but when we arrived at the gates of Jerusalem, he sent them back home. First we went to Irisa's house. We knocked on the door and a servant let us in.

I stood in the atrium, surrounded by a peculiar atmosphere: quiet but tense. Irisa was not yet at home, although the servant presumed that she would soon return. When she finally returned Irisa said, "Oh, my God. How wonderful that you are here." I asked her, What is the matter?" She was almost hysterical. "Jesus returned to Jerusalem two days ago. It is the time of the Passover festival and Jerusalem is filled with people. When I heard that he was coming, Salome and I went out into the crowded streets of Jerusalem and waited for Jesus, who we had not seen for some months. He appeared in the town riding on the back of a donkey, as if he was a king. The inhabitants and visitors waved to him and called, 'Here comes David's son, the King of Israel. Hosanna to heaven, praised be he who comes to us.'

"There was a powerful atmosphere in the town, and the Roman soldiers were aware of their responsibility to keep the peace. But the soldiers could not hold back the enormous crowd. Jesus rode ahead of the crowd with his disciples next to him. We could not keep up with him as he made his way to the Mount of Olives. He had withdrawn to a house that had been placed at his disposal, together with his disciples. Later I asked Joseph of Arimathea where he was, and he replied that he was staying in the house with his disciples for the time being. Miriam, I am afraid of what might happen. I know what Jesus has done, and that it will have serious consequences for him. The priests have challenged him and have their spies and henchmen everywhere. To make matters worse he had stopped at various points and spoken to the people and preached. I have heard that the priests place their henchmen in the crowds and ask repeatedly: 'Are you the King of the Jews?'"

I asked where Salome was and she replied, "She is with the others. But we could not find Jesus." I asked, "Could we not ask Joseph of Arimathea where he is?" She said, "I will send a servant to him, although I have heard that he has withdrawn for the time being. He has not contacted any of us." "And Lazarus?" I asked. "Lazarus, Martha and a few others are together in the house of your parents. I don't know where the rest of them are. I am disquieted, Miriam. It is as if great bells are ringing above me, telling me that the unimaginable is going to happen." I asked, "Have you seen Magda?" Irisa said, "No I haven't. But if you wish I could send a messenger to her. We have not met for a long time. After the evening in Canaan everybody has been trying to find peace and tranquillity. A few of us have met occasionally, but we have always been careful not to draw attention to ourselves. We try to be calm and collected, but I must admit that the last months have not been very relaxing. But I am very glad to see you again." In answer to my question, she added, "Mary is here in the town; she came with Jesus. I have seen the two of them simultaneously, but Mary kept herself at a distance from Jesus. He entered Jerusalem as King, as was prophesied, in the line of David. The scriptures also prophesied that he would ride on a donkey in the Passover festival. It was rather curious, and I had the feeling that he intended to provoke the authorities. He had never previously so earnestly participated in prophecies or predictions in the scriptures. The whole scene was very unusual to me, although the people were much affected. It was if he was an actor playing his part on the stage."

I looked at Simon quizzically and he said seriously, "Miriam, let things happen the way they should. We needed to come to

Jerusalem, and we have done so. Be patient until we know what has happened and what we have to do." I needed to rest, as my belly was getting heavier and I needed to lie down after the journey to Jerusalem.

Some hours later a servant arrived from Joseph of Arimathea. Jesus wished to see us, but we were to tell nobody that he was in Joseph's house. The servant would bring us to the house in the evening. Joseph instructed the servant that only he, Simon, Miriam and Irisa should come. At the chosen time, the servant led us to Joseph's house on a hill in Jerusalem. It was a beautiful, spacious building, and Joseph said, "Come in. Jesus is waiting for you."

Jesus was surrounded by his disciples and had somehow changed. Mary Magdalene and Magda were also there. He embraced Simon and said, "I am glad to see you, my friend. It is nice that you came to visit me." Then he came to me and embraced me, saying, "Miriam, it is lovely to see you again. I see you have to carry a heavy load." Then he asked me if he might put his hand on my abdomen, to which I agreed. It was a peculiar sensation; it was as if the child in my womb started communicating with Jesus. Jesus looked at me and said, "Everything is allright. You have a healthy child. It is a boy." I looked at Simon and saw that he was delighted. We ventured to ask Jesus what his plans were, and in the presence of his disciples he asked, "Would you like to join me for the meal this evening?" He was quite calm and composed. He radiated benevolence, and when I looked into his eyes I could only see pure truth in them. Nothing showed in his eyes, apart from his authentic godliness. One could sense the unity of the moment, as if past and future did not exist.

The disciples were very quiet. Much had happened to them. They were withdrawn and spoke little with us. We remained near Jesus, and only Joseph of Arimathea conversed with us. Jesus said, "Come. Our host has prepared a meal for us." We entered a fine room in the upper story of the house, within which was a great table. Jesus bade us to be seated. His disciples sat around him, and he requested the traditional Passover bread to be brought.

Jesus looked at us all and it became very quiet in the room. He said, "That which shall come to pass is what should come to pass. I have given you all what was due to you. You now know what to do when something happens to me." Then he spoke to Joseph of Arimathea. "Joseph, my old friend. You have helped me so often, and I beg of you one more thing. I do not think that what is happening in Israel will end well. The hate and persecution that have followed me will also follow you when I am no longer here. The land in which you have all grown up will no longer be a safe home for you all. The Lord has sent me many visions, but I cannot see very far into the future at present. Joseph, you once told me that you have a large property in a southern land across the sea. If the situation deteriorates further and Israel is no longer safe, I beg you to bring those I love to safety in another land, particularly Mary Magdalene. Let them find a new home when the old one is no longer favorable. I have not followed this course and fulfilled this mission to see my loved ones suffer under the sword of hate.

"I beg you all to save yourselves and bring that which I love away from here. This is my wish. I do not want you to be persecuted. I would like you to leave this country as worthy human beings and worthy servers of my mission. The inheritance I have left here on Earth should not be lost; please save it in my name." Then he spoke to each of his twelve disciples saying, "Your vision is strong and you are well prepared for your missions. I do not want any of you to be in danger. The authorities fear me, and I think they will name me an enemy of the state. I would like you to promise me today that, in that event, you are prepared to renounce me. You still have great things to do on Earth, and I do not want your missions to be endangered. Please save your own lives, even if you must renounce me." Some of the disciples were upset and said, "We could never renounce you. Nor could we deny being your followers."

Jesus replied, "You will have to do it, since it is my wish. I do not want to see your lives endangered. I want to save you so that you remain alive to complete our missions." Then he looked at Peter and said, "Even if you soul is tormented by the thought, I want you to promise me that you are willing to renounce me. Otherwise all that I have built up with you will be destroyed by the priests and their henchmen. Please promise me, Peter." Peter shook his head. "I cannot believe that I would be able to renounce you." Jesus was very loving when he said, "But believe me, you will do it. And I assure you here and now that it is my wish, and not yours." Then he turned to Judas, who looked at the floor, embarrassed, and said, "What do you want me to do, Lord? From what you have said, you seem prepared to go to your death. You should try to reconcile yourself with the priests. They are not really taking steps against you. Why do you present us with a scenario which would be avoidable, if you were to seek reconciliation?"

Jesus answered him, "Judas, I am not here to seek reconciliation with everyone, and to live in peace with murderers; that is also the will of my Father. I am here at the zenith of barbarism and brutality on this Earth. For that cause I am willing to sacrifice my life. Even if I wished to avoid death, it is not my Father's wish that I seek reconciliation with murderers. It is my Father's will that the irreconcilable is evident, clear for all, also comprehensible for you. But you can help me, Judas." Judas knelt before Jesus, who went on, "Judas, my trustworthy friend, what I beg of you is the greatest sacrifice that you can imagine." Judas looked at hime and said, "Lord, I am prepared to die with you. Let me go with you when you choose death, however you choose it. I am willing to go with you. Then I will meet my death with you."

Jesus said, "No, Judas. What I expect from you will be even worse than that. You must help me speed my own sacrifice." Judas said, "Then tell me Lord, what I should do for you, and how." Jesus explained, "You know the priests from earlier times. Go to them and say that you have defected from me and reinforce all of the arguments they are spreading around Jerusalem. Support them and ask for money in exchange for renouncing me in public. Bring them to my place of residence." Jesus spoke with stifled voice. Everyone in the room held their breath. There was no sound in the room. Then Judas broke into tears and knelt before Jesus, crying, "Lord, what do you demand of me?" Jesus lifted him on to his feet and said lovingly, "Judas, please help me. The images of what awaits me are so clear to me. How much longer can I tolerate them? Let yourself be courageous, as heroic as I want to be, without having to be a hero. Please let us accept our destinies and not delay them further." Judas said, "I do not think my strength is sufficient to do this." Jesus replied, "Then let me be your strength. The Father and I will be your strength. What should happen must be fulfilled. It was written in the scriptures a long time ago, and now it must come to pass." Judas tried to escape from his fate, saying, "Lord, I can no longer remain here when you demand something like that from me. Can I go now? But how can I do what you wish?" Jesus replied, "Judas, stay with us a bit longer. This evening you should leave us, knock on the temple door and do what I requested from you." Jesus began to cry. "Judas, believe me, every one of you in this room shall be redeemed in the future, through that which is happening here. I would have liked to find another way to wipe clean the sins of the Earth, but I too follow the will of my Father."

The only person who remained calm in the room was Simon. I recognized it when I sensed what he was feeling. An infinite peace emanated from him, and he listened impassively to everything that was said. He seemed to be calm in the face of all that happened. That was also a source of comfort to me. Nevertheless, it was not clear to all of us what was going to happen to us. Jesus had described the unimaginable to us, which we would experience in the next days and which would be more ghastly than anything we could imagine. Jesus said, "You are all my friends in Heaven as on the Earth. You are loyal companions of God. My friends, I would like to celebrate the traditional Essene communion with you, those who have prepared my way and accompanied me on it. You guard the Light of Christ in all worlds and have let it be resurrected in this world. Stay with me this evening. Don't leave me now. After the meal I would request you to leave me alone with my disciples. Mary Magdalene, you should also leave with them."

He looked at Simon, Irisa and me and said, "Please take her with you. There will be no rest tonight." I can scarcely describe how empty the room suddenly seemed. Jesus was the most incredible soul that I had ever met. He was no human being: he was my God. Any normal person would have attempted to avoid such a tragic fate, would have hesitated or attempted to flee, but Jesus encouraged fate to run its course, without a spark of fear or pain.

On the contrary, this evening I sensed that he was more anxious about those he loved than he was about himself. He was more concerned about where we were going and what we were doing than about his own fate. Only his strength helped us to make this time tolerable. Everything took its course, and Jesus began to pray in this emptiness. Then he began to break bread, as I had experienced with the Essenes. He handed it to each of us with the words, "Eat from the bread of eternal life, that you are healed forever."

It suddenly occurred to me that Mary was not there. I later learned that Jesus did not want her to be there. I asked myself where she was, but in the next instant Jesus took the goblet he had used in Canaan and filled it again. Once more he prayed intensely, within himself. I saw how he was in close communion with God. Then he passed the wine around with the words, "This is my blood, which will be spilled for you and for all humanity. Drink the blood of the ancient alliance of God's rule, to eternity, in the name of our Lord." He gave us wine, and everything he did reminded me of the last evening I spent with the Essenes. It was a rebirth of the memory. But this time it was different: Jesus blessed the ritual with the seal of eternity.

As the goblet was passed around we were all conscious of the oneness of our community. We all served the same master. As we drank I saw visions that showed me that we did not serve the will of the Earth or humanity, but that we served only the will of one who leads us — who always was and will always be. With the wine I felt my infinite love of the Father in Heaven and of his Son, who was at that moment more present than ever before. Jesus then went to his disciples with a basin of water, and knelt before them in the old Essene tradition. As he commenced washing their feet they protested, "No Lord. We cannot accept that from you." But Jesus replied, "If not from me, from whom then?" Then he continued until he had washed all their feet, after which he also washed ours. When he came to me, he regarded me with the same love that he had shown to his own disciples. As he knelt before me I wept, since I also saw vulnerability in him. I knew that Jesus would not permit anyone to touch the pain in him. He was determined to sacrifice himself and requested nothing from others.

When he had washed all our feet he said, "Now all is accomplished. I beg the rest of you to go, and to leave me alone with my disciples. Judas, it is time to go. Fulfill that which you have to." Judas then came to Jesus and they embraced one another. Despairingly Judas said, "Will I ever see you again, Lord?" Jesus answered, "We will meet again there where we are all united with God. Now go, Judas! Don't delay another moment, and forget your doubts. Do that which must be done." It was a terrible moment for me as Judas left the room. I could not imagine what a great burden he carried in his heart as he left. But he did that which his master had requested from him. Jesus had also named a place where they could meet secretly, and where Jesus would wait for him.

Then Jesus said to us, "It is time for you to go." Jesus and Simon embraced one another long and tenderly, and we left him. Joseph of Arimathea and Mary Magdalene also came with us. We left in complete silence, since nobody was able to speak. We walked silently through the streets of Jerusalem until Joseph left us with the words: "I will remain in contact with you. I know where I can find you." Then we went home.

It was a sleepless night for all of us. Simon remained outside, and as I wandered sleeplessly through the house I saw him outside meditating. It was as if he was not here, but in another world. I saw his body, but his spirit was somewhere else. I tried to regain my equilibrium and my tranquillity, and thought of the child in my womb. But the being within me seemed unperturbed by the events, as if it understood. This gave me strength, which carried me through the night. Waiting for the inevitable was a ghastly experience. Irisa could not sleep either, and we just looked at one another wordlessly as we met each other wandering through the house. Next morning there was a loud banging on the front door. It was Lazarus. He told us what he had heard in the town: after we had left Jesus he had gone to the Mount of Olives. Judas had appeared later, after he had renounced Jesus. As Lazarus spoke, we were silent. It was as if our mouths were sealed. Lazarus was naturally very angry about what Judas had done, and we were unable to calm him; we could not tell him the truth. He reported that Jesus was led away, and I asked him how he knew. He replied that the younger Jacob had come and told him. Lazarus said, "But nobody came to help him! When I asked why not, he told me that it was Jesus' wish. He let himself be arrested without resistance. He is now in the hands of the priests' henchmen."

Simon looked at Lazarus calmly and asked, "And what happens next?" Lazarus said, "I don't know. But I think we should go to the temple. Nobody seems to know what is going to happen."

We got dressed rapidly and walked hurriedly to the temple. Irisa said, "I will try to discover what is happening. I know a lot of people here, even the wife of Pontius Pilate, Prefect of Judea. I will attempt to meet her, to hear more about the situation." We waited on the forecourt of the temple, where great crowds had collected. The sun was hot and pitiless.

Irisa returned after a while and said, "Claudia told me that the high priests had accused Jesus of being a traitor in the presence of Pilate. They alleged that Jesus intended to overthrow the state, and that he declares himself to be the rightful King of Israel. They have apparently persuaded Pilate that Jesus advocated overthrowing the Roman occupation. He is purported to be the chief agitator of the people." Simon asked Irisa, "And what does Pilate say to this?" Irisa replied, "Claudia said that Pilate wants nothing to do with the whole thing, but the priests keep pressuring him. Jesus is in prison and the priests demand that Jesus should appear before him. They are accusing him of everything possible. How can they be so wicked? How can they be so untrue?"

We returned home, since there was no further news. We just waited to hear of further developments. Mary Magdalene was with us, and she seemed to be suffering from shock. She hardly spoke and repeatedly withdrew to her room. Irisa was impatient. "I am going to go into town again, and see what I can find out." When she returned, she reported, "The high priests, Annas and Caiaphas, wouldn't let up and continued to press for Jesus' conviction, appearing before Pilate every single hour. Jesus is imprisoned, but I don't know where." Simon asked, "Do you think it would be possible to visit him?" Irisa replie, "I'll try to find out. But it's all so ghastly. Hundreds of people are gathered in front of Pilate's palace. You wouldn't believe what the high priests are doing; they're distributing money to the people, bribing them to shout, 'Convict him! Convict him!' Ordinary citizens and the police have been bribed to demand the conviction and death of Jesus, because they claim that he is a sinner, a warlock and an enemy of the state."

I was sick when I heard this, and went outside to vomit. The high priests had finally accomplished the conviction of an innocent person by intrigue, treachery and bribery, so that he was going to have to appear before a Roman tribunal. They exaggerated and lied to provoke the Romans. Jesus had done nothing to deserve that. Simon remained calm and said, "Those priests are treacherous. They know the Roman belief in straightforward thinking — everything is black and white to them. In the end, the Romans have only one aim: to retain their power and their empire in Israel. Jesus is being presented as a rebel, and the priests are trying to persuade Pilate that Jesus is a threat to the Roman occupiers. They are clever. Pilate is going to have to act, in order to pacify Rome."

Joseph of Arimathea arrived just as Irisa left again to obtain more current information. Joseph was politically influential and had contacts in at the highest level in the city. He too had news: "The Council of Temple Elders has been strongly influenced by Annas and Caiaphas. Every hour they come with some slander or insults against Jesus, and try to bring him to justice as a traitor. Nicodemus and I are powerless. Now they're demanding that Jesus be put to death, finally, just to get rid of him. They're to convince Pilate that Jesus should die by crucifixion." Irisa returned and said, "I've spoken to Claudia and asked if it might be possible to speak to Jesus. She told me that her husband would probably have no objection to visitors, though no more than two, and she'd ask him to agree to a visit." Simon looked at Mary Magdalene and said, "When we're allowed to visit him in jail, then you and me should try to see him. Will you come with me?"

Irisa accompanied the two of them, and the rest of us remained in the house, waiting anxiously. In the meantime, I had begged Salome to collect Lazarus, Martha and others who were at our house, since Irisa's house was certainly safer: as a Roman citizen, she enjoyed a particular status, and was less likely to be molested by the temple bullies or Roman soldiers. When Lazarus arrived, I asked him, "Do you know where the disciples are?" He did not know, but said, "They've all disappeared and nobody knows where they are. They're in hiding, and, apparently, they've informed nobody of their whereabouts." I was at first slightly offended, but then I remembered what Jesus had said in the previous night — that they should remain hidden somewhere in the town. I could imagine how they felt, now that Jesus was in prison: they knew that the master they loved was incarcerated within the mighty walls of the Roman prison, without any way of knowing what was happening to him. We were also kept in suspense. We had hours of waiting in front of us.

In the early hours of the morning, Simon and Mary Magdalene returned. Mary Magdalene was crying and I asked, "Have you seen Jesus?" Simon replied, "Yes, we saw him. But they'd really mistreated him." I asked, "How is he and what did he say?" Mary Magdalene replied, "Fortunately, thanks to Pilate's wife, we were able to speak to him alone for a while. He had a few requests of Simon and me, but I don't want to go into them at present." I observed that Joseph of Arimathea and Simon discreetly left the room together, to discuss the matter further. Jesus' mother, Mary, had also come to join us, since she had been staying with Lazarus. She accepted the situation with infinite composure. But her gaze was completely empty. Mary Magdalene was in deep despair and I tried to comfort her and give her my support.

Then she said, "Miriam, you have no idea how disrespectfully they have treated him. He really was in a terrible state. His face was swollen, and he had black eyes and other marks of mishandling. They treated him as if he was a wild animal. How can human beings be so barbarous and unfeeling?"

Then Mary Magdalene went to sleep on my knee, thoroughly exhausted. Simon and Joseph remained outside of the room a long time. When they returned to the room, Joseph left the house immediately and Simon did not say anything about what they had been discussing. He then sent somebody to fetch Magda, and she arrived shortly afterwards. Simon embraced her and she said, "I could not believe that my vision would be fulfilled. I predicted each of the things that has taken place. Sometimes I don't know whether the gift of second sight is a blessing or a curse." Simon said, "It is better when you stay with us. You would no longer be safe in your own house. We want to stay together for the time being, and see how things develop."

Joseph returned a short time later and knocked on the door. He said, "The priests have gotten their way. Annas and Caiaphas have succeeded with their evil tongues, so Jesus must appear before Pilate's tribunal. Pilate agreed since he was pledged to loyalty to the Roman occupiers; he is the liaison between the Jewish people and the Roman state. They charge Jesus with being a traitor and rebel against the Roman people. Pilate had no alternative." Simon asked, "Where will the trial take place? Can we be present at the tribunal?" Joseph replied, "Every Roman tribunal is open to the public. Every citizen has the right to attend. You should know, however that there will be a great number of Roman soldiers present, so we should remain anonymous as long as possible. Tomorrow morning Jesus will appear before the tribunal." We resolved to remain together for the night and to accompany Joseph discreetly to the place of the tribunal. We did not sleep that night. Simon was in another room, where I heard him pacing up and down, sorting out his thoughts for the next day.

The next morning we divided ourselves into small groups, to prevent us being identified. We intended to meet at the prefect's palace, to try to get into the public gallery. I went with Simon and Irisa. In the forecourt we saw Peter, who was completely deranged but tried to remain unidentified. We went to him and asked, "What is it, Peter?" He was in despair, and cried out, "You cannot imagine what I did last night. When they arrested Jesus, the others fled. I remained in the streets with the citizens, who were still out in great numbers and torches were burning everywhere. One of them asked me, 'Are you not one of them? Don't you belong to him who calls himself the Messiah?' I had no idea that I could do it, but I renounced Jesus three times. I acted as if I didn't know him!" Simon took him by the shoulders and said, "Peter, stop feeling guilty. That is what Jesus asked you to do. Your guilty conscience doesn't help any of us. We shall need our strength for that lies ahead of us. However, it is better when we don't remain together." Peter said, "I want to stay and see what happens." Simon replied, "Then you stay in the crowd to avoid recognition. We will attempt to enter the hall for the tribunal. Afterwards we will return to Irisa's house. Come to her house, irrespective of how long the tribunal lasts. We don't know what these murderers are planning."

Great crowds had assembled in the tribunal hall. Many Roman soldiers were present to keep order. Joseph negotiated passes for us to enter the hall. A raised platform was provided for the prefect. In the midst of the great crowd of spectators, I saw the Jewish high priests, as I had often seen them before. With expressionless faces, like conspirators, they waited silently as Pilate arrived and took his place where all could see him. He raised his voice and demanded, "High Priests of Jerusalem, voice of the people, what are your allegations against the prisoner?" "We request the indictment and the conviction of Jesus of Nazareth." Pilate seemed impatient, and asked, "But what have you to bring against him?" One of the priests stood and shouted, "He is a traitor to the Roman and Jewish people. He tries to turn the Jewish folk against us, we who always keep the peace in accordance with the wishes of the Roman Empire. He tries to bribe the Jewish people with the idea of a new king. He wants to overthrow the Roman Empire in Israel."

Pilate asked, "Can you prove this?" The priest answered, "He describes himself as the King of the Jews." "And what other accusations have you?" "He heals on our holy Sabbath. He breaks our laws. The people outside demand his death!" Pilate was astonished, and pressed for more. "His death? Has he really done anything really bad?""He is a magician and turns the heads of the people. He wants to become King of Israel, and depose the present king. When you are really the servant of the Roman state you have no alternative to sentencing him to death. He is an enemy of the state." Pilate said, "I have read the evidence which you have submitted to me; even my own wife says he is innocent. She is convinced that he is honest and blameless, and has only done good. I have inquired about him in detail and see nothing dangerous about him; on the contrary, he heals and helps people. He has never called himself King of Israel, or demanded taking over power in Jerusalem. Nothing like that is known to me."

Then the priests became really angry, and said, "We do not agree. Ask the people." Pilate said, "I would like to speak to the man myself." He ordered, "Let the prisoner be brought in. He should present his own case, whether he is innocent of guilty. That is his right in this tribunal." He gave a signal and I thought I would faint when Jesus was brought in between two armed guards: he had been so badly treated that he was unrecognizable. But he walked upright and ignored his injuries. As Jesus passed through the door into the room a man sprang forward and laid his cloak on the floor in front of Jesus, for him to walk on. But Jesus drew back and avoided the cloak. Pilate was very angry and screamed, "What are you doing?" The man answered, "I do that which I have seen others doing for him. I only want to spread my cloak out as a sign of my veneration for him. I saw how he came into Jerusalem." Pilate said, "Withdraw your cloak immediately."

Jesus looked at the man lovingly and spoke a few words to him — as if he wanted to explain to him that it was not necessary, and that he should not endanger his life. Then Jesus proceeded through the hall toward Pilate.

Then something extraordinary occurred: the imperial banners that the Roman soldiers held aloft to the left and right of Pilate's platform slowly lowered themselves as Jesus approached Pilate. Everybody in the room noticed it. Pilate was extremely angry with the soldiers holding the banners. "What are you doing there? Stop it immediately!" The soldiers carrying the banners were perplexed, but did not dare to reply. Then one of them had the courage to say, "Honorable Prefect Pilate. Believe us. We didn't do anything." The priests shouted from the other end of the room, "You have all seen the magician, that he manipulates the people; and how he himself influences the banners in this room!" Pilate roared, "Silence! I do not believe that a magician is so powerful. If you think he is a magician, then exchange our soldiers with your own men!" Jesus stood still, in the middle of the hall. The high priests exchanged their own men for the Roman soldiers carrying the banners. Then Pilate said to Jesus, "Come nearer."

Once again, the banners dropped almost to the floor in front of Jesus, as if they were they were bowing to the Messiah. Pilate was livid. Helpless, he lay back in his seat and put his hands over his face. He tried to get control of himself. Then he stood up and disappeared behind curtain.

A few seconds later he reappeared, fighting for control. He looked at Jesus. "So you are the Nazarene. You cause a lot of unrest in the town." Jesus did not reply, and Pilate continued,

"You stand before me because you are accused by your own people." Jesus only looked at him calmly, but did not reply. "They accuse you of claiming to be the King of the Jews. Tell me, are you a king?" Jesus answered quietly and calmly, "If I were a king I would have an army like you, Pilate. My army would have fought for me, and I would not stand before you as a destitute beggar, oppressed, mistreated and in chains. So what are your accusations against me?" Pilate swallowed hard and one could hear his sigh to the end of the room. "Don't make it so difficult for me. You have an advocate even in my own house. You appear in the dreams of my own wife. She does not miss a single opportunity to declare your innocence. You can make life easier for both of us."

The high priests started screaming again, almost as one: "You see, Pilate, how the magician influences the dreams of your own wife." Pilate struck the table in front of him with a hammer and shouted, "Silence! If you are not silent this instant I will have the hall cleared and continue behind closed doors." He bent forward and looked at Jesus. "Are you a king or are you not? Say that you are not, and I can release you here and now." Jesus said, "I am a king, but my kingdom is not of this world." Pilate stood up, relieved and said, "Then we have concluded the proceedings. You all heard? As he has explained he will attack neither the Roman Empire nor the Jewish state. Have you further accusations against him?"

The high priests protested, "He violates the laws of our people. He heals on the Sabbath. He is unclean, ignores our customs and violates Jewish law, for which the penalty is death by stoning. We demand this penalty from you." Pilate replied, "I cannot see any violation of our laws. It is up to you to judge him by your laws." The priests were furious and shouted, "We cannot accuse him under our laws! We are not empowered to sentence someone to death on the Sabbath. Only you can do that. We want to leave that to you." Pilate leaned back in his chair and said, "Jesus of Nazareth, don't make it so difficult for me. Defend yourself with one word and I will let you go free. According to my laws you are innocent. I have nothing to accuse you of."

Jesus looked at him calmly and said, "Pilate, I cannot help you. You must serve your master as I serve mine. I will not change our destinies. Do what you have to do. I will neither defend my innocence nor admit my guilt." Pilate stood up, saying, "Due to your lack of cooperation and your general behavior, I sentence you to forty lashes of the whip. Thus the requirements of Roman law are fulfilled. The proceedings are closed. You can now have him back again." Then he left the hall. Jesus was led away, and was completely calm.

We who had witnessed it all were miserable and distressed, apart from Simon and Joseph of Arimathea. An official entered the room and called, "The tribunal is closed." The high priests screamed, "We demand the right to have another trial!" The official replied, "Pilate is unwilling to continue the proceedings." Then the priests called out, "Then listen to the people outside. The Jews demand his conviction!"

Following the disturbance, Pilate appeared again. He demanded silence and said, "I leave the decision to you. Let the Jewish people decide." Then he descended to the hall and went outside on to the steps, followed by the crowd. He said, "Citizens of Israel, what are your demands?" I heard the people screaming, "Put him to death, put him to death." There were some voices shouting, "Let him go free. Hosanna to God let our Messiah go free." But the voices demanding Jesus' death drowned everything else, so that it seemed as if the citizens were almost unanimous.

Irisa stood next to me and said, "They have all been bribed. The priests spent a lot of money buying public opinion and using the people for their own purposes. Now Pilate is in a corner." Pilate stood there, perplexed, and said, "Tomorrow morning I will reappear here. Until then, you have time to reach a decision. At Passover I always let you choose one prisoner to be freed. Tomorrow morning I will ask you who it will be. I shall accept, if I must, the will of the Jews." As he returned to the hall he called, "Bring me a bowl of water." His soldier did as he requested. Pilate stood in front of the high priests Annas and Caiaphas, and said, "In the name of the gods, I have done what I could. I now in the presence of this crowd wash my hands of the whole affair." He threw the basin on the floor and left the room.

I was angry and fearful for Jesus. Simon took me outside so that I could breathe freely again. We returned silently to Irisa's house. Jerusalem was in an uproar. The people were discussing and arguing. Every street was in turmoil, so it was difficult to make progress. When we finally reached the house we were all exhausted. Simon withdrew into a side room.

After a while there was a knock at the door and Peter entered. Irisa went to him, took his hands and said, "Peter, whatever happens now, do not feel guilty. This was Jesus' wish. Now you can stay here. Are you hungry? Or have you had something to eat and drink?" Peter replied, "Dear lady, I could not eat anything. I just want a quiet place to sleep, and perhaps a cup of water." He sat in the corner, completely confused and exhausted, a picture of misery. We were all of us in not much better condition. Mary Magdalene had also attended the tribunal and was in a state of shock. We were all silent and depressed.

In all the years we had known Jesus we had experienced only love and forgiveness from him. None of us could understand in our hearts how someone so full of love and understanding could be subjected to so much cruelty and disrespect. I went to my room, and when I had quieted down somewhat, I felt my understanding grow. It was as if Jesus and the child inside me were saying to me, "Forgive those misled people you saw today, despite their cruelty and hate, so that you do not carry the burden of their guilt." I murmured continuously words of forgiveness and slept. When I awoke from a dreamless sleep, I went to Simon in the next room. He was calm and collected and took me in his arms. "My dear Miriam, now you must be brave. The unspeakable will happen." I asked him, "Can I stay with you for a while?" He said, "Of course you can." I stayed until Joseph of Arimathea returned.

Joseph arrived, out of breath. "I have prepared everything. If the priests and their henchmen think they can persuade the people by paying them to achieve their aims, then we can do the same, so that people help us instead." Then he and Simon disappeared into another room, where they remained for several hours. We heard them talking, but none of us wanted to know the details. We were too occupied with our own feelings.

411

I could scarcely look at Peter, sitting in a corner looking completely bereft and staring into space. I sat next to him, just to show that someone was there to support him. He began to speak despairingly: "You cannot conceive what a magnificent man Jesus is. On the evening we went to the Mount of Olives, he withdrew and left us alone, spending his time in prayer and with God intermittently throughout the night. Blood and sweat dripped from his forehead. He suffered a great deal that evening. He had accepted his lot. Later that night Judas appeared with some Roman soldiers and demanded to know Jesus' whereabouts.

"Jesus offered no resistance, and said, 'Here is he whom you seek.' The Romans said, 'We are here to arrest you. There is a charge against you.'" Peter swallowed hard before he could go on. "Miriam, I was so angry I tore the sword out of the soldier's hand and struck him on the head with it. I couldn't do anything else, because I couldn't bear it. Jesus' voice commanded me, 'Leave him alone, Peter. Nobody should be able to accuse us of injuring or otherwise harming others.' The soldier was injured and his ear bled. Jesus went to him and said, 'Don't worry. Your ear is healthy.' Then he turned to the soldiers and said, 'I shall not offer any resistance. Do what you have to do.' He didn't even look at us. But it appeared as if the soldiers were his prisoners, not the other way round. Nevertheless they forced him to his knees, hit him and chained his hands, and led him away like a common criminal. I tried to follow him, but lost sight of him and then lost my way in the streets of Jerusalem. So I was unable to find out where they had took him. Since that time I have not seen the others. But I think that is what he told them to do. My last impression of them was their despairing postures when

412

they left the house, scattering in all directions. I don't know how I am going to live with the thought that we could not protect him."

"Peter," I said. "He did not train you to be a fighter, one who kills his enemies. You have done the right thing. Let the moment go. We must save our strength for what is important. Everybody assumes the worst will happen. But what is that? Better think of Him and what he had taught you. Think of what he has left you as an inheritance. You must only believe in that and nothing else. Would you like something to eat or drink?" He replied, "I cannot eat anything, but I would like some water." I was happy that he was feeling at least a bit better. He had pulled himself together after he was able to describe his experiences to someone. I was also happy that he told me, since it was a part of the story that might otherwise not have been known to me. The more I heard about Jesus' attitude toward his position, the greater was my respect for him. He truly showed that he loved his enemies from the bottom of his heart, regardless of what they had done to him. My love for the Messiah was only increased further, and I was determined more than ever to defy the world in his name. The mass of the public was blind, and I was willing to combat this blindness with my love. That was my revolution in his name and for his honor.

That night we again did not sleep. Only occasionally did we close our eyes and doze out of exhaustion. My child carried me through the night. Simon and Joseph of Arimathea seemed to have been awake the whole night, until they opened the doors early next morning and Simon said, "It is time to go." They were evidently prepared for some action.

413

We split up into several groups, as we had before. Jerusalem was in turmoil. The streets were full of people, even at this early hour. In front of prefect's house the crowd was so dense that one could scarcely move. At the allotted time Pilate appeared. The aggressive crowd, incited by the priests, shouted, "Crucify him, crucify him!" Evidently many hundreds of citizens had been paid by the priests, from money donated by generous and devout believers — unknowingly donated to finance the treacherous activities of the high priests, so that they could suppress all opposition! The people were blind to the dishonesty of the priests since nobody had opened their eyes. They were prisoners in the darkness of their small world. I felt sympathy for these people, who had become even more enslaved than they had already been. They were unable to recognize those who had come to give them the gift of freedom; they were forced to ignore or despise him.

I was certain that many of those who demanded his death had been the same ones who had shouted, "Hosanna, welcome to the King" as Jesus rode into Jerusalem on a donkey. Now they shouted, "Nail him to the cross!" These people were absolutely capricious. They sought to crucify their own prophets, as they have always done. I knew that the history of this people was a product of God's anger. They attracted the wrath of the heavens.

My reflections were interrupted as Pilate appeared and said, "Today is the day when the people of Israel make their choice. You may elect one of the prisoners to regain his freedom. In the name of the law, whom do you choose? Whom will the people see in their midst as free man?" Then he added,

"People of Israel, with the honest feelings of my heart I say to you, the man from Nazareth, the one you want to crucify, is completely innocent of all crimes, and is only guilty of being himself. I would not condemn him. Do not forget what his message is and how much good he has done. He healed your children. He seems to have awakened the dead. He has only brought good to you. What is now your verdict? Who should go free?" But the people were so blind. It had grown dark and gloomy around them, and I could see how their eyes reflected this gloom. They insisted on liberating one of the leaders of the Zealots. As if with one voice they shouted, "Barabbas! We want him free, and not the preacher from Nazareth."

We were at the back of the crowd, and Simon and I looked at one another. Jesus and Barabbas were led in front of the crowd and Pilate asked again, "I will free immediately the one who you want. Whom do you choose?" The crowd screamed, "Barabbas!" Then Pilate said something that completely surprised me: "A treacherous people want to have a traitor! You can have him." Then the warder threw Barabbas in front of the people, and the crowd cheered in jubilation. It was a gruesome rejoicing.

Jesus stood there and I could only cry. They had tortured and beaten him, and the blood ran down his face as he bowed his head. He did not look at the crowd. He, who had always turned his eyes lovingly to the people, bowed his head and only looked at the ground in front of him. I knew that that was the greatest punishment that could strike the people — not to experience the loving gaze of the Messiah. Pilate said to Jesus, "I cannot do any more for you. The people have decided." He was miserable, and one could see his sadness and resignation. Then he said quietly, "Then he must be crucified, along with those who have been condemned today."

Then I saw the warders approach Jesus. A Roman soldier placed a crown of thorns on his head and blood streamed down his face anew. The soldier shouted, jeeringly, "See the King of the Jews. He cannot even help himself out of this situation, the miserable fool!" Then he kicked Jesus. Our Messiah broke down in front of us and fell to his knees. Then they dragged him down the steps. The crowd was so thick that we had to fight our way through the surging mass of people to reach him. He was hauled to another place, where he was publicly whipped. The warders brought a massive wooden cross. The crowd was whipped into a sadistic uproar as the warder mocked, "Carry your cross yourself. If you are truly a king, then stand upright and show what you can do. You have awakened the dead but you can't help yourself, oh feeble king!"

Mary Magdalene was next to me and collapsed completely. Simon went to her, held her head in his hands until she had recovered somewhat, and said, "When you want to, we can go home." As she opened her eyes, she said, "I cannot leave him now. But what I have just seen tears my heart in two."

I took her in my arms and said, "Mary Magdalene, it has broken all of our hearts. But let us stay with him. Here he has nobody but us. We will not leave him, don't worry. Simon, help us please. Mary Magdalene and I wish to go to him." Simon said, "You are crazy. You cannot get to the front of this enormous crowd. And you risk being trampled to death." I said, "No, Simon. But let us at least try to get to him."

The crowd pushed Jesus up the hill to Golgotha, where the Romans crucified their enemies. We could see Jesus drag his cross up the hill. We tried to get nearer to him but there were so many onlookers who pushed past us when we tried to move forward. I really did not know whether we were in the midst of animals or human beings. They were blood-thirsty, with no motivation other than evil glee. There were occasionally a few who were distraught and weeping, and I could not do anything other than say to them, "Don't cry for him; pray for him." Time seemed to stand still. But the sadistic crowd surged up the hill behind Jesus, greedy for bloody satisfaction. Suddenly a cry rang out: "Jesus has fallen! He has collapsed."

Mary Magdalene let out a heart–rending cry. "I will go to him!" I held her hand and said, "Come, we will get to him, even if we have to kill the whole pack here, we will not leave him alone." Simon helped us to push our way through to Jesus. He was suddenly filled with incredible power and took us both by the hand and pulled us through the horde until we could finally get near to Jesus. I would have liked to have avoided the sight before me: Jesus dragged his cross up the hill, and the sadistic warders continued to whip him, even as he fell to his knees. But again he got to his feet and continued to drag his cross, as if he had some superhuman power in him.

As we approached the plateau where several crosses had already been erected, something extraordinary happened: the crowd suddenly became silent and there were no more shouts of "Crucify him!" Great masses of people fell on their knees and started to pray. Andrew emerged from the crowd and was foolhardy enough to try to take the cross from Jesus and carry it himself. But he was immediately attacked by a warder, who threw him back and struck him, unconscious, to the ground. Simon was able to get to Andrew, and lifted him up and carried him on his shoulders. We followed Simon.

We were finally able to get near Jesus. His eyes were so swollen that he could scarcely see. It seemed that he oriented himself based entirely on the whip–lashes of the warder, to define the direction in which he should drag his cross. We final ly came near enough to him that, despite his swollen eyes, he was able to recognize us. Then he raised his head and said, "There you are." But there was no possibility for us to help him, since our path was blocked by Roman soldiers. Suddenly, he appeared to have summoned additional strength, probably due to Simon's presence, and was able to drag his cross to the top of the hill. At the same time I saw Magda, who came to us and held my hand as we climbed to the place of his martyrdom, which was sealed off by the soldiers. Then Joseph of Arimathea suddenly appeared, and I caught sight of Mary and John in the crowd. Simon appeared to generate some particular energy, so that the crowd did not seem to dare to follow Jesus any farther. We were then able to proceed to the top of the hill of Golgotha, only to be stopped by the soldiers. Meanwhile Jesus had reached the place of his crucifixion — a gruesome sight and one we could not approach any closer.

Suddenly, as if from nowhere, the Roman soldier that I had seen in Canaan was there. Simon went to speak to him, and the soldier recognized him. After the short conversation Simon beckoned to us. Mary, John, Mary Magdalene and I went to Simon. The cross was erected next to the others with ropes. Just down the hill from the place of his planned crucifixion, there was a tremendous clap of thunder that shook the whole hill and spooked the crowd. Mary Magdalene fainted, and I had to support her; I do not know which was louder, her scream or the sound of hammering as Jesus was nailed to the cross.

Simon said, "The Roman has kept his promise to Jesus. He is letting us go and stay nearer to him." The Roman soldier then let us through and prevented others from approaching, but he said, "I am afraid you cannot approach closer than that. You will have to remain there. If you stay there you have my protection. Nobody will contradict me." I looked at him and said, "You also believe in him." He answered, "Yes, I do. And I am ashamed of my people. But my hands are tied. All that I can do is to let you be near to him and protect you as long as you remain here."

He was our sentinel, he allowed us to remain a few feet from the Messiah. Jesus was alone and nobody came into contact with him apart from the slaves appointed by the Romans. Mary, Mary Magdalene and I knelt and prayed. We saw how he hung from the cross, and prayed to God and to heaven, whence he had come to us. Joseph of Arimathea took our sentinel to one side and spoke to him, after which the soldier nodded. Then Magda appeared beside me. She radiated a particular energy, which was familiar to me, and said, "Not long to wait, and then our special knowledge will be called for. Forget what you see here, Miriam. Collect your inner God–given powers together. Remember what you have learned with the Essenes. Nothing is decided. God's wonder is still with us." At that moment everything was suddenly still, as if the world were holding its breath. The picture of Jesus on the cross somehow changed. Simon just stood there and looked at Jesus with his infinite patience. One could sense the love that flowed between them.

Curiously, I no longer saw the man on the cross, only Jesus as a God–like being. There were no people behind us; the Romans had pushed them all back down the hill. We were with him on the mountain of his destiny. In the seventh hour Jesus suddenly spoke. "Lord, I give my spirit into your hands. It is done!" Then his head fell to one side and we were petrified in that moment. My heart almost stood still, but Magda took my hand and shook her head, saying, "Just wait." Joseph of Arimathea gave our Roman sentinel a signal, and the Roman went to Jesus, took a lance with a saturated sponge on it and drove it between Jesus' ribs. Then he called out loud, so that everyone could hear him: "He is dead."

Joseph of Arimathea looked at us significantly. The others who hung on their crosses were not yet dead. Jesus had died astonishingly quickly, and in this hour the heavens gave their signal: everything came to a standstill and time did not exist anymore. After some minutes Joseph said, "Simon, as agreed!" Simon spoke to Mary and me and said, "Joseph will try to get Jesus' body down from the cross as quickly as possible. He will use his connections to take it to Joseph's family grave. Joseph will request that the corpse be transferred to the graveyard." Then Simon looked at us knowingly and said quietly, "Jesus is not dead. He is still alive. But we must now move quickly."

We left Golgotha, and Simon brought us to a place near the cemetery. He said, "Wait here! The women dare not be seen in the graveyard." I asked Simon, "What is planned?" He replied, "Nothing is permanently predictable yet. Since Jesus is still alive we will do all that is humanly possible to revive him." I protested, "But the Roman's lance penetrated right through his body." Simon smiled and said, "The sponge was soaked in anesthetic. Have we not learned from the great Essene magicians since time immemorial, what one can do with the human body? You have surely not forgotten. But now I must go. I leave you alone for a while."

After some time Simon returned and said, "Joseph of Arimathea had arranged that Jesus would be taken down from the cross so rapidly. He was able to persuade the high priests that Jesus was indeed dead, and begged for his body could be released for burial." We returned to the cross where Jesus hung, and the sympathetic Roman soldier ordered a colleague to assist in gently lowering the cross to the ground. We extracted the nails and removed Jesus from the place of his indignity. The Romans were very cooperative and helped us carry him. Together we placed him gently on a stretcher.

As we carried him to the family grave of Joseph of Arimathea, which was behind the hill, Jesus' mother Mary enveloped his near–lifeless body with all her love. Simon touched Jesus and said, "He is alive. We must act quickly now." Our benevolent Roman soldier ordered two of his company to come with us to watch over the grave. He said, "You are responsible for seeing that nobody comes near the grave."

As we carried Jesus I noticed that he emitted a singular energy, but was apparently not breathing. Nevertheless, I was sure that he was still alive.

We laid Jesus in a stone tomb, and the Roman ordered his two soldiers to go down the hill to the town administration and certify that Jesus of Nazareth was dead. He would remain there and watch over the grave discreetly from a distance while we would ostensibly take leave of Jesus. When we were alone, Joseph of Arimathea said, "So, now you all have to show what you can do to revive him." Joseph had hidden elixirs, herbs, and ointments in the grave. First he gave Jesus a special potion to drink, which he administered in small sips, and we all suddenly realized what he was doing. I had spent long enough learning with the Essenes to know what we were truly capable of: allowing a person to lapse into an apparent death, and then reviving them by expelling the poison out of the body again with a special potion. I knew what Joseph had given him. Jesus then began to vomit, and quivered due to cramps. Before our very eyes life returned to his body, even though he was weak and scarcely conscious. But he was with us again!

His whole being had been revived. Each one of us played a part in healing him: restarting his breathing, his heart rhythm and his full blood circulation. Magda was magnificent; she applied ointment and oil to his whole body so that his wounds gradually closed. Mary summoned all of her extraordinary healing powers. I returned to the full consciousness of our godly state, and was also able to assist Jesus' reanimation. Then Simon completed the healing of his wounds, so that only slight scars remained. Jesus was almost fully restored to health: his breathing was normal and there was color in his cheeks. But he had still not returned to consciousness. Then we decided to close the tomb in which Jesus lay with a large rock. We enlisted the help of the two soldiers, who had been watching over the grave outside, and with an almost super-human effort we closed the grave.

Then Joseph of Arimathea said to the Roman soldier, "Now you can take over the watch. We have taken our leave of him and anointed him following our traditions." Then the two soldiers returned and stated that they had reported the death officially to the town administration. Then our Roman friend ordered, "You two can keep watch over the grave now. I will relieve you later." He gave us the signal that it was time for us to leave the tomb. I do not think he knew what he had done for us by permitting us to revive Jesus. Joseph discussed with our friend the times of changing the guard. Then we left together, leaving the two soldiers watching over his burial place.

Joseph said, "Now we have to return home, that's the most important thing, and we have to behave as if we knew nothing about Jesus' recovery." Simon added, "He will now sleep. The divine forces will now regenerate his body. We will meet again here tonight. Then he will be fully conscious and sufficiently recovered." We returned home and told nobody what we had done, and let them believe that Jesus was indeed dead. We went to bed but after a few hours Simon awakened us. He said simply, "Come. We must return to Jesus." Nobody asked where we were going, and Simon and I left the house with Mary Magdalene and Magda, in the direction of the tomb.

Joseph had not yet arrived, but our Roman friend had relieved the two soldiers and was watching over the grave. He looked at us and said, "I don't know what is happening in the grave, but I don't think I want to know." Simon asked him, "Did your two soldiers notice anything? Were they suspicious?"

The Roman replied, "For a moment they were not sure. But they are not smart enough to draw any conclusions. Perhaps you should give them a nice sum of money, and say it was in gratitude for their looking after the grave and letting you have access to it." Simon asked, "Where are they now?" The Roman replied, "I sent them away and told them that the family would generously reward them for staying at the grave with the corpse."

Simon gave him money, enough to satisfy the soldiers. Our Roman friend left us and we were alone, waiting for Joseph of Arimathea. After some hours he eventually appeared, very out of breath. Simon asked him, "What happened. Why are you so late?" Joseph replied, "You cannot imagine what happened to me. The high priests forced me into a room and locked me in. They wanted to imprison me." We gasped, "How did you escape?" He replied, "It was a miracle: After they had left me, the door suddenly burst open all on its own, and I was able to leave without hindrance. That's why I'm so late."

Simon only laughed knowingly. "Come now. We must act. There is no time to lose." Together we managed to remove the stone behind which Jesus was lying, and Joseph gave Jesus another drink. Mary, Mary Magdalene, Simon, Joseph and I were there as Jesus returned to life. He had returned to us. Slowly he sat up and we helped him out of the grave. He smiled as if nothing had happened. But he had changed. Something about him was different. Simon had brought him fresh clothes, and Jesus dressed himself. He stood in front of us in silence, and Mary Magdalene moved towards him. He looked at her and said, "Please do not try to tie me down. You will not find me the same being as the one who left you."

Simon was very quick-witted and said, "I think we should leave this place as quickly as possible."

Simon helped Jesus, who was still somewhat weak. Together we walked around the outskirts of the town, avoiding busy streets, to avoid being identified. Eventually we reached Joseph of Arimathea's house. We heard later that the two soldiers returned to find the grave empty, and let themselves be persuaded by our Roman friend that we had stolen the body. To avoid a disgrace, the high priests bribed the two soldiers to spread the word that we had stolen the corpse of Jesus but that they had no interest in finding it, so we appeared to be the culprits, but so that using all our discretion we could stay out of danger.

We were at least safe for the time being in Joseph's house. We were all silent until Jesus spoke. "We do not have much time in Jerusalem. We must leave here as soon as possible. Do you know where my twelve disciples are, Joseph?" Joseph replied, "I informed them that, after the crucifixion, they should come to my house so that I would be able to tell them what really happened." Jesus said, "They believe I am dead." Joseph replied, "We thought it best not to tell them of our plans. We did not know whether our plans would be successful." Jesus answered, "God's plans always succeed."

Simon went to Jesus and said, "Jesus, my friend. Would you like us to remain or would you like to be alone?" Jesus replied, "Please leave me alone with my disciples. I would like to talk to them in private. Come back tomorrow evening. We must decide how we can leave this place as quickly as possible."

We returned to Irisa's house, and for the first time in many days were able to sleep peacefully through the night. Simon also slept deeply and peacefully. We did not inform any of the others where we had been, and nobody dared to ask us. They all thought we had only helped Mary at Jesus' grave. We slept well, and at breakfast Simon finally broke the news to Irisa: "Irisa, the Messiah is not dead." Irisa seemed not the least surprised and calmly said, "I was sure the whole time that you had done something that the world should not yet know about." Then she asked, "What have you planned for the future?" "We will meet him this evening at Joseph of Arimathea's house, and will plan how to leave Jerusalem unnoticed as fast as possible." Irisa sighed and said, "What a story! My God, my God, what we have all witnessed." Then she looked at Simon and said, "You are all superhuman. You have grown to a stature for which the world is not yet prepared."

Mary, Mary Magdalene, Simon and I went to Joseph of Arimathea's house in the evening. I could not restrain a smile as I saw the expressions on the faces of the disciples who were present. Joseph told us that none of them could believe that Jesus was standing before them. They had indeed believed that Jesus was resurrected as a ghost, until they saw his remaining scars, and were able to touch them. Jesus had spent the whole night with them, during which no one had slept. He had given every disciple specific instructions as to where they should go and how they could best leave the country. Jesus had told them about the various countries where their futures lay, the visions he had for them and their missions. There was a curious atmosphere in the room and it seemed that they all wanted to lose no time and to leave immediately. It was the beginning and the end of very particular epochs, and we were sad to take leave of the disciples. Only the younger Jacob remained.

When they left at last, Jesus said, "Some of them face arduous destinies, but they are prepared to face the future. The world is full of disbelief and persecution. At present it is better that all believe I am dead. The high priests themselves paid to reinforce this belief. Otherwise the people might burn down the temple in their anger. Let us be happy to leave things the way they are."

Jesus sat down and reflected. After several quiet minutes he said, "Joseph, I believe you should all leave soon. None of you can remain here any longer. Mary Magdalene, you should go with them." Joseph and Simon discussed the idea of going to Egypt, where Joseph would find a ship to transport us to another country far removed from Israel. I was dismayed at the prospect, in view of my state. Simon noticed it and said, "Don't worry Miriam. We have three months before the baby will be born. Perhaps we can wait for the birth in Egypt. Perhaps we will already be sailing. We don't know when we will charter a ship and a crew capable of bringing us to our chosen destination. Joseph and I have enough contacts to arrange everything." Jesus said, "You should take my brother Jacob with you. Also Lazarus, Salome and all others who want to accompany you. Too much has happened here."

I asked, "And you, Jesus? What of you?" He replied, "I must first speak to my Father. In those hours on the cross I did not know myself whether my life on Earth was ended or whether it should continue. When I was in a state of trance, while I

427

was being tortured, I saw the visions of your plans, but I did not know at that time whether they would be successful. The hours alone with my Father on the cross have clarified many things for me."

I asked, "Are you not coming with us?" Jesus answered, "I believe I would endanger your lives if I were to accompany you. My face and my person are now known in many countries. I think I will return to the East. I will know where I can find you. But now you should also leave as soon as you can." I asked, "Jesus, you are leaving us after all that we have been through together?" He answered, "I will never leave you. I am always with you." I protested, "But now you can come with us, in a distant country, far removed from your enemies and far removed from our enemies, and make a new start." Jesus said, "I am afraid that is not my life. I think that I would like to use the rest of my life, which the Lord has given me, reaching out to people in other lands, redeeming and liberating them. My message and my mission on Earth require my freedom, since there is still much to do." I asked, "Should someone accompany you?" Jesus replied, "No, not for the moment."

Simon clapped him on the shoulder and said, "Well, for the near future, I know where I can find you; send my greetings to the great master in the Himalayas."

We returned to Irisa's house and made our plans. Except for Irisa and Magda, all of our friends decided to come with us to Egypt and take the boat to our ultimate destination. Magda was determined to remain in Jerusalem and said, "I have fulfilled that for which I am on Earth. Now I will seek only my silence and my God. I am too old to start a new life. I have received a great gift from the Lord, the task I have been able to complete in His name. But you are all young. Your lives and your missions are certainly not complete. Israel is a small part of this world. Hence it is good when you move to other lands and carry the seeds of what was born here into the world outside."

Simon decided that we should return to our house in Canaan before we left Israel forever. He wanted to settle some business matters, and see his sister. Everything went quickly. Joseph of Arimathea wanted to leave already, but remained for a few days to be with Jesus. Since Simon and Joseph seemed to know the country, they arranged to meet in Egypt.

The beginning and end blend together into one. Joseph of Arimathea and all the others were preparing for the journey from Jerusalem to Egypt, in separate groups with separate itineraries. We discussed final details with Jesus in Joseph's house. The man I had observed several times with Jesus was also there; he sat quietly in a corner observing and radiating his distinctive light. Jesus said, "I will travel to India again. I feel most attracted to that country. This is my friend, whom I will take with me as pupil and prepare him to carry the Light of Christ in the future. We do not have much more time." Then he paused for a moment and said, "I have sad news for you all, which disturbs me too. I have heard that Judas has hanged himself outside the gates of the city. He was not informed that I am indeed alive and well." We were all shocked by the news, and many of us wept. I did. Jesus was quiet for a moment and then said quietly, "Just one more life and he will be free. He was a true friend. Everything on Earth has its shadowy side, even if there is no sun. We pray to God that one day it will be different."

That evening we said farewell to Jesus. It was curious, as if we would never be parting again, and this was just a blessing for the journey, which each one of us received. This evening, though, I knew that from then on we would all go in different directions, toward new lives and different destinies. But the glorious time we'd had with Jesus and all the others would remain with us always. Somehow it was simultaneously sad and a relief. Jesus had left us.

It was later we heard the rumor from Israel, that Jesus was seen ascending to Heaven as a glowing white manifestation. Everybody assumed that they had seen Jesus resurrected. In a certain sense it was true: Jesus died and then came to life again. But the people did not want to know our secret — which was a good thing, since it protected us. As we bade Jesus farewell we knew that it was not a parting forever, but nobody knew when, where and how we would meet again.

Simon and I left for Canaan, and we knew that we would meet the others in Egypt a few weeks later. Simon wanted us to travel secretly at night. He asked often whether it was not too exhausting for me, but I replied, "Don't worry about me. Everything is in order. I just want to get to our house again. We must say farewell to our house."

With this thought we arrived at Canaan. Simon needed a week to settle all his affairs. He did not tell me what he did, but I knew that he was preparing some business. I asked him, "What will happen to the house? We cannot return here." He said, "I have passed the house on to Helena Salome and her husband. They are not involved with Jesus, and will have no problems with the authorities." "When do we start," I asked, holding his hand, "I am anxious about the journey and where we are going." He was calm and explained, "You don't have to worry about anything. I have enough money and enough business connections in many countries that we don't have to worry wherever we go. I am accustomed to travelling. I learned about foreign lands on my journeys with my father, and how to establish business connections in strange countries. Don't worry about such things. We will live a good life." Then he stroked my swollen abdomen affectionately.

A week later we left Canaan. Simon made arrangements so that we could travel to Egypt in comfort. He took into account that my abdomen was swollen and heavy with the child, and that I could no longer tolerate the heat. Our journey lasted three weeks before we arrived at a seaport in Egypt. There we met the others. Simon seemed to know his way around and accommodated us in a splendid house, which he had rented for us. He and Joseph of Arimathea concerned themselves with finding a ship and crew for us, in order that we could sail in a few days or weeks. I asked him, "Will we sail before the baby arrives?" He answered, "I don't know yet. We have not yet found the right ship. There are not so many ships here that one can rent privately. But we have used all our contacts, and I am sure we will find something soon."

Several weeks passed and my pregnancy was nearly over. I had only one month before the baby was due when the men said, "We can travel in a week's time." I was shocked. "I just can't board the ship in this condition!" Simon said, "The sea voyage lasts around three weeks. I think we should risk it." I assented and, in the Egyptian seaport, we said farewell to Mary, who didn't want to come with us. She and John wished

431

to settle together in another country. I was unsettled and begged, "Don't leave me alone, Mary." She replied, "There is no need for you to be afraid. Every step we take is decided by God. I don't think you need me anymore. Everything will be all right." It was, naturally, a sad moment for me as she left. It was as if I had lost my mother a second time. Mary had led me through so much of my life, taught me so much and given me so many gifts. She, in turn, had lost so much — her husband and her son – but she was still a perpetual source of radiant love, shining every moment throughout the world.

As we sat together one evening, Simon and Joseph told us that we would be sailing next day. They had hired a ship, a crew and bought sufficient provisions for the voyage. Everyone had to decide whether they wished to sail with us. Mary Magdalene had changed, becoming more composed. She said to us, "Jesus picked me as an apostle, and commissioned me to travel to foreign lands. So I would like to come with you." Jesus' younger brother, Jacob, along with Lazarus, Joseph of Arimathea, Seraphim, Salome and several others also wished to sail with us, to which I agreed. If our child was going to be born during the voyage, I would have excellent support from the women travelling with us too. We weighed anchor and set sail for our new life, leaving our past life behind us. We were on a voyage into an unknown future, on a sea that I had never experienced.

All I could do was put my trust in the sea that carried us to our new life. Every day, I thought of the sea as God, who carries us through life without us knowing where we are going. Sometimes wild storms and rough seas shook the ship. But we had a good crew and a good ship.

We had travelled about three weeks when Joseph suddenly called out, "Look, in the distance! There's land dead ahead of us. We're nearly there. That's the country we're travelling to; I know it. I've got a house there." Within a day, we had landed and Joseph explained that his house was on the outskirts of a large trading town, about two days journey from our landing place. As we set foot on land, my child began to move in my womb, as if it had a message for our new homeland. That was a sign, and I told Simon. He looked at me helplessly for a moment and then said, "I will see to it that we find the best possible accommodation in this town. Stay here and I'll collect you when we have a house." The women estimated that I had a few hours before the birth, and should not worry. And thus it was.

I gave birth to our son and was bathed in light. The light streamed through all worlds and through us, and I knew that I was bringing a very special child into this land, just as Jesus had predicted. Simon was very happy, and as he looked at our child, saying:,"This child comes out of a world that only Jesus and I know."

We gave our son the name John, after the younger John, who had prophesied the child's birth. I needed some days to recover from the birth. During those nights, I dreamed that this land, a very ancient country, had some connection with God's realm on Earth, and that we had come here to fulfill the prophecy, and to awaken that which had long been buried deep within the Earth. I dreamed of a golden land, and that our son had a very special mission here. I had many visions of this land, where we now lived. A long time ago, we had mislaid our original purpose, which we would rediscover on our journey here. Simon was next to me and said, "We'll see what life has in store for us. The future is unknown, but I know that we are at the place where we should be."

Sometimes we did speak about the wonderful times we had been permitted to experience. But here our story ends ... and begins anew.

Index of events

Index of events

Index of events

Index of names

Index of names

For your personal notes

444

445

Contact the authors

The authors work and lecture internationally, holding workshops, seminars, retreats and meditations.

Their advice is sought worldwide by individuals and businesses for guidance in this difficult but enlightening time.

You may want to contact them. You are cordially invited to do so.

Please visit their web sites at:

www.cl-publishing.com

www.jesus-the-book.com

www.fengshuivision.com

Coming soon

Jesus The Book – Part Two

· Mary Magdalene gives birth to Sara

· Jesus returns from the Himalayas

· The Essenes are guided to a new community

· Meeting Masters from Atlantis

· Jesus travels to many European countries teaching

· Wedding of Jesus and Mary Magdalene

· Meeting Peter and Andrew in Rome

· Mary in Greece

· New schools of healing

· The holy bloodline – wedding of Sara and John

And many other seeds, Jesus planted at that time to grant us a rich harvest of blessing and light today.

Prayer of Jesus

Lord and Father in heaven.
Hallowed be thy name.
Born out of love and enveloped in that love,
you reign throughout eternity.
You are the beginning and the end.
You are our birth and our death.

Lord in heaven,
forgive us our sins
and forgive those who have sinned against us.
Lead us to redemption,
not by seeking revenge, but by donating forgiveness.
Let us know that we are children of thy kingdom.
Forgive us every moment when we forget you.
For yours is the kingdom, the love, the power and the glory.
You carry the name of eternity,
which you have imprinted in our hearts and in our souls.
Raise us up so that we can see your face.
Lead us into the light, from the finite into the infinite.
Let love be the law of our lives,
so that peace and joy reign.

Father in heaven,
let we the children of the Earth
be the messengers of your glory and your name.
For you are the birth of our souls,
and so we can see your eternal light, your peace
and your glory, forever and ever.

Amen.